Words of Praise for the Teachings of Abraham
and *Ask and It Is Given*

*"This is, plain and simply, one of the most powerful books I have
ever read. One's entire life can change because of what is found here.
And all given with such love! This book is a Life Treasure."*
— **Neale Donald Walsch**, the author of *Conversations with God*

*"I've been a huge fan of the teachings of Abraham for
ten years. They've helped me and my family tremendously."*
— **Christiane Northrup, M.D.**, the author of
Women's Bodies, Women's Wisdom

"One of the most valuable things about **Ask and It Is Given**
*is that Abraham gives us 22 different powerful processes to achieve
our goals. No matter where we are, there's a process that can make
our lives better. I love this book, and I love Esther and Jerry Hicks!"*
— **Louise L. Hay**, the author of *You Can Heal Your Life*

*"This is a great book! My wife and I have enjoyed these profound
and extremely practical Abraham teachings for several years. We
trust that you will benefit as well. We recommend it to all our friends!"*
— **John Gray, Ph.D.**, the author of
Men Are from Mars, Women Are from Venus

*". . . a publishing milestone. . . . you'll be fortunate to tap in to the
thinking of those who are permanently connected to Source Energy.
Moreover, these voices of Spirit speak in a language you'll understand
and be able to instantly translate into action. They offer you no less
than a blueprint for understanding and implementing your own destiny."*
— **Dr. Wayne W. Dyer**, the author of *The Power of Intention*

Ask

and It Is

Given

Also by Esther and Jerry Hicks
(The Teachings of Abraham)

Card Deck, Calendar, and Books

*The Amazing Power of Deliberate Intent (also in Spanish)

*The Teachings of Abraham Well-Being Cards

The Science of Deliberate Creation Daily Planning
Calendar/Workbook

A New Beginning I: Handbook for Joyous Survival

A New Beginning II: A Personal Handbook to Enhance Your
Life, Liberty, and Pursuit of Happiness

*Sara, Book 1: The Foreverness of Friends of a Feather

*Sara, Book 2: Sara & Seth: Solomon's Fine Featherless Friends

*Sara, Book 3: A Talking Bird Is Worth a Thousand Words

Audiocassettes and CDs

*Introduction to Abraham

Abraham-Hicks Starter Set

Abraham's Greatest Hits

Special Subjects Vol. I & II

A New Adventure (Music)

Videocassettes

The Art of Allowing

The Science of Deliberate Creation

Relationships & Co-creation

Health & Well-Being

Money & Manifestation

Death & Life

Paranormal Concepts

*Available from Hay House

ها ها ها

Please visit Hay House USA: www.hayhouse.com®
Hay House Australia: www.hayhouse.com.au
Hay House UK: www.hayhouse.co.uk
Hay House South Africa: orders@psdprom.co.za
Hay House India: www.hayhouse.co.in

Ask
and It Is
Given

Learning to Manifest Your Desires

Esther and Jerry Hicks

(The Teachings of Abraham)

HAY HOUSE, INC.
Carlsbad, California
London • Sydney • Johannesburg
Vancouver • Hong Kong • New Delhi

Published and distributed in the United States by: Hay House, Inc.: www.hay house.com • *Published and distributed in Australia by:* Hay House Australia Pty. Ltd.: www.hayhouse.com.au • *Published and distributed in the United Kingdom by:* Hay House UK, Ltd.: www.hayhouse.co.uk • *Published and distributed in the Republic of South Africa by:* Hay House SA (Pty), Ltd.: orders@psdprom.co.za *Distributed in Canada by:* Raincoast: www.raincoast.com • *Published in India by:* Hay House Publishers India: www.hayhouse.co.in

Editorial supervision: Jill Kramer   *Design:* Amy Gingery

Library of Congress Cataloging-in-Publication Data

Abraham (Spirit)
 Ask and it is given : learning to manifest your desires / [channelled by] Esther and Jerry Hicks.
  p. cm.
 ISBN 1-4019-0459-9 (trade pbk.) • 1-4019-0799-7 (hardcover)
 1. Spirit writings. I. Hicks, Esther. II. Hicks, Jerry. III. Title.
 BF1301.A17 2004
 133.9'3—dc22

                    2004006622

Hardcover ISBN 13: 978-1-4019-0799-0
Hardcover ISBN 10: 1-4019-0799-7
Tradepaper ISBN 13: 978-1-4019-0459-3
Tradepaper ISBN 10: 1-4019-0459-9

10 09 08 07   27 26 25 24
1st printing, September 2004
24th printing, March 2007

Printed in the United States of America

ல. ல. ல

This book is dedicated to all of you who, in your desire for
enlightenment and well-being, have asked the questions this
book has answered, and to three delightful children of our
children, who are examples of what the book teaches:
Laurel (5); Kevin (3); and Kate (2), who are not yet asking
because they have not yet forgotten.

And these teachings are especially dedicated to Louise Hay,
whose desire to ask and learn—and disseminate around
this planet—the principles of Well-Being, has led her to
ask us to create this comprehensive book of the
teachings of Abraham.

ல. ல. ல

Contents

PART I: Things That We Know, That You May Have Forgotten, Which Are Important for You to Remember

* You Only Hear What You Are Ready to Hear

* You Said, "I Will Live in Joy!"
* We Know Who You Are
* There Is Nothing That You Cannot Be, Do, or Have

* The Basis of Your Life Is Absolute Freedom
* No One Else Can Create in Your Experience
* You Are Eternal Beings in Physical Form

* Well-Being Is Lined Up Outside Your Door
* You Are a Physical Extension of Source Energy
* The Evolutionary Value of Your Personal Preferences

* A Consistent Formula Gives You Consistent Results
* You Are a Vibrational Being in a Vibrational Environment
* Your Emotions As Vibrational Interpreters

Foreword

by Dr. Wayne W. Dyer, the best-selling author of *The Power of Intention*

The book you're holding in your hands at this moment contains some of the most powerful teachings available to you on our planet today. I've been profoundly touched and influenced by the messages that Abraham offers here in this book, and through the tapes that Esther and Jerry have been providing over the past 18 years. In fact, I'm deeply honored that Abraham has asked me to provide a brief Foreword to this book, which I consider to be a publishing milestone. It is unique in all of publishing—you'll be fortunate to tap in to the thinking of those who are permanently connected to Source Energy. Moreover, these voices of Spirit speak in a language you'll understand and be able to instantly translate into action. They offer you no less than a blueprint for understanding and implementing your own destiny.

My first thought is that if you're not yet ready to read and apply this great wisdom, then I urge you to simply carry this book with you for a few weeks. Allow the energy that it contains to permeate through any resistance that your body/mind might offer, and let it resonate with that inner place that is formless and boundaryless—this is what is often called your *soul,* but Abraham would call it your *vibrational connection to your Source.*

This is a universe of vibration. As Einstein once observed, "Nothing happens until something moves"—that is, everything vibrates to a particular measurable frequency. Break the solid world down to smaller and tinier components and you see that what appears to be solid is a dance—a dance of particles and empty spaces. Go to the tiniest of these quantum particles, and you discover that it emanated from a source that vibrates so fast that it defies the world of beginnings and endings. This highest/fastest energy is called Source Energy. You and everyone and everything originated in this vibration and then moved into the world of things, bodies, minds, and egos. It was in the leaving of this Source Energy in our body/minds that we took on our entire world of problems, illnesses, scarcities, and fears.

The teachings of Abraham, essentially, are focused on helping you to return, in all respects, to that Source from which all things originate and all return to as well. This Source Energy has a look and a feel to it that I've touched upon in my book *The Power of Intention*. Abraham, however, can offer this enlightening wisdom to you by having the benefit of being 100 percent connected to that Source and never ever doubting that connection—it's evident in every paragraph of this book. That's why I call this a publishing milestone.

You're in direct, conscious contact with a cadre of honest, no-nonsense beings who have only your well-being in mind. They'll remind you that you came from a Source of well-being and that you can either summon that higher vibrational energy to yourself and allow it to flow unimpeded in every aspect of your life, or you can resist it, and by doing so stay disconnected from that which is all-providing and all-loving.

The message here is quite startling and yet oh-so-simple—you came from a Source of love and well-being. When you're matched up to that energy of peace and love, you then regain the power of your Source—that being the power to manifest your desires, to summon well-being, to attract abundance where scarcity previously resided, and to access Divine guidance in the form of the right people and the precisely correct circumstances. This is what your

Source does, and since you emanated from that Source, you can and will do the same.

I've spent a full day with Abraham in person, I've dined with Esther and Jerry, and I've listened to hundreds of Abraham's recordings, so you can take it from me firsthand—you're about to embark on a life-changing journey offered to you by two of the most authentic and spiritually pure people I've ever encountered. Jerry and Esther Hicks are as much in awe of their role in bringing these teachings to you as I am in writing this Foreword for Abraham.

I encourage you to read these words carefully and apply them instantly. They summarize an observation I've offered for many years now: "When you change the way you look at things, the things you look at change." You're about to see and experience a whole new world changing right before your eyes. This is the world created by a Source Energy that wants you to reconnect to it and live a life of joyful well-being.

Thank you, Abraham, for allowing me to say a few words in this precious, precious book.

I love you—ALL OF YOU.

— **Wayne**

Preface

by Jerry Hicks

Sunlight is beginning to spill across the Malibu coastline as I begin this Preface. And the deep indigo tint of the Pacific Ocean at this time of the morning seems to match the depth of pleasure I'm feeling as I'm imagining the value you're about to receive from the revelations within this book.

Ask and It Is Given is certainly a book about our "asking" being answered by All-That-Is. But it's primarily about *how* whatever we're asking for is being given to us—and it's also the first book to ever, in such clear terminology, give us the simple practical formula for *how* to ask for, and then *how* to receive, whatever we want to be, do, or have.

Decades ago, while searching for plausible answers to my never-ending quest to know what "It" is all about, I discovered the word *ineffable* (meaning "incapable of being expressed in words"). *Ineffable* coincided with a conclusion I'd formed relative to It. I had decided that the closer we get to knowing the "Non-Physical," the fewer words we have for clearly expressing It. And so, any state of complete knowing would also, therefore, be a state of ineffability. In other words, at this point in our time-space reality the Non-Physical cannot be clearly expressed with physical words.

Throughout physical history, we've evolved to, through, and into billions of philosophies, religions, opinions, and beliefs. Yet, with the billions upon billions of thinkers thinking, concluding, and passing their beliefs on to the next generations, we have not—at least not in any words we can agree on—found physical words to express the Non-Physical.

Recorded history has retained some form of documentation of but a few of the many Beings who have consciously communicated with Non-Physical Intelligence. Some were revered, while some were damned by others. Most, however, who have been conscious of personal communication with the Non-Physical (perhaps in fear of being damned or even institutionalized) have decided to go and tell no one about their revelations.

Moses, Jesus, Muhammad, Joan of Arc, Joseph Smith . . . to name but a few of those better known to the English-speaking world . . . were each outspoken recipients of Non-Physical Intelligence, most of whom met with quite untimely and horrible physical ends. And so, although each of us is directly receiving some form of Non-Physical guidance, only a few receive blocks of Non-Physical thought that are clear enough to be translated into our physical words—and of those few, fewer still are willing to disclose their experience to others.

I remind you of this information as a preface to what you're about to read, for my wife, Esther, is one of those rare persons who can, at will, relax her conscious mind enough to allow the reception of Non-Physical answers to whatever is asked. Somehow Esther receives blocks of thought (not words) and, just as a Spanish-English translator would hear a thought projected in Spanish words and then translate the thought (not the actual words) into English words, Esther instantly translates the Non-Physical thought into its closest physical (English) word equivalent.

Please note that since there aren't always physical English words to perfectly express the Non-Physical thought that Esther receives, she sometimes forms new combinations of words, as well as using standard words in new ways (for example, capitalizing them when normally they would not be) in order to express new ways of looking at life. And for that reason, we've created a brief Glossary at the back of this book in order to clarify our uncommon usage of some common words. In other words, there is the common term, *well-being,* meaning the state of being happy, healthy, or prosperous. But the basis of Abraham's uncommon philosophy is translated into English as *Well-Being.* It's about the broader Universal, Non-Physical Well-Being that flows naturally to all of us unless we do something to pinch it off. (Also, within the text, we will initially put in quotation marks any coined words that you wouldn't find in any dictionary but whose meanings are obvious—such as "overwhelment" or "endedness.")

Since 1986, Esther and I have traveled to about 50 cities a year presenting workshops, and any of the attendees can discuss or pose questions on whatever subject they want to talk about; no subjects are off-limits. People have come by the thousands: from different ethnic groups, from different walks of life, from different philosophical backgrounds . . . all wanting to improve life in some way, either directly for themselves, or indirectly by assisting others. And to those thousands who have asked for more, the answers have been given—through Esther Hicks, from Non-Physical Intelligence.

And so, in response to the asking by those, like you, who want to know more, this philosophy of Well-Being has evolved into the creation of this book.

At the heart of these teachings is the most powerful Law of the Universe, the *Law of Attraction.* Over the past decade, we've published much of Abraham's teachings in our quarterly journal, *The Science of Deliberate Creation,* which has highlighted the newest perspectives gleaned from questions posed by the attendees of our *Art of Allowing Workshops.* As such, this philosophy is continually evolving as more of you bring to our attention your newest questions and perspectives.

This book offers you a hands-on course in spiritual practicality. It's a how-to book in the broadest sense of the term—that is, how to be, do, or have anything that pleases you. This book also teaches you how *not* to be, do, or have anything that displeases you.

— Jerry

᠅ ᠅ ᠅ ᠅ ᠅ ᠅

An Introduction
to Abraham

by Esther Hicks

"

S

he speaks with spirits!" our friends said. "She'll be here next week, and you can make an appointment with her and ask her anything you like!"

That's about the last thing on this earth that I would ever want to do, I thought, but at the same time I heard Jerry, my husband, saying, "We really would like to make an appointment. How do we go about doing that?"

ᐤ ᐤ ᐤ

That was 1984, and in the four years that we'd been married, we'd never had an argument or even exchanged cross words. We were two joyous people, living happily ever after with each other, and compatible on nearly every subject that came up. The only discomfort that I ever felt was when Jerry would entertain friends with one of his stories from 20 years earlier, relating his experiences with the Ouija board. If we were at a restaurant or some other public place when I sensed one of those stories coming on, I would politely (or sometimes not so politely), excuse myself and retreat to the ladies' room, sit in the bar, or take a walk to the car until I believed that sufficient time had passed and the account would be over. Happily, Jerry eventually stopped telling those stories when I was around.

I wasn't what you'd call a religious girl, but I'd attended enough Sunday-School classes to develop a very strong fear of evil and the devil. Thinking back, I'm not really sure if our Sunday-School teachers had actually devoted a greater proportion of our classes to teaching us to fear the devil or if that's simply what stood out in my mind. But that is, for the most part, what I remember from those years.

So, as I'd been taught, I carefully avoided anything that could possibly have any connection to the devil. One time when I was a young woman, I was sitting in a drive-in theater and happened to look out the back window of the car at the other movie screen and saw a horrible scene from *The Exorcist* (a movie that I'd purposely avoided seeing), and what I saw, without hearing the sound, affected me so strongly that I had nightmares for weeks.

☙ ☙ ☙

"Her name is Sheila," our friend told Jerry. "I'll make the appointment for you and let you know."

Jerry spent the next few days writing down his questions. He said he had some that he'd saved up since he was a small child. I didn't make a list. Instead, I struggled with the idea of going at all.

As we pulled into the driveway of a beautiful house in the heart of Phoenix, Arizona, I remember thinking, *What am I getting myself into?* We walked up to the front door, and a very nice woman greeted us and showed us into a lovely living room where we could wait for our scheduled appointment.

The house was large, simply but beautifully furnished, and very quiet. I remember feeling a sort of reverence, like being in a church.

Then a big door opened, and two pretty women dressed in fresh, brightly colored cotton blouses and skirts entered the room. Apparently we were the first appointment after lunch; both women looked happy and refreshed. I felt myself relax a little bit. Maybe this wasn't going to be so weird after all.

Soon we were invited into a lovely bedroom where three chairs were situated near the foot of the bed. Sheila was sitting on the edge of the bed, and her assistant sat in one of the chairs with a small tape recorder on the table beside her. Jerry and I sat in the other two chairs, and I braced myself for whatever was about to happen.

The assistant explained that Sheila was going to relax and release her consciousness, and then Theo, a Non-Physical entity, would address us. When that happened, we'd be free to talk about anything we desired.

Sheila lay across the end of the bed, only a few feet from where we were seated, and breathed deeply. Soon, an unusual-sounding voice abruptly said, "It is the beginning, is it not? You have questions?"

I looked at Jerry, hoping that he was ready to start, because I knew that I was *not* ready to talk with whoever was now speaking to us. Jerry leaned forward; he was eager to ask his first question.

I relaxed as Theo's words slowly came out of Sheila's mouth. And while I knew that it was Sheila's voice we were hearing, I somehow also knew that something far different from Sheila was the source of these marvelous answers.

Jerry said he'd been saving his questions up since he was five years old, and he asked them as rapidly as he could. Our 30 minutes passed so quickly, but during that time, somehow, without my speaking a word, my fear of this strange experience lifted, and I was filled with a feeling of well-being that surpassed anything that I'd ever felt before.

Once back inside our car, I told Jerry, "I'd really like to come back tomorrow. There are some things *I* would now like to ask." Jerry was delighted to make another appointment because he had more questions on his list as well.

About halfway through our allotted time on the following day, Jerry reluctantly relinquished the remaining minutes to me, and I asked Theo, "How can we more effectively achieve our goals?"

The answer came back: "Meditation and affirmations."

The idea of meditation didn't appeal to me at all, and I wasn't aware of anyone who practiced it. In fact, when I thought of the word, it brought to mind people lying on beds of nails, walking on hot coals, standing on one foot for years, or begging for donations at the airport. So I asked, "What do you mean by *meditation?*"

The answer was short, and the words felt good as I heard them: "Sit in a quiet room. Wear comfortable clothing, and focus on your breathing. As your mind wanders, and it will, release the thought and focus upon your breathing. It would be good for you to do it together. It will be more powerful."

"Could you give us an affirmation that would be of value for us to use?" we asked.

"*I* [say your name] *see and draw to me, through divine love, those Beings who seek enlightenment through my process. The sharing will elevate us both now.*"

As the words flowed from Sheila/Theo, I felt them penetrate to the core of my being. A feeling of love flowed to me and through me like nothing I'd ever felt before. My fear was gone. Jerry and I both felt wonderful.

"Should we bring my daughter, Tracy, to meet you?" I asked.

"If it is her asking, but it is not necessary, for you, too (Jerry and Esther), are channels."

That statement made no sense to me at all. I couldn't believe that I could be this old (in my 30s), and not already know something like that, if it were true.

The tape recorder clicked off, and we both felt mild disappointment that our extraordinary experience was finished. Sheila's assistant asked us if we had one last question. "Would you like to know the name of your spiritual guide?" she asked.

I would have never asked that, for I had never heard the term *spiritual guide,* but it sounded like a good question. I liked the idea of guardian angels. So I said, "Yes, please, could you tell me the name of my spiritual guide?"

Theo said, "We are told it will be given to you directly. You will have a clairaudient experience, and you will know."

What is a clairaudient experience? I wondered, but before I could ask my question, Theo said with a tone of finality, "God's love unto you!" and Sheila opened her eyes and sat up. Our extraordinary conversation with Theo had ended.

After Jerry and I left the house, we drove to a lookout point on the side of one of the Phoenix mountains and leaned against the car, staring off into the distance watching the sunset. We had no idea of the transformation that had taken place within us that day. We only knew that we felt wonderful.

When we returned home, I had two powerful new intentions: I was going to meditate, whatever in the world *that* meant, and I was going to find out the name of my spiritual guide.

So, we changed into our robes, closed the curtains in the living room, and sat in two large wingback chairs, with an étagère between us. We'd been encouraged to do this together, but it felt odd, and the étagère helped to mask the strangeness for some reason.

I remembered Theo's instructions: *Sit in a quiet room, wear comfortable clothing, and focus on your breathing.* So we set a timer for 15 minutes, and I closed my eyes and began to breathe consciously. In my mind, I asked the question: *Who is my spiritual guide?* and then I counted my breath, in and out, in and out. Right away, my entire body felt numb. I couldn't distinguish my nose from my toes. It was a strange but comforting sensation, and I enjoyed it. It felt as if my body was slowly spinning even though I knew that I was sitting in a chair. The timer rang and startled us, and I said, "Let's do it again."

Once more, I closed my eyes, counted my breaths, and felt numb from head to toe. Again, the timer rang and startled us. "Let's do it again," I said.

So we set the timer for another 15 minutes, and again I felt numbness overtake my entire body. But this time, something, or someone, began to "breathe my body." From my vantage point, it felt like rapturous love, moving from deep inside my body outward. What a glorious sensation! Jerry heard my soft sounds of pleasure and later said that, to him, I appeared to be writhing in ecstasy.

When the timer went off and I came out of the meditation, my teeth chattered like never before. *Buzzed* would be a better word for the experience. For nearly an hour, my teeth buzzed as I tried to relax back into my normal state of awareness.

At that time, I didn't realize what had happened, but I know now that I'd experienced my first contact with Abraham. While I didn't know *what* had happened, I did know that whatever it was—*it was good!* And I wanted it to happen again.

So Jerry and I made the decision to meditate every day for 15 minutes. I don't think we missed a day in the next nine months. I felt the numbness, or feeling of detachment, each time, but nothing else extraordinary happened during our meditations. And then, right before Thanksgiving of 1985, while meditating, my head began to move gently from side to side. For the next few days, during meditation, my head would move in that gentle flowing motion. It was a lovely sensation that sort of felt like flying. And then, on about the third day of this new movement, during meditation, I realized that my head was not randomly moving about, but it was as if my nose was spelling letters in the air. "M-N-O-P" is what I realized it was.

"Jerry," I shouted, "I'm spelling letters with my nose!" And with those words, the rapturous feelings returned. Goose bumps covered my body from head to toe as this Non-Physical Energy rippled through my body.

Jerry quickly took out his notebook and began writing down the letters, as my nose wrote them in the air: "I AM ABRAHAM. I AM YOUR SPIRITUAL GUIDE."

Abraham has since explained to us that there are many gathered there with "them." They refer to themselves in the plural because they're a Collective Consciousness. They've explained that, in the beginning, the words "I am Abraham" were spoken through me only because my expectation for my spiritual guide was singular, but that there are *many* there with them, speaking, in a sense of the word, with one voice, or a consensus of thought.

To quote Abraham: *Abraham is not a singular consciousness as you feel that you are in your singular bodies. Abraham is a Collective Consciousness. There is a Non-Physical Stream of Consciousness, and as one of you asks a question, there are many, many points of consciousness that are funneling through what feels to be the one perspective (because there is, in this case, one human, Esther, who is interpreting or articulating it), so it appears singular to you. We are multidimensional and multifaceted and certainly multi-consciousness.*

Abraham has since explained that they're not whispering words into my ears, which I am then repeating for others, but instead they're offering blocks of thoughts, like radio signals, which I'm receiving at some unconscious level. I then translate those blocks of thoughts into the physical word equivalent. I "hear" the words as they're spoken through me, but during the translation process itself, I have no awareness of what is coming, or time for recollection of what has already come.

Abraham explained that they had been offering these blocks of thoughts to me for quite some time, but I was so strictly trying to follow Theo's instructions—which said, "When your mind wanders, and it will, release the thoughts and focus on your breathing"—that whenever one of these thoughts would begin, I would release it as quickly as possible and focus back upon my breathing. I guess the only way they could get through to me was to spell letters in the air with my nose. Abraham says that those wonderful sensations that rippled through my body when I realized that I was spelling words was the joy they felt upon my recognition of our conscious connection.

Our communication process evolved rapidly over the next few weeks. The spelling of letters in the air with my nose was a very slow process, but Jerry was so excited about this clear and viable source of information that he would often wake me up in the middle of the night to ask Abraham questions.

But then, one night I felt a very strong sensation moving through my arms, hands, and fingers, and my hand began thumping on Jerry's chest as we lay in bed together watching television. As my hand continued to thump, I felt a very strong impulse to go to my IBM Selectric typewriter, and as I put my fingers on the keyboard, my hands began moving quickly up and down the keys as if someone was quickly discovering what this typewriter was all about and where the specific letters were placed. And then my hands began to type: Every letter, every number, again and again. And then the words began to take form on the paper: *I am Abraham. I am your spiritual guide. I am here to work with you. I love you. We will write a book together.*

We discovered that I could put my hands on the keyboard and then relax, much in the same way that I did during meditation, and that Abraham (whom we will now refer to as "they" from here on in) would then answer questions about anything that Jerry would ask. It was an amazing experience. They were so intelligent, so loving, and so available! Anytime, day or night, they were there to talk to us about anything that we wanted to discuss.

Then, one afternoon, while driving on a Phoenix freeway, I felt a sensation in my mouth, chin, and neck, similar to the familiar feeling of getting ready to yawn. It was a very strong impulse, so strong I couldn't stifle it. We were rounding a corner between two big trucks, and both of them seemed to be crossing the line into our lane at the same time, and I thought for a moment that they were going to drive right over the top of us. And in that very moment, the first words that Abraham spoke through my mouth burst out, "Take the next exit!"

We exited the freeway and parked in a lot underneath an overpass, and Jerry and Abraham visited for hours. My eyes were closed tightly, and my head moved up and down rhythmically as Abraham answered Jerry's stream of questions.

ତ ତ ତ

How is it that this wonderful thing has happened to me? At times, as I think about it, I can hardly believe that it's true. It seems like the kind of thing that fairy tales are made of—almost like making a wish as you rub the magic lantern. At other times, it seems like the most natural, logical experience in the world.

Sometimes I can barely remember what life was like before Abraham came into our lives. I have, with few exceptions, always been what most would call a happy person. I had a wonderful childhood, with no major traumas, and along with two other sisters, I was born to kind and loving parents. As I mentioned, Jerry and I had been blissfully married for about four years, and I was, in every sense, living happily ever after. I wouldn't have described myself as someone filled with unanswered questions. In fact, I really wasn't asking many questions at all, and I hadn't formulated any strong opinions about much of anything.

Jerry, on the other hand, was filled with passionate questions. He was a voracious reader, always looking for tools and techniques that he could pass along to others to help them live more joyous lives. To this day, I've never known anyone who wants more to help others live successful lives.

Abraham has explained that the reason why Jerry and I are the perfect combination for doing this work together is because Jerry's powerful desire summoned Abraham, while my absence of opinions or angst made me a good receiver for the information that Jerry was summoning.

Jerry was so enthusiastic, even in his first interactions with Abraham, because he understood the depth of their wisdom and the clarity of their offering. And throughout all these years, his enthusiasm for Abraham's message hasn't waned in the least. No one in the room ever enjoys what Abraham has to say more than Jerry.

In the beginning of our interactions with Abraham, we didn't really understand what was happening, and we had no real way of knowing whom Jerry was talking with, but it was still thrilling and amazing and wonderful—and weird. It seemed so strange that I was certain that most people I knew wouldn't understand; they probably wouldn't even *want* to understand. As a result, I made Jerry promise that he would tell no one about our amazing secret.

I guess it's now obvious that Jerry didn't keep that promise, but I'm not sorry about that. There's nothing that either of us would rather do than be in a room filled with people who have things they'd like to discuss with Abraham. What we hear most often, from people who meet Abraham through our books, videos, audio series, workshops, or Website, is: "Thank you for helping me remember what I've somehow always known," and "This has helped me tie together all the pieces of truth that I've found along the way. This has helped me make sense of everything!"

Abraham doesn't seem interested in forecasting our future, as a fortune-teller might, although I believe that they always know what our future holds, but instead they're teachers who guide us from wherever we are to wherever we want to be. They've explained to us that it's not their work to decide what we should want, but it *is* their work to assist us in achieving whatever we desire. In Abraham's words: *Abraham is not about guiding anyone toward or away from anything. We want you to make all your decisions about your desires. Our only desire for you is that you discover the way to <u>achieve</u> your desires.*

My favorite thing that I've ever heard spoken about Abraham came to us from a teenage boy who had just listened to a recording in which Abraham was addressing some questions that teens had been asking. The boy said, "At first, I didn't believe that Esther was really speaking for Abraham. But when I heard the tape, and heard Abraham's answers to these questions, I then knew that Abraham was real, because there was no judgment. I don't believe that any person could be so wise, so fair, and without judgment."

For me, this journey with Abraham has been more wonderful than I can find words to explain. I adore the sense of Well-Being I've achieved from what I've learned from them. I love how their gentle guidance always leaves me with a feeling of self-empowerment. I love seeing the lives of so many of our dear friends (and new friends), improving through the application of what Abraham has taught them. I love having these brilliant and loving Beings pop into my head whenever I ask, always ready and willing to assist in our understanding of something.

(As an aside, several years after our meeting with Sheila and Theo, Jerry looked up the name *Theo* in our dictionary. "The meaning of *Theo*," he joyously announced to me, "is *God*"! How perfect that is! I smile as I reflect back on that wonderful day, which was such an extraordinary turning point for us. There I was, worried about interacting with evil, when I was, in fact, on my way to having a conversation with God!)

In the early days of our work with Abraham, our audiences wanted us to explain our relationship with Abraham. "How did your meeting occur? How do you maintain your relationship? Why did they choose you? What is it like to be the speaker of such profound wisdom?" So, Jerry and I would spend a few minutes at the beginning of every speaking engagement or radio or television interview trying our best to satisfy those questions. But I always felt impatient with that part of our presentation. I just wanted to relax and allow Abraham's Consciousness to begin flowing, and to get on with what Jerry and I felt was the true reason we were standing there to begin with.

Eventually, we created a free *Introduction to Abraham* recording that people could listen to at their leisure, which explains the details of how our Abraham experience began and evolved. (We've now posted that 74-minute *Introduction* as a free download at **www.abraham-hicks.com**, our interactive Website to explain who we are and what we were doing before meeting Abraham.) We both very much enjoy our part in the process of getting Abraham's message into a format that can be heard and utilized by others, but to us, Abraham's message has always felt like the main event.

This morning, Abraham said to me, *Esther, we are aware of the questions that are radiating from the mass consciousness of your planet, and here, through you, we will joyously offer the answers. Relax and enjoy the delicious unfolding of this book.*

So I'm going to relax here, and allow Abraham to immediately begin writing this book to you. I imagine that they will explain to you, from their perspective, who they are, but more important, I believe that they will help you come to understand who *you* are. It is my desire that your meeting with Abraham will be as meaningful for you as it continues to be for us.

— With love, Esther

PART 1

Things That We Know,
That You May Have Forgotten,
Which Are Important for You
to Remember

Chapter 1

The Power of Feeling Good Now

We are called Abraham, and we are speaking to you from the Non-Physical dimension. Of course, you must understand that you also have come forth from the Non-Physical dimension, so we are not so different from one another. Your physical world has come forth from the projection of the Non-Physical. In fact, you and your physical world are extensions of the Non-Physical Source Energy.

In this Non-Physical realm, we do not use words, for we do not require language. We also do not have tongues with which to speak or ears with which to hear, although we do communicate perfectly with one another. Our Non-Physical language is one of vibration, and our Non-Physical communities, or families, are those of intention. In other words, we radiate that which we are, vibrationally, and others of like intent assemble. That is also true of your physical world, although most of you have forgotten that this is so.

Abraham is a family of Non-Physical Beings naturally assembled by our powerful intention to remind you, our physical extensions, of the Laws of the Universe that govern all things. It is our intention to help you remember that you are extensions of Source

Energy; that you are blessed, loved Beings; and that you have come forth into this physical time-space-reality to joyously create.

All who are physically focused have Non-Physical counterparts. There is no exception to that. All who are physically focused have access to the broader perspective of that which is Non-Physical. There is no exception to that. But most physical Beings have become so distracted by the physical nature of your planet that you have developed strong patterns of resistance that thwart your clear connection to your own Source. It is our intention to help those who are asking to remember that connection.

While all physical humans have access to the clear communication from the Non-Physical, most are not consciously aware of it. And often, even when you are aware that it is possible, you hold habits of thought that act as resistance hindering your ability to consciously interact.

However, on occasion, a clear channel of communication opens and we are able to convey our understanding, vibrationally, to someone who can clearly receive it and translate it. And that is what is happening here through Esther. We offer our knowing, vibrationally, in a way that is similar to what you understand as radio signals, and Esther receives those vibrations and translates them into the physical word equivalent. There are not, however, adequate physical words to convey our satisfaction and joy in being able to offer our knowing to you, in this way, at this time.

It is our powerful desire that you be pleased with where you are right now, in this moment—no matter where you are. We understand how strange these words must sound to you if you are standing in a place that seems far from where you want to be. But it is our absolute promise to you that when you understand the power of feeling good now, no matter what, you will hold the key to the achievement of any state of being, any state of health, any state of wealth, or any state of anything that you desire.

These pages are specifically written to give you a better understanding of yourself and of everyone else around you, and you may find some of that helpful, but words really do not teach. Your true knowledge comes from your own life experience. And while you will be a constant gatherer of experience and knowledge, your life is not only about that—it is about fulfillment, satisfaction, and joy. Your life is about the continuing expression of who you truly are.

You Only Hear What You Are Ready to Hear

We are talking to you at many levels of your awareness, all at the same time, but you will only receive whatever you are now ready to receive. Everyone will not get the same thing from this book, but every reading of this book will net you something more. This is a book that will be read many times by those who understand its power. It is a book that will help physical Beings understand their relationship to GOD and to ALL-THAT-THEY-REALLY-ARE.

This is a book that will help you understand who you really are, who you have been, where you are going, and all that you continue to be.

This book will help you understand that you never, ever get it done. It will help you understand your relationship with your history and with your future—but, most important, it will awaken within you your awareness of the potency of your powerful *now*.

You will learn how you are the creator of your own experience and why all of your power is in your *now*. And ultimately this book will lead you to an understanding of your *Emotional Guidance System* and to an understanding of your *vibrational set-point*.

Here you will find a series of processes that will assist you in reconnecting with the "Non-Physical" part of yourself, processes that will help you in achieving anything you desire. And as you apply these processes, and as your memory awakens to the powerful Laws of the Universe—*your naturally joyful zest for life will return*.

❧ ❧ ❧ ❦ ❦ ❦

Chapter 2

We Are Keeping Our Promise to You— We Are Reminding You of Who You Are

*D*o you know what you want? Do you know that you are the creator of your own experience? Are you enjoying the evolution of your desire? Do you feel the freshness of a new desire pulsing within you?

If you are among the rare humans who answered, "Yes, I'm enjoying the evolution of my desire. I feel wonderful as I stand in this place where many things that I desire have not yet come to me," then you understand who you are and what this physical life experience is really all about.

But if you are, as most humans are, feeling unhappy about your unfulfilled desires; if you have a desire for more money, but you find yourself in a continual state of shortage; if you are not satisfied with your job situation, but you feel stuck and cannot see any way of improving it; if your relationships are not satisfying, or if the dream relationship that you have desired for as long as you can remember continues to be just out of reach; if your body does not feel or look the way you would like . . . then there are some very important and rather easy-to-understand things that we would like to convey to you here.

We want to give you this information because we want you to find your way to all things that you desire. But that is really only a small part of our reason, for we understand that even when you have achieved everything on your current list of things that you desire, there will be another list, even longer and more expansive, to take its place. So, this book is not being written to assist you in getting everything you want checked off your list, for we understand the impossible nature of that endeavor.

We write this book to reawaken within you your memory of the power and inevitable success that pulses through the core of that which you really are. We write this book to assist you in returning you to your place of optimism, positive expectation, and expanding joy; and to remind you that there is nothing that you cannot be, do, or have. We write this book because we promised you we would. And now, as you hold this book in your hands, you are completing a promise you made as well.

You Said, "I Will Live in Joy!"

You said, *"I will go forth into the physical time-space-reality among other Beings, and I will assume an identity with a clear and specific perspective. I will learn to see myself from that point of view, and I will enjoy being seen as that point of view."*

You said, *"I will observe what surrounds me, and my response to what I observe will cause my own valuable personal preferences to be born."*

You said, *"I will know the value of my preferences. I will know the value of my perspective."*

And then you said (and this is the most important part of all), *"I will always feel the power and value of my own personal perspective, for the 'Non-Physical Energy' that creates worlds will flow through my decisions, my intentions and my every thought, for the creation of that which I set into motion from my perspective."*

You knew then, before your physical birth, that you were "Source Energy" specifically focused in this physical body, and you knew that the physical person you would become could never be separated from that which you came from. You understood then, your eternal connection to that Source Energy.

You said, *"I will love pouring myself into this physical body, into physical time-space-reality, for that environment will cause me to focus the powerful Energy that is me into something more specific. And in the specifics of that focus, there will be powerful motion forward—and joy."*

We Know Who You Are

So, you came forth into this wonderful body, remembering the joyous, powerful nature that is you, knowing that you would always remember the splendor of the Source from which you came, and knowing that you could never lose your connection to that Source.

So now, here we are, helping you remember that no matter how you may feel right now, you cannot lose your connection to that Source.

We are here to help you remember the powerful nature that is you, and to assist you in returning to that confident, joyful, always-looking-for-something-else-wonderful-to-turn-your-attention-to person that is you.

Since we know who you are, we will easily help you remember who you are.

Since we are where you came from, we will easily remind you of where *you* have come from.

Since we know what you desire, we will easily guide you to help yourself to that which you desire.

There Is Nothing That You Cannot Be, Do, or Have

We want you to remember that there is nothing that you cannot be, do, or have, and we want to assist you in achieving that. But we love where you are right now, even if you do not, because we understand how joyful the journey (from where you are to where you want to go) will be.

We want to help you leave behind any perceptions you have picked up along your physical trail that are thwarting your joy and power, and we want to help you reactivate the powerful knowing that pulses within the very core of that which you are.

So relax, and enjoy this easy-paced journey to rediscovering who you really are. It is our desire that by the time you reach the end of this book, you will know yourself as we know you, that you will love yourself as we love you, and that you will be enjoying your life as we are enjoying your life.

Chapter 3

You Do Create Your Own Reality

Not so very long ago, our friends Jerry and Esther were introduced to this phrase: "You are the creator of your own reality." (They had discovered the *Seth* books by Jane Roberts.) For them, it was both an exciting prospect and a troubling one, for, like so many of our physical friends, they did desire creative control of their own experience, but they were plagued with some basic questions: "Is it *really* all right for us to choose the reality that we create? And if it *is* appropriate for us to do so, *how* do we go about doing it?"

The Basis of Your Life Is Absolute Freedom

You were born with an innate knowledge that you do create your own reality. And, in fact, that knowledge is so basic within you that when someone attempts to thwart your own creation, you feel an immediate discord within yourself. You were born knowing that you are the creator of your own reality, and although that desire to do so pulsed within you in a powerful way, when you began to integrate into your society, you began to accept much of the same picture that others held of the way your life should unfold. But still, within you today lives the knowledge that you *are* the creator of your own life experience, that absolute freedom exists as the basis of your true experience, and that ultimately the creation of your life experience is absolutely and only up to you.

You have never enjoyed someone else telling you what to do. You have never enjoyed being dissuaded from your own powerful impulses. But over time, with enough pressure from those who surrounded you who seemed convinced that their practiced way was more valid than your way (and, therefore, ultimately better), you gradually began to release your determination to guide your own life. You often found it easier just to adapt to their ideas of what was best for you rather than trying to figure it out for yourself. But in all this adapting to your society's attempts to make you fit in, and in your own attempt to find less trouble, you have unwittingly relinquished your most basic foundation: your total and absolute freedom to create.

You have not given up this freedom easily, however, and, in fact, you can never truly release it, for it exists as the most basic tenet of your very being. Still, in your attempt to release it for the sake of getting along, or in your hopeless resignation that you have no other choice than to give up your powerful right to choose . . . you have gone crossways to your natural current, and contrary to your very soul.

No One Else Can Create in Your Experience

This book is about your realignment with Source Energy. It is about your reawakening to the clarity, goodness, and power that is really who you are. It is written to assist you in consciously returning to the knowledge that you *are* free and that you always *have been* free—and that you always *will be* free to make your own choices. There is no satisfaction in allowing someone else to attempt to create your reality. In fact, it is not *possible* for anyone else to create your reality.

Once you have realigned with eternal forces and Universal Laws, and with that which is truly the Source of that which you are, then joyous creation, beyond physical description, awaits you, for you *are* the creator of your own experience, and there is such satisfaction in intentionally guiding your own life.

You Are Eternal
Beings in Physical Form

You are eternal Beings who have chosen to participate in this specific physical life experience for many wonderful reasons. And this time-space-reality on Planet Earth serves as a platform in which you are able to focus your perspective for the purpose of specific creation.

You are eternal Consciousness, currently in this wonderful physical body for the thrill and exhilaration of specific focus and creation. The physical being that you define as "you" stands on the Leading Edge of thought, while Consciousness, which is really your Source, pours through you. And in those moments of inexpressible elation, those are the times when you are wide open and truly allowing your Source to express through you.

Sometimes you are fully allowing the true nature of your Being to flow through you, and sometimes you do not allow it to flow. This book is written to help you understand that you have the ability to always allow your true nature to pour through you, and that as you learn to *consciously* allow your full connection with the You that is your Source, your experience will be one of absolute joy. By consciously choosing the direction of your thoughts, you can be in constant connection with Source Energy, with God, with joy, and with all that you consider to be good.

Absolute Well-Being
Is the Basis of Your Universe

Well-Being is the basis of this Universe. Well-Being is the basis of All-That-Is. It flows to you and through you. You have only to allow it. Like the air you breathe, you have only to open, relax, and draw it into your Being.

This book is about <u>consciously</u> allowing your natural connection to the Stream of Well-Being. It is about remembering who you really are so that you can get on with the creation of your life experience in the way you intended before you came forth into this physical body, and into this magnificent Leading-Edge experience . . . where you fully intended to express your freedom in endless, joyous, co-creative ways.

Can you understand how much Well-Being is flowing to you? Do you understand how much orchestration of circumstances and events on your behalf is available to you? Do you understand how adored you are? Do you understand how the creation of this planet, the creation of this Universe, fits together for the perfection of your experience?

Do you understand how beloved you are, how blessed you are, how adored you are, and what an integral part of this creative process you are? We want you to. We want you to begin to understand the blessed nature of your Being, and we want you to begin to look for the evidence of it, because we are showing it to you in every moment that you will allow yourselves to see it: in the lining up of lovers, money, fulfilling experiences, and beautiful things for you to see; in the lining up of circumstances and events; and in the lining up of amazing co-creative experiences where you are rendezvousing with one another for no other reason than for the fantastically important reason of fulfilling, satisfying, and pleasing yourself and giving yourself joy in the moment.

Your motion forward is inevitable; it must be. You cannot help but move forward. But you are not here on a quest to move forward—you are here to experience outrageous joy. That is why you are here.

Chapter 4

How Can I Get There from Here?

Perhaps the question we hear most often from our physical friends is: *Why is it taking me so long to get what I want?*

It is not because you do not want it enough.
It is not because you are not intelligent enough.
It is not because you are not worthy enough.
It is not because fate is against you.
It is not because someone else has already won your prize.

The reason you have not already gotten what you desire is because you are holding yourself in a vibrational holding pattern that does not match the vibration of your desire. That is the only reason—ever! And an important thing for you to now understand is that if you will stop and think about it, or, more important, stop and *feel* about it, you can identify your very discord.

So now, the only thing you need to do is gently and gradually, piece by piece, release your resistant thoughts, which are the only disallowing factors involved. Your increasing relief will be the indicator that you are releasing resistance, just as your feelings of increased tension, anger, frustration, and so on, have been your indicators that you have been adding to your resistance.

Well-Being Is Lined
Up Outside Your Door

We want to remind you of the basic premise that must be understood before any of this will make sense to you: Well-Being flows; Well-Being wants you! Well-Being is lined up outside your door. Everything you have ever desired, whether spoken or unspoken, has been transmitted by you vibrationally. It has been heard and understood by Source and has been answered, and now you are going to *feel* your way into allowing yourself to receive it, one feeling at a time.

You Are a Physical
Extension of Source Energy

You are an extension of Source Energy. You are standing on the Leading Edge of thought. Your time-space-reality was set into motion through the power of thought long before it manifested in the physical form in which you see it now. *Everything in your physical environment was created from Non-Physical perspective by that which you call Source. And just as Source created your world, and you, through the power of focused thought, you are continuing to create your world from your Leading-Edge place in this time-space-reality.*

You and that which you call Source are the same.
You cannot be separated from Source.
Source is never separated from you.
When we think of you, we think of Source.
When we think of Source, we think of you.
Source never offers a thought that causes separation from you.

You cannot offer a thought that would cause total separation (*separation* is actually far too strong of a word), but you can offer thoughts that are different enough in vibrational nature to hinder your natural connection with Source. We refer to that condition as *resistance*.

The only form of resistance, or hindrance of your connection to that which is Source, is offered by you from your physical perspective. Source is always fully available to you, and Well-Being is constantly extended to you, and often you are in the state of *allowing* this Well-Being, but sometimes you are not. *We want to assist you in* <u>*consciously*</u> *allowing your connection, more of the time, to Source.*

As extensions of Non-Physical Energy, you are taking thought beyond that which it has been before—and through contrast, you will come to conclusions or decisions. And once you align with your desire, the Non-Physical Energy that creates worlds will flow through you . . . which means enthusiasm, passion, and triumph. That is your destiny.

From the Non-Physical, you created you; and now from the physical, you continue to create. We all must have objects of attention, desires that are ringing our bells, in order to feel the fullness of who we are flowing through us for the continuation of All-That-Is. That desire is what puts the eternalness in eternity.

The Evolutionary Value of
Your Personal Preferences

Do not underestimate the value of your preferences, for the evolution of your planet depends upon those of you on the Leading Edge of thought continuing to fine-tune your desires. And the contrast, or variety, in which you are standing provides the perfect environment for the formation of your personal preferences. As you are standing in the midst of contrast, new desires are radiating constantly from you in the form of vibrational signals that are received and answered by Source—and in that moment, the Universe is expanding.

This book is not about the expanding Universe, or about Source answering your every request, or about your worthiness—for all of that is a given. This book is about you putting yourself in a vibrational place of receiving all that you are asking for.

The Science of Deliberate Creation

We want to assist you in the deliberate realization of the things that your environment has inspired within you, for we want you to experience the exhilaration of joyously, *consciously,* creating your own reality. You *do* create your own reality. No one else does. And, you create your own reality even if you do not understand that you do so. For that reason, you often create by default. *When you are consciously aware of your own thoughts, and you are deliberately offering them, then you are the <u>deliberate</u> creator of your own reality*—and that is what you intended when you made the decision to come forth into this body.

Your desires and beliefs are just thoughts: "Ask and it is given." You ask through your attention, through your wanting, through your desire—that is the asking (whether you desire it *to* happen, or you desire it *not* to happen, you are asking. . . .). You do not have to use your words. You just have to feel it in your being: *I desire this. I adore this. I appreciate this,* and so on. That desire is the beginning of all attraction.

You never grow tired of expansion or of creation, for there is no ending to the new ideas of desires that flow. With every new idea of something you would like to experience, possess, or know . . . will come its actualization or manifestation—and with that manifestation will also come a new perspective from which you will desire. The contrast, or variety, never ends, so the sprouting forth of new desires will never end, and as that "asking" never ends, the "answering" never ceases to flow. And so, new perspectives will always be yours. New contrasts, and new inspiring desires and perspectives, will be laid out eternally before you.

Once you relax into the idea that you will never cease to be, that new desires will be constantly born within you, that Source will never stop answering your desires, and that your expansion is, therefore, eternal, then you may begin to relax if, in this moment, there is something that you desire that has not yet come to fruition. *It is our desire that you become one who is happy with that which you are and with that which you have—while at the same time being eager for more. That is the optimal creative vantage point: To stand on the brink of what is coming, feeling eager, optimistic anticipation—with no feeling of impatience, doubt, or unworthiness hindering the receiving of it—that is the Science of Deliberate Creation at its best.*

Chapter 5

This Simple Basis of Understanding Makes It All Fit Together

There is a current that runs through everything. It exists throughout the Universe, and it exists throughout All-That-Is. It is the basis of the Universe, and it is the basis of your physical world. Some are aware of this Energy, but most humans are unaware of it. However, everyone is affected by it.

As you begin to understand the basis of your world, and you begin to look for, or better said, *feel for,* your awareness of this Source Energy that is the basis of all things, you will then understand everything about your own experience. You will also more clearly understand the experiences of those around you.

A Consistent Formula Gives You Consistent Results

Like learning to understand the basics of mathematics and then having the successful experience of understanding the results of their applications, you will now have a formula for understanding your world that will always be consistent, and which will yield consistent results to you. They will be so consistent that you will be able to predict your future experiences with absolute accuracy, and you will be able to understand your past experiences with a knowing that was unavailable to you before.

You will never again feel like a victim, in the past or future, cowering from the idea of unwanted things pouncing into your life experience. You will finally understand the absolute creative control that you have of your own life experience. And then, you will be able to turn your attention to your own creative power, and you will experience the absolute bliss of watching all manner of things converging to assist you in the creation of your own specific desires. Everyone has this potential . . . and some are realizing it.

It will be an extremely satisfying experience to identify your own personal desires, which will be rising from the contrasting life experiences that you are living, and to know that each of those desires can be fully realized. From that place of belief; from that place of understanding the basics that are always consistent: You will now shorten the time between the inception of your idea of desire and its full and absolute manifestation.

You will come to know that all things you desire can come easily and swiftly into your experience.

You Are a Vibrational Being in a Vibrational Environment

You can *feel* whether you are allowing your full connection to Source Energy or not. In other words, the better you feel, the more you are allowing your connection; the worse you feel, the less you are allowing your connection. Feeling good equals allowing the connection; feeling bad equals not allowing the connection—feeling bad equals resisting the connection to your Source.

You are, even in your physical expression of flesh, blood, and bone, a "Vibrational Being," and everything you experience in your physical environment is vibrational. And, it is only through your ability to translate vibration that you are able to understand your physical world at all. In other words, through your eyes, you translate vibration into that which you see. Using your ears, you translate vibration into the sounds that you hear. Even your nose, tongue, and fingertips are translating vibrations into the smells, tastes, and touches that help you understand your world. But your most sophisticated of vibrational interpreters by far are your emotions.

Your Emotions As Vibrational Interpreters

By paying attention to the signals of your emotions, you can understand, with absolute precision, everything you are now living or have ever lived. And, with a precision and ease that you may have never before experienced, you can use this new understanding of your emotions to orchestrate a future experience that will please you in every way.

By paying attention to the way you feel, you can fulfill your reason for being here, and you can continue your intended expansion in the joyful way that you intended. By understanding your emotional connection to who you really are, you will come to understand not only what is happening in your own world and why, but you will also understand every other living Being with whom you interact. Never again will you have unanswered questions about your world. You will understand—from a very deep level, from your broader Non-Physical perspective, and through your own personal physical experience—everything about who you are, who you have been, and who you are becoming.

❧ ❧ ❧ ❧ ❧ ❧

Chapter 6

The Law of Attraction, the Most Powerful Law in the Universe

Every thought vibrates, every thought radiates a signal, and every thought attracts a matching signal back. We call that process the *Law of Attraction.*

The *Law of Attraction* says: *That which is like unto itself is drawn.* And so, you might see the powerful *Law of Attraction* as a sort of Universal Manager that sees to it that all thoughts that match one another line up.

You understand this principle when you turn on your radio and deliberately tune your receiver to match a signal from a broadcasting tower. You do not expect to hear music that is being broadcast on the radio frequency of 101FM to be received on your tuner when it is set at 98.6FM. You understand that radio vibrational frequencies must match, and the *Law of Attraction* agrees with you.

So, as your experience causes you to launch vibrational rockets of desires, you must then find ways of holding yourself consistently in vibrational harmony with those desires in order to receive their manifestation.

To What Are You
Giving Your Attention?

Whatever you are giving your attention to causes you to emit a vibration, and the vibrations that you offer equal your asking, which equals your point of attraction.

If there is something you desire that you currently do not have, you need only put your attention upon it, and, by the *Law of Attraction,* it will come to you, for as you think about this thing or experience that you desire, you offer a vibration, and then, by *Law,* that very thing or experience must come to you.

However, if there is something that you desire that you currently do *not* have, and you put your attention upon your current state of *not having it,* then *Law of Attraction* will continue to match that *not having it* vibration, so you will continue to *not have that which you desire.* It is Law.

How Can I Know
What I Am Attracting?

The key to bringing something into your experience that you desire is to achieve vibrational *harmony* with what you desire. And the easiest way for you to achieve vibrational harmony with it is to imagine having it, pretend that it is already in your experience, flow your thoughts toward the enjoyment of the experience, and as you practice those thoughts and begin to consistently offer that vibration, you will then be in the place of allowing that into your experience.

Now, by paying attention to the way you *feel,* you can easily know if you are giving your attention to your desire or if you are giving it to the *absence* of your desire. When your thoughts are a vibrational match to your desire, you feel good—your emotional range would be from contentment to expectation to eagerness to joy. But if you are giving your attention to the lack, or absence, of your desire—your emotions would range from feelings of pessimism to worry to discouragement to anger to insecurity to depression.

And so, as you become *consciously* aware of your emotions, you will always know how you are doing with the *allowing* part of your *Creative Process,* and you will never again misunderstand why things are turning out the way they are. Your emotions provide a wonderful guidance system for you, and if you will pay attention to them, you will be able to guide yourself to anything that you desire.

You Get What You Think About, Whether You Want It or Not

By the powerful Universal Law of Attraction, you draw to you the essence of whatever you are predominantly thinking about. So if you are predominantly thinking about the things that you desire, your life experience reflects those things. And, in the same way, if you are predominantly thinking about what you do not want, your life experience reflects those things.

Whatever you are thinking about is like planning a future event. When you are appreciating, you are planning. When you are worrying, you are planning. (Worrying is using your imagination to create something you do not want.)

Every thought, every idea, every Being, every thing, is vibrational, so when you focus your attention on something, even for a short period of time, the vibration of your Being begins to reflect the vibration of that which you are giving your attention to. The more you think about it, the more you vibrate like it; the more you vibrate like it, the more of that which is like it is attracted to you. That trend in attraction will continue to increase until a different vibration is offered by you. And when a different vibration is offered, things that match *that* vibration are then drawn to you, by you.

When you understand the *Law of Attraction,* you are never surprised by what occurs in your experience, for you understand that you have invited every bit of it in—through your own thought process. *Nothing can occur in your life experience without your invitation of it through your thought.*

Because there are no exceptions to the powerful *Law of Attraction,* a thorough understanding of it is easy to achieve. And once you understand that you get what you think about, and, equally important, when you are aware of what you are thinking, then you are in the position to exercise absolute control of your own experience.

How Big Are Your Vibrational Differences?

Here are some examples. There is a very big vibrational difference in your thoughts of *appreciation* of your mate, and in your thoughts of what you would like to be *different* about your mate. And your relationship with your mate, without exception, reflects the preponderance of your thoughts. For, while you may not have done it consciously, you have literally thought your relationship into being.

Your desire for an improved financial condition cannot come to you if you often feel jealous of your neighbor's good fortune, for the vibration of your desire and the vibration of your jealous feelings are different vibrations.

An understanding of your vibrational nature will make it possible for you to easily, deliberately create your own reality. And then, in time and with practice, you will discover that all desire that you hold can be easily realized—for there is nothing that you cannot be, do, or have.

You Are a Summoner of Vibrational Energy

You are Consciousness.
You are Energy.
You are Vibration.
You are Electricity.
You are Source Energy.
You are Creator.
You are on the Leading Edge of thought.

You are the most specific, most active summoner and utilizer of the Energy that creates worlds, that exists anywhere in this always evolving, eternally becoming Universe.

You are creative genius expressing here in this Leading-Edge time-space-reality for the purpose of taking thought beyond that which it has ever been before.

Even though it may seem odd to you at first, it will be helpful for you to begin to accept yourself as a Vibrational Being, for this is a Vibrational Universe in which you are living, and the Laws that govern this Universe are Vibrationally based.

Once you become consciously at one with the Universal Laws, and gain an understanding of why things respond in the way they do, all mystery and confusion will be replaced by clarity and understanding. Doubt and fear will be replaced with knowledge and confidence, uncertainty will be replaced with certainty—and joy will return as the basic premise of your experience.

When Your Desires and Beliefs Are a Vibrational Match

That which is like unto itself is drawn, so the vibration of your Being must match the vibration of your desire in order for your desire to be fully received by you. You cannot desire something, predominantly focus on the absence of it, and then expect to receive it, because the vibrational frequency of its absence and the vibrational frequency of its presence are very different frequencies. Another way of saying that is: *Your desires and your beliefs must be a vibrational match in order for you to receive that which you desire.*

Here is a glimpse of the bigger picture: You are here having experiences that cause you, in your divinely specific perspective, to identify, consciously or unconsciously, your personal preferences. Now, as that happens, Source, who hears you and adores you, immediately answers your vibrational, electronic request, whether you are able to put conscious, verbal words to it or not.

So no matter what you ask for—whether you ask for it with your words, or with just a subtle impression of your desire—your request is heard and answered every time, no exceptions. When you ask, it is always given.

All-That-Is . . . Is Benefiting
from Your Existence

Because of your exposure to your specific experience, which causes your specific desire to be formulated within you, and because Source hears and answers your request—the Universe, in which we are all focused, expands. What a wonderful thing!

Your current time-space-reality, your current culture, your current ways of looking at things—all of the things that make up your perspective—have evolved over countless generations. In fact, it would not be possible to retrace all the desires, conclusions, and perspectives that have resulted in your unique point of view right here and now. But what we want very much for you to hear is that no matter what has caused your unique point of view to come about—it *has* come about. You do exist; you are thinking; you are perceiving; you are asking—and you are being answered. And All-That-Is is benefiting from your existence and from your point of view.

So your importance is not in question, not to us anyway. We completely understand your immense value. Your worthiness is not in question, not to us anyway. We know that you deserve to have the Energy that creates worlds responding to your every desire—and we know that it does, but many of you, for many reasons, hold yourself apart from receiving the very things you are asking for.

Rediscover the Art of
Allowing Your Natural Well-Being

We want you to rediscover your innate ability to *allow* the Well-Being of this Universe to flow steadily and unrestricted into your experience, and we call this discipline the *Art of Allowing.* It is the *Art of Allowing* the Well-Being—which makes up every particle of that which you are and that which you come from—to continue to flow through you as you continue to be. The *Art of Allowing* is the art of no longer resisting the Well-Being that you deserve; the Well-Being that is natural; the Well-Being that is your legacy, your Source, and your very Being.

Now there are no preliminary courses for you to study in preparation for understanding what is presented here. This book is written so that you can begin to receive value from right where you are. You are ready for this information, right now, and this information is ready for you.

Chapter 7

You Are Standing on the Leading Edge of Thought

We like to refer to the place where you are standing as the *Leading Edge of Thought,* for as you stand there—in your physical body, in your physical environment, having your physical experience—you are the furthermost extension of that which we are.

All that has ever been before is culminating into that which you now are. And just as all of *your* experience, from the time of your birth into your physical body until now, has culminated into who *you* now are, *all that has ever been experienced by All-That-Is has culminated into all that is now being experienced in the physical life experience on Planet Earth.*

As every person on your planet is having experiences that are causing their desires to be born, a sort of mass summoning is occurring, which literally equals the evolution of your planet. And so, the more you interact, the more your personal preferences are being identified and radiated . . . and the more of your preferences that are being radiated, the more are being answered. As such, a powerful Stream of Source Energy is now stretched out before you from which *your* individual, personal preferences will be received.

In other words, because of what so many have lived and are living, and because of the summoning power of so many of *their* desires, the Well-Being of *your* future experience is well in place. And, in like manner, *your* current desires will, in turn, provide an Energy stream for future generations to benefit from.

If You Can Desire It, the Universe Can Produce It

If your involvement in your time-space-reality inspires within you any sincere desire, then the Universe has the means to supply the results that you seek. Because your ability to reach for more expands with each achievement that came before, the expansion may feel breathtaking to those just coming to understand the power of it, but it may feel absolutely normal to those who have already come to understand and expect Well-Being to flow constantly into their experience. The Stream of Well-Being flows even if you do not understand that it does, but when you *consciously* become aligned with it, your creative endeavors become so much more satisfying, for then you discover that there is absolutely nothing that you desire that you cannot achieve.

It Works, Whether You Understand It or Not

It is not necessary that you fully understand the complexities of this eternally expanding environment in order to reap the benefits of that which it has become, but it *is* necessary that you find a way to go with the flow of the Well-Being that is stretched out before you. So, in that effort, we offer these words: *There is only a Stream of Well-Being that flows. You can allow it or resist it, but it flows just the same.*

You would not walk into a brightly lit room and look for the "dark switch." In other words, you would not expect to find a switch that would flood an inky darkness into the room to cover the brightness of the light—you would find a switch that would resist the light, for in the absence of the light there is darkness. And, in like manner, there is not a Source of "evil," but there could be a resisting of that which you believe is Good, just as there is not a Source of sickness, but there could be a resisting of the natural Well-Being.

Without Asking, You Will Receive No Answer

Sometimes people will compliment Esther for being able to receive the wisdom of Abraham, and for putting it into written or spoken word for others to experience and receive benefit from, and we also add our appreciation to that. But we also want to point out that Esther's receiving and translation of our vibration is only part of the equation. Without the asking that precedes it, there could be no answering.

The people of your times are benefiting dramatically from the experiences of those generations that preceded you, for through the experiences that they lived, and the desires that were generated within them, the summoning began. And today, you are the ones on the Leading Edge of reaping the benefits of what those past generations asked for; at the same time, *you* are continuing to ask, and *you* are now summoning . . . and on it goes. So can you see how, if you can find a way to allow it, there is an avalanche of Well-Being at your fingertips, ripe for your plucking—provided you are in vibrational alignment with it? (And can you not see why—since there is never a crowd on the Leading Edge—you are not going to have a lot of people you can talk to about this?)

These days, there are some people experiencing intense hardships or traumas, and because of how they are living right now, their asking is in a heightened and intense place. And because of the intensity of their request, Source is responding in kind. And although the person who is doing the asking is usually so involved in the trauma that they are not personally receiving the benefit of their own asking, future generations—or even current generations who are not, right now, disallowing—are receiving the benefit of that asking.

We are giving this to you by way of helping you understand: *There is an unlimited Stream of Well-Being and an abundance of all manner of things available to you at all times—but you must be in alignment with the receiving of those things. You cannot stand in resistance of them and receive them at the same time.*

Open the Floodgates and
Let Your Well-Being Flow In

See yourself, right where you are now, as the beneficiary of the powerful Stream of Well-Being. Try to imagine that you are basking in the flow of this powerful stream. Make an effort to feel yourself as the Leading-Edge beneficiary of this unlimited stream, and smile and try to accept that you are worthy of it.

Your ability to feel your worthiness of the powerful Stream of Well-Being will undoubtedly depend on what is happening in your life right now. Under some conditions you feel utterly blessed, and under others you feel not so blessed, and it is our desire that, as you read this book, you will come to understand that to the degree you feel blessed and expect good things to flow to you, this indicates the level of your state of *allowing*; and to the degree that you do not feel blessed, where you do not expect good things to come to you, this indicates your degree of resistance. And it is our desire that, as you continue to read, you will feel able to release any habits of thought that have resulted in your disallowing of the Stream.

We want you to understand that if it were not for resistant thoughts you have picked up along your physical trail that are not in vibrational alignment with the Stream of Well-Being, you would be, right now, a full receiver of that Stream—for you are a literal extension of it.

You (and how you feel) is all that is responsible for whether you let in your inheritance of Well-Being or not. And while those around you may influence you, more or less, to allow or not allow that Stream, it is ultimately all up to you. You can open the floodgates and let in your Well-Being, or your can choose thoughts that keep you pinched off from what is yours—but whether you allow it or resist it, the stream is constantly flowing to you, never ending, never tiring, always there for your reconsideration.

You Are in the Perfect Position to Get There from Here

Nothing has to change in your environment or in the circumstances that surround you for you to begin to deliberately allow your own connection to the Stream of Well-Being. You could be in prison, you could have been diagnosed with a terminal illness, you could be facing bankruptcy, or you could be in the middle of a divorce. Still, you are in the perfect place, right now, to begin. And we also want you to understand that this will not require a great deal of time, for it only requires a simple understanding of the Universal Laws, and a determination to move toward a state of *allowing*.

When you drive your vehicle from place to place, you have an awareness of your starting place as well as an awareness of where you are going. You accept that you cannot get there instantaneously; you accept that you will travel the distance, and in time, you will arrive at your destination. And while you may feel anxious to get there, and maybe even tire of the journey, you do not get so discouraged at the midway mark that you just turn around and go back to your starting place. You do not drive back and forth and back and forth from your starting point to the midway point and then finally collapse from the never-ending journey.

You do not announce your inability to accomplish your journey. You accept the distance between your starting place and where you desire to be—and you continue to move in the direction of your destination. You understand what is required—and you do it. And we want you to come to know that the journey between where you are and where you want to be—on all subjects—can be just as easily understood.

❧ ❧ ❧ ❧ ❧ ❧

Chapter 8

You Are a Vibrational Transmitter and Receiver

Now you are ready to understand the most essential part of controlling, creating, and enjoying your physical life experience.

Even more than the material being that you have come to know as you—you are a *Vibrational Being.* When someone looks at you, they see you with their eyes and hear you with their ears, but you are presenting yourself to them, and to the Universe, in a much more emphatic way than can be seen or heard: *You are a vibrational transmitter, and you are broadcasting your signal in every moment of your existence.*

As you are focused in this physical body, and while you are awake, you are constantly projecting a very specific, easily identifiable signal that is instantly received, understood, and answered. Immediately, your present and future circumstances begin to change in response to the signal you are offering *now.* And so, the entire Universe, right now, is affected by what you are offering.

You Are an Eternal Personality, Focusing in the Now

Your world, present and future, is directly and specifically affected by the signal that you are now transmitting. The personality that is You is really an eternal personality, but who you are right now, and what you are thinking right now, is causing a focusing of Energy that is very powerful. This Energy that you are focusing is the same Energy that creates worlds. And it is, in this very moment, creating your world.

You have a built-in, easy-to-understand *guidance system* within you, with indicators that help you understand the strength or power of your signal, as well as the direction of your focus. And, most important, it is this very same *guidance system* that helps you understand the alignment of your chosen thought with the Energy Stream itself.

Your feelings are the representatives of your guidance system. In other words, the way you feel is your true indicator of your alignment with your Source, and of your alignment with your own intentions—both pre-birth and currently.

Your Powerful Beliefs Were Once Gentle Thoughts

Every thought that has ever been thought still exists, and whenever you focus upon a thought, you activate the vibration of that thought within you. So, whatever you are currently giving your attention to is an activated thought. But when you turn your attention away from a thought, it becomes dormant, or no longer active. The only way to consciously deactivate a thought is to activate another. In other words, the only way to deliberately withdraw your attention from one thought is to give your attention to another.

When you give your attention to anything, the vibration, at first, is not very strong, but if you continue to think about it or speak about it, the vibration gets stronger. So, with enough attention to any subject, it can become a dominant thought. As you give more and more attention to any thought, and as you focus upon it and therefore practice the vibration of it—the thought becomes an even bigger part of your vibration—and you could now call this practiced thought a *belief.*

The Longer You Think Thoughts, the Stronger They Become

Because the *Law of Attraction* is behind the expansion of your thoughts, it is not possible to give your attention to something without achieving an alignment with it to some degree. And so, the longer you ponder the thought, and the more frequently you return to the thought, the stronger your vibrational alignment becomes.

As you achieve a stronger alignment with any thought, you then begin to feel emotions that indicate your increased or decreased alignment with your own Source. In other words, as you give more of your attention to any subject, your emotional reading of either harmony or disharmony with who you really are becomes stronger. If the subject of your attention is in alignment with what the Source of your Being knows, you would feel the harmony of your thoughts in the form of good feelings. But if the subject of your attention is not in alignment with what your Source knows it to be, you would feel the disharmony of your thoughts in the form of bad feelings.

Your Attention to It Invites It In

Every thought that you give your attention to expands and becomes a bigger part of your vibrational mix. Whether it is a thought of something you want or a thought of something you do not want—your attention to it invites it into your experience.

Since this is an attraction-based Universe, there is no such thing as exclusion. Everything is about inclusion. So, when you see something that you would like to experience and you focus upon it, shouting *yes* to it, you include it in your experience. But when you see something that you would not want to experience, and you focus upon it, shouting *no* at it, you also include that in your experience. You do not invite it in with your *yes* and exclude it with your *no*, because there is no exclusion in this attraction-based Universe. Your focus is the invitation. Your attention to it is the invitation.

And so, those who are mostly observers thrive in good times but suffer in bad times because what they are observing is already vibrating, and as they observe it, they include it in their vibrational countenance; and as they include it, the Universe accepts that as their point of attraction—and gives them more of the essence of it. So, for an observer, the better it gets, the better it gets; or the worse it gets, the worse it gets. However, one who is a visionary thrives in *all* times.

With your practiced attention to any subject, the Law of Attraction delivers circumstances, conditions, experiences, other people, and all manner of things that match your habitual dominant vibration. And as things begin to manifest around you that match the thoughts you have been holding, you now develop stronger and stronger vibrational habits or proclivities. And so, your once small and insignificant thought has now evolved into a powerful belief—and your powerful beliefs will always be played out in your experience.

⁂ ⁂ ⁂ ⁂ ⁂ ⁂

Chapter 9

The Hidden Value Behind
Your Emotional Reactions

Your sense of sight is different from your sense of hearing, and your sense of smell is different from your sense of touch, but even though they are different, they are all vibrational interpretations. In other words, when you approach a hot stove, your sense of sight does not necessarily tell you that the stove is hot; your sense of hearing and your senses of taste or smell are not usually the way you recognize a hot stove either. But as you approach the stove with your body, the sensors in your skin let you know that the stove is hot.

You were born with sensitive, evolved, sophisticated translators of vibrations that help you understand and define your experience. And in the same way that you utilize your five physical senses to interpret your physical life experience, you were born with other sensors—your emotions—which are further vibrational interpreters that help you understand, in the moment, the experiences that you are living.

Emotions Are Indicators
of Your Point of Attraction

Your emotions are your indicators of the vibrational content of your Being, in every moment. And so, when you become aware of the feeling of your emotions, you can also be aware of your vibrational offering. And once you combine your knowledge of the *Law of Attraction* with your in-this-moment awareness of what your vibrational offering is, then you will have full control of your own powerful point of attraction. With this knowledge, you can now guide your life experience in any way you choose.

Your emotions—simply, purely, and only—are about your relationship with your Source. And since your emotions tell you everything that you would ever want or need to know about your relationship with your Source, we often refer to your emotions as your *Emotional Guidance System.*

When you made the decision to come forth into this physical body, you fully understood your eternal connection to Source Energy, and you knew that your emotions would be constant indicators that would let you know, in every moment, your current relationship with Source Energy. And so, understanding the powerful guidance that you have eternal access to, you felt no sense of risk, no sense of confusion—only a sense of adventure and true exhilaration.

Emotions Are Indicators of Your
Alignment with Source Energy

Your emotions indicate the degree of your alignment with Source. Although you can never achieve such a complete misalignment with Source that you disconnect from it altogether, the thoughts that you choose to give your attention to do give you a substantial range in alignment or misalignment with the Non-Physical Energy that is truly who you are. And so, with time and practice, you will come to know, in every moment, your degree of alignment with who you really are, for when you are in full allowance of the Energy of your Source, you thrive, and to the degree that you do not allow this alignment, you do not thrive.

You are empowered Beings; you are utterly free to create, and when you know that, and are focused upon things that are in vibrational harmony with that, you feel absolute joy. But when you think thoughts that are contrary to that truth, you feel the opposite emotions of disempowerment and bondage. And all emotions fall somewhere within that range, from joy to disempowerment.

Use Your Emotions to
Feel Your Way Back to Well-Being

When you think a thought that rings true with who you really are, you feel harmony coursing through your physical body: Joy, love, and a sense of freedom are examples of that alignment. And when you think thoughts that do *not* ring true with who you really are, you feel the disharmony in your physical body. Depression, fear, and feelings of bondage are examples of that misalignment.

In the same way that sculptors mold clay into the creation that pleases them, you create by molding Energy. You mold it through your power of focus—by thinking about things, remembering things, and imagining things. You focus the Energy when you speak, when you write, when you listen, when you are silent, when you remember, and when you imagine—you focus it through the projection of thought.

Like the sculptors who, with time and practice, learn to mold the clay into the precise desired creation, *you can learn to mold the Energy that creates worlds through the focus of your own mind.* And, like the sculptors who, with their hands, *feel* their way as they re-create their vision—you will use your emotions to *feel* your way to Well-Being.

Chapter 10

The Three Steps to Whatever
You Want to Be, Do, or Have

The *Creative Process* is conceptually a simple one. It consists of just three steps:

- **Step 1** (your work): You ask.

- **Step 2** (not your work): The answer is given.

- **Step 3** (your work): The answer, which has been given, must be received or allowed (you have to let it in).

Step 1: You Ask

Because of the wonderful and diverse environment in which you are focused, **Step 1** comes easily and automatically, for this is how your natural preferences are born. Everything—from your subtle or even unconscious desires to clear, precise, vivid ones—results from the contrasting experiences of your day-to-day life. Desires (or *asking*) are the natural by-product of your exposure to this environment of fantastic variety and contrast. And so, **Step 1** comes naturally.

Step 2: The Universe Answers

Step 2 is a simple step for you, for it is not your work at all. **Step 2** is the work of the Non-Physical, the work of the GOD Force. All things that you ask for, large and small, are immediately understood and fully offered, without exception. Every point of Consciousness has the right and the ability to ask, and all points of Consciousness are honored and responded to immediately. When you ask, it is given. Every time.

Your "asking" is sometimes spoken with your words, but more often it emanates from you vibrationally as a constant stream of personally honed preferences, each building on the next, and each one respected and answered.

Every question is answered. Every desire is given. Every prayer is answered. Every wish is granted. But the reason that many would argue with that truth, holding up examples of unfulfilled desires from their own life experiences, is because they have not yet understood and completed the very important **Step 3**—for without the completion of this step, the existence of **Steps** 1 and 2 could go unnoticed.

Step 3: You Allow It In

Step 3 is the application of the *Art of Allowing*. It is really the reason your guidance system exists. It is the step whereby you tune the vibrational frequency of your Being to match the vibrational frequency of your desire. In the same way that your radio tuner must be set to match the frequency of the broadcasting station you desire to hear, the vibrational frequency of your Being must match the frequency of your desire. And we call that the *Art of Allowing*—that is, allowing what you are asking for. Unless you are in the receiving mode, your questions, even though they have been answered, will seem unanswered to you; your prayers will not seem to be answered, and your desires will not be fulfilled—not because your wishes have not been heard, but because your vibrations are not a match, so you are not letting them in.

Every Subject Is Two Subjects: Wanted and Not Wanted

Every subject is really two subjects: There is that which you desire, and the lack of it. *Often—even when you believe you are thinking about something that you desire—you are actually thinking about the exact opposite of what you desire.* In other words, "I want to be well; I don't want to be sick." "I want to have financial security; I don't want to experience a shortage of money." "I want the perfect relationship to come to me; I don't want to be alone."

What you think and what you get is always a perfect vibrational match, so it can be very helpful to make a conscious correlation between what you are thinking and what is manifesting in your life experience, but it is even more helpful if you are able to discern where you are headed even before you get there. Once you understand your emotions and the important messages they are giving you, you will not have to wait until something has manifested in your experience to understand what your vibrational offering has been—you can tell, by the way you feel, exactly where you are headed.

Your Attention Must Be on It, Not on the Lack of It

The *Creative Process* is occurring whether you are consciously aware of it or not. Because of the variety and contrast of your experience, continual new preferences are being born within you, and you are, even without knowing it, broadcasting them as requests. And in the moment that you broadcast a preference, Source Energy receives your vibrational request and, by the *Law of Attraction,* offers immediate responses, which you must then align to vibrationally.

The reason that you are not always aware that your desires have been answered is because there is often a time gap between your asking **(Step 1)** and your allowing **(Step 3)**. *Even though a clear desire has emanated from you as a result of the contrast you have considered,* *you often, rather than giving your attention purely to the desire itself, focus back on the contrasting situation that gave birth to the desire. And in doing so, your vibration is more about the reason you have launched the desire than it is about the desire itself.*

For example, your automobile is getting older and is beginning to require frequent repairs . . . and as you begin to notice its fading beauty, you find yourself desiring a new car. And as you very much wanted that feeling of confidence that a dependable new car brings, a vibrational rocket of desire emanated from you, and Source received it fully and responded, in kind, immediately.

But because you were not consciously aware of the Laws of the Universe and the *Three-Step Process of Creation,* that fresh, exhilarating feeling was short-lived for you. So, instead of immediately turning your attention toward your fresh new desire and continuing to ponder the idea of this delicious *new* vehicle (thus achieving vibrational harmony with your own *new* idea) you look back at the vehicle you currently own, pointing out the reasons that you desire the new car. "This old car no longer pleases me," you conclude, not realizing that in looking at the unpleasing car, you are tuning your vibration back to *it,* and not forward to the new car you desire. "I really need a new car," you explain, pointing out the dents, the cracks, and the undependable performance of the old one.

With each statement of need and justification for a new car, you unwittingly reinforce the vibration of your current unpleasant situation, and in doing so, you continue to hold yourself out of vibrational alignment with your new desire, and out of the receiving mode of what you are asking for.

As long as you are more aware of what you <u>do not</u> want regarding this situation, what you <u>do</u> want cannot come to you. In other words, if you are predominantly thinking about your beautiful new car, then it is steadily making its way to you, but if you are predominantly thinking about your undependable current car, your dependable new car cannot move toward you.

It may seem difficult to make the distinction between actually thinking about your new car and beating the drum of the old car, but once you are aware of your *Emotional Guidance System,* this distinction will be very easy for you to make.

**Now You Hold the Key to
Creating Your Every Desire**

Once you understand that your thoughts equal your point of attraction and that the way you *feel* indicates your level of *allowing* or *resisting,* you now hold the key to creating anything that you desire.

It is not possible for you to consistently feel positive emotion about something and have it turn out badly, just as it is not possible for you to consistently feel bad about something and have it turn out well—for the way you feel will tell you if you are allowing your natural Well-Being or not.

Although there is no source of sickness, you may offer thoughts that disallow the natural flow of your wellness just as you may offer thoughts that disallow the natural flow of your abundance, although there is no source of poverty. Well-Being is constantly making its way to you, and if you have not learned thoughts that slow it or restrict it, you are experiencing it in all areas of your life.

It does not matter where you currently stand in relationship to anything you desire. By paying attention to the way you *feel,* and by directing your thoughts to better-feeling thoughts, you can again achieve vibrational harmony with the Well-Being that is natural to you.

Remember, as extensions of pure, positive Non-Physical Energy, the more in vibrational harmony you are with You, the better you feel. For example, when you are appreciating something, you are a vibrational match to who you really are. When you love someone, or yourself, you are a vibrational match to who you really are. But if you are finding fault with yourself or another, you are, in that moment, offering a vibration that does not match who you really are, and the negative emotion you feel is your indicator that you have introduced a vibration of resistance and that you are no longer in the state of *allowing* your pure Connection between the physical you and the Non-Physical part of You.

We often refer to that Non-Physical part of You as your *Inner Being,* or your *Source.* It is not important what you call that Source of *Energy,* or *Life Force,* but it *is* important that you are consciously aware of when you are allowing a full connection to it and when you are restricting it in some way—and your emotions are your constant indicators of your degree of allowing or resisting that connection.

Chapter 11

With Practice, You Will Become a Joyous, Deliberate Creator

As you consciously consider the way you feel, you will get better and better at directing the Source Energy, and you will become a disciplined and joyous *deliberate creator*. With practice, you will be able to achieve a focused control of this *Creative Energy*, and, like the skilled sculptor, you will take delight in the molding of this Energy, which creates worlds, and direct it toward your individual creative endeavors.

As you focus *Creative Energy*, there are two factors to consider: first, the intensity and speed of the Energy; and second, your level of allowing or resisting it. The first factor has to do with the amount of time you have spent considering your desire, and to what degree you have become specific. In other words, when you have been wanting something for a long time, your summoning power is much greater than if you are thinking about it for the first time today. Also, whenever you have considered it for some time, having experienced contrast that helped you to become even more specific about it, your desire summons it in an even more powerful way. Once a desire has achieved that sort of power or speed, it is quite easy for you to *feel* how you are doing with the second factor: the *allowing* or *resisting* part of the equation.

When you are thinking about something that you have been wanting for a very long time, and, in this moment, you are noticing that it has not yet happened, a strong negative emotion would be present within you, for you are thinking about something that has very strong energy that you are not in vibrational alignment with. However, if you are thinking about something that you have been wanting for a long time and you are imagining that it *is* happening, then your emotion would be one of anticipation or eagerness.

And so, you can tell by the way you *feel* whether, in this moment, you are a match to your desire or a match to its absence; whether you are allowing or resisting your desire, or whether you are, in this moment, helping or hindering.

It Is Not about Controlling Thoughts, It Is about Guiding Thoughts

In your highly technologically evolved society where you have immediate access to almost everything that is happening around your planet, you are bombarded with thoughts and ideas that, at times, feel invasive to your personal experience. And so, the idea of controlling your thoughts when there are so many other thoughts coming forth seems impossible. It seems, instead, rather normal to just give your attention to whatever is in front of you.

We are not encouraging you to make an effort to control your thoughts, but instead, to make an effort to, more or less, *guide* your thoughts. And it is not even so much about guiding your thoughts as it is about reaching for a *feeling*, because reaching for the way you would like to *feel* is an easier way to hold your thoughts in vibrational alignment with that which you believe is good.

The *Law of Attraction* is already magnetically attracting and organizing your thoughts, so having an understanding of, and deliberately working with the *Law of Attraction* is extremely helpful in an effort at guiding your own thoughts.

Remember, whenever you give your attention to a thought, that thought immediately becomes activated within you, so the *Law of*

Attraction immediately responds, which means that other thoughts, in vibrational harmony with the thought that you have just activated, now join your activated thought, making it a more pronounced, more powerful, and more attractive thought. And as you continue your focus, and as your thought expands, that more powerful thought that you have just activated is joined by others like it . . . and on it goes.

When Your Practiced Thought Becomes a Dominant Thought

Whenever you have consistently focused upon a subject, causing a consistent vibrational activation of it within you, it becomes a practiced or dominant thought. And once that happens, *things* that match it will begin to manifest around your dominant thought. In the same way that your earlier thought was joined by other *thoughts* that matched it—now *things* that match your dominant thought will begin to show up in your experience: magazine articles, conversations with friends, personal observations . . . the attraction process will become very apparent. *Once your focused attention has sufficiently activated a dominant vibration within you, things—wanted or unwanted—will begin to make their way into your personal experience. It is Law.*

How to Effectively Become a Deliberate Creator

Remember, before you can effectively benefit from paying attention to your emotions, you must first accept that Well-Being is the only Stream that flows. You can allow or disallow this Stream, but when you allow it, you are well; and when you disallow it, you are sick. In other words, there is only a Stream of wellness, which you are allowing or resisting, and you can tell by the way you *feel* which you are doing.

You are supposed to thrive. You are supposed to feel good. You *are* good. You *are* loved, and Well-Being is constantly flowing to you, and if you will allow it, it will manifest in all manner of ways in your experience.

Whatever you are giving your attention to is already pulsing an Energy vibration. And as you hold your attention upon it, you begin to vibrate as it is vibrating. Each time you focus upon it, and each time you offer the vibration, it feels easier for you to do it the next time, until, in time, you develop a sort of vibrational proclivity. It is like practicing anything; it can get easier and easier. And with enough focusing on this thought, and therefore practicing this vibration, you form what you call a *belief*.

A *belief* is only a practiced vibration. In other words, once you have practiced a thought long enough, then anytime you approach the subject of that thought, the *Law of Attraction* will take you easily into the full vibration of your belief. So now, the *Law of Attraction* accepts that belief as your point of attraction, and brings to you things that match that vibration. And so, as you have life experience that matches those thoughts you were pondering, you conclude, "Yes, this is truth." And while it may be accurate to call it "truth," we would prefer to call it attraction, or creation.

Anything that you give your attention to will become your "truth." The Law of Attraction says that it must. Your life, and everyone else's, too, is but a reflection of the predominance of your thoughts. There is no exception to this.

Have You Made a Decision to Direct Your Thoughts?

To be the *deliberate creator* of your own experience, you will be the one who has decided to direct your thoughts, for only when you deliberately choose the direction of your thoughts can you deliberately affect your own point of attraction.

You cannot continue to discuss, observe, and believe things in the same way you always have and make changes in your point of attraction, any more (as we mentioned previously) than you can set your radio dial to 630AM and receive the broadcast from 101FM. Your vibrational frequencies have to match.

Every emotion that you feel is about your alignment or misalignment with the Energy of your Source. Your emotions are your indicators of the vibrational variance between your physical Being and your Inner Being, and when you pay attention to these emotions and try to focus on good-feeling thoughts, you are then using your *Emotional Guidance System* in the way that you intended when you decided to come into this physical body.

Your *Emotional Guidance System* is the key to helping you understand what your vibrational content is and therefore exactly what your current point of attraction is. *Distinguishing between the actual thought of what you want, compared to the thought of its absence, is sometimes difficult. But distinguishing between your emotional response to your thought of your desire, and your emotional response to your thought of the absence of your desire, is a very easy thing to do. Because, when you are fully focused upon your desire (and your vibrational offering purely reflects that), you feel wonderful. And when you focus upon the absence of something that you truly want, you feel awful. Your emotions always let you know what you are doing with your vibration; your emotions always let you know exactly what your point of attraction is; and so, by paying attention to your emotions and by <u>deliberately</u> offering thoughts that affect the way you feel, you can <u>consciously</u> guide yourself into the vibrational frequency that will allow the fulfillment of any desire you hold.*

Can You Accept Yourself
As a Vibrational Being?

Most of our physical friends are unaccustomed to viewing their lives in terms of vibrations, and they are certainly not accustomed to thinking of themselves as radio transmitters and receivers—but you do live in a *Vibrational Universe,* and you are more *Energy, Vibration,* or *Electricity* than you realize. *Once you allow this new orientation and begin to accept yourself as a Vibrational Being who attracts all the things that come into your experience, then you will begin the delicious journey into Deliberate Creation. Once you begin to understand the correlation between what you are thinking, what you are feeling, and what you are receiving, now you have it. Now you hold all the keys that are necessary to get from wherever you are to wherever you want to be, on all subjects.*

Chapter 12

Your *Emotional Set-Points* Are Within Your Control

Most people do not believe they have control over what they believe. They observe things happening around them and evaluate them, but they usually feel that they have no control whatsoever about the belief that is formulating within them. They spend their lives sorting events into categories of good or bad, wanted or unwanted, right or wrong—but rarely do they understand that they have the ability to control their personal relationship with these events.

It Is Impossible to Control Conditions That Others Have Created

Since many people approve of some of the conditions that others have created but disapprove of others, they set out on the impossible mission of trying to control conditions. Through personal force or strength, or gathering together in groups to gain the feeling of more power or control, they seek to preserve their own Well-Being by attempting to take control of any circumstances that they believe could threaten it. But, in this attraction-based Universe where there is no such thing as exclusion, the harder they push against unwanted things, the more they achieve vibrational alignment with unwanted things—and in doing so, the more they invite unwanted things into their own experience. And as more unwanted things now manifest in their experience, they shore up their own belief (they "prove it" to themselves) that they were right all along about how bad and invasive that unwanted thing was to begin with. In other words, the more you defend your own beliefs, the more the *Law of Attraction* helps you live them out.

"But Whose 'Truth' Is the True TRUTH?"

With enough attention to anything, the essence of what you have been giving thought to will eventually become a physical manifestation. And then as others observe your physical manifestation, through their attention to it, they help it to expand. And then, in time, this manifestation, whether it is one that is wanted or not, is called "Truth."

We want you to remember that you have absolute choices about the "Truths" that you create in your own experience. Once you understand that the only reason anyone ever experiences anything is because of their attention to the subject, then it is easy to see that "Truth" only exists because someone gave their attention to it. So when you say, "I should give my attention to such and such, because it is true," that is the same thing as saying, "Another gave their attention to something that *they* did not want, and by *their* attention to it they have invited it into *their* experience. And since *they* have attracted something unwanted into *their* experience, I should do it, also."

There are many wonderful things that you are making your Truths, and there are many not-so-wonderful things that you are making your Truths—*Deliberate Creation* is about *deliberately* choosing those experiences you make your Truths.

Your Point of Attraction
Is Being Affected

When your activated thoughts are general and not very focused, those early vibrations are still very small and do not yet have much attraction power or pulling power, so to speak. And so, in these early stages, you would not likely see any manifested evidence of your attention to the subject. But even though you do not yet *see* the evidence, the attraction of other thoughts that are a vibrational match to these is occurring. In other words, the thought is becoming stronger; its pulling power is getting stronger, and other similar thought vibrations are joining it. And, as the thought gains momentum, you now begin to get an emotional reading on how well this growing thought-vibration is matching the Energy of your Source. If it matches who you are, your good-feeling emotions indicate that. If it does *not* match who you are, your bad-feeling emotions indicate that.

For example, when you were little, your grandmother may have said to you, "You are such a wonderful child. I love you so very much. You will have a fulfilling and happy life. You have so many talents, and the world will benefit by your presence." These words felt good because they were a vibrational match to what was at the very core of you. But when someone says to you, "You are bad. You should be ashamed of yourself. You have displeased me. You are inappropriate," these words feel awful because your attention to them has caused you to become vibrationally different from who you really are and what you really know.

The way you feel is a clear and accurate indication of your alignment, or misalignment, with your Source Energy. In other words, your emotions let you know if you are *allowing*, or if you are in a current state of resistance to, your connection with Source.

Moods As Indicators of
Your <u>Emotional Set-Points</u>

When you continue to focus upon any thought, it becomes increasingly easy to continue to focus upon it because the *Law of Attraction* is making more thoughts like it available to you. And so, emotionally speaking, you are developing a mood or an attitude. Vibrationally speaking, you are achieving a habitual vibrational groove, so to speak—or a *set-point*.

Your mood is showing you a good representation of what you are inviting into your experience. Your mood, or your general feeling about something, is a clear indication of your practiced vibration. In other words, whenever any subject is activated within you through your exposure to your environment, your vibration jumps immediately to your most practiced vibrational place, or *set-point*.

For example, let us say that when you were a child, your parents experienced severe financial difficulty. And so, the lack of money and the inability to purchase desired things was often discussed in your home, with the accompanying emotions of worry and fear. Often, in response to your request for something, you were told that "money doesn't grow on trees," and that "just because you want it doesn't mean you'll get it," and that "you, like everyone else in this family, should learn to do without. That is just the way that it is. . . . " Because of years of exposure to these thoughts of "lack," your habit of thought around the subject of money—your *Emotional Set-Point*— became one of low expectation of financial success. And so, whenever you thought about money or abundance, your mood or attitude would immediately shift to disappointment, worry, or anger.

Or, when you were a child, maybe your friend's mother was killed in an automobile accident, and then your close association with someone who was experiencing such severe childhood trauma made you fearful for the Well-Being of your own parents. Whenever they traveled somewhere by automobile, you would be gripped by fear until they returned. And so, bit by bit, you developed a habit of worry about the Well-Being of those you loved. Your *Emotional Set-Point* became that of insecurity.

Or, when you were a teenager, perhaps your grandmother suddenly died of a heart attack. And in the years that followed her death, you often heard your mother expressing her concern about the high probability of the same thing happening to her and her children (including you!). Nearly every time any conversation about your grandmother came up, her untimely heart attack became an emotional—and fear-producing—part of the conversation. Even though *your* body was strong and you continued to feel physically good, a concern about your own physical vulnerability rumbled under the surface. And so, over time, you achieved an *Emotional Set-Point* of physical vulnerability.

Your Emotional Set-Points *Can Be Changed*

In the same way that your Emotional Set-Points *can change from feeling basically good or secure to feeling bad or insecure, your set-points can change from not feeling good to feeling good, for your set-points are achieved simply by attention to a subject, and through your practiced thought.*

However, most people do not *deliberately* offer thought, but instead, they let their thoughts gravitate to whatever is happening around them: Something happens. They observe. They have an emotional feeling response to what they are observing. And since they usually feel powerless in controlling what they are observing, they conclude that they have no control over their emotional response to what they are observing.

We want you to understand that you do have absolute control over the set-points that you achieve. And we want you to understand the extreme value in deliberately achieving your own set-points. Because, once you expect something, it will come. The details of it may play out differently—but the vibrational essence will always be an exact match.

⌁ ⌁ ⌁ ⌁ ⌁ ⌁

Chapter 13

Allow Your Feelings
to Be Your Guide

Another important premise that is valuable to remember is that you are a physical extension of Source Energy, and that an eternal Stream of Source Energy flows to you and through you—and that it *is* you. This Stream flowed before the physical Being that you know as you was born, and it will continue to flow once the physical Being that you know as you experiences what you call "death."

Every living thing, animal, human, or plant, experiences that which is called death, with no exception. Spirit, which is who we really are, is eternal. So what death must be is but a changing of the perspective of that eternal Spirit. If you are standing in your physical body and consciously connected to that Spirit, then you are eternal in nature and you need never fear any "endedness," because, from that perspective, there is none. (You will never cease to be, for you are eternal Consciousness.)

Your emotions let you know how much Source Energy you are summoning in this moment by virtue of the desire you hold in this moment. They also let you know whether your preponderance of thought on the subject matches your desire, or matches the absence of your desire. For example, a feeling of passion or enthusiasm indicates that there is a very strong desire focused in the moment; a feeling of rage or revenge also indicates that there is a very strong desire; however, a feeling of lethargy or boredom indicates very little focused desire in the moment.

When you really, really want something, and you are thinking about your desire and feeling pleasure from the thought, your thought vibration is now in alignment with your desire—and the current from your Source is flowing through you toward your intended desire with no restriction or resistance. We call that: *allowing*. But when you really, really want something and are feeling anger or fear or disappointment, that means you are focused upon the opposite of your desire, and in doing so, you are introducing another non-matching vibration to the mix—and the degree of negative emotion that you are now experiencing indicates the degree of your resistance to your receiving of your desire.

Learn to Pay Attention to Your Feelings

When emotions are strong—whether they feel good or feel bad—your desire is strong. When emotions are weak, your desire is not so strong.

When emotions feel good—whether they are strong or weak—you are allowing the fulfillment of your desire.

When emotions feel bad—whether they are strong or weak—you are in the state of disallowing the fulfillment of your desire.

Your emotions are *absolute* indicators of your vibrational content. Therefore, they are the perfect reflection of your current point of attraction. They help you know, in any moment, whether or not you are currently allowing the fulfillment of your desire.

You may believe that you cannot control your emotions, or you may believe that you should control your emotions, but we would like you to approach your emotions in a different way: It is our encouragement that you pay attention to how you feel and allow your emotions to be the valuable indicators they are.

An Empty Feeling Is Telling
You Something Important

When the fuel gauge on your vehicle indicates that the tank is empty, you do not criticize the indicator. You receive the information that it has offered you, and you do something about adding more fuel to your tank. Similarly, a negative feeling is an indicator that your current choice of thoughts has you offering a vibration that is so out of harmony with your Source Energy that you are currently disallowing your full connection to that Energy Stream. (You could say your tank is approaching empty.)

Your emotions do not create, but they do indicate what you are currently attracting. If your emotions are helping you know that your choice of thoughts is not taking you in the direction that you desire to go, then do something about that: *Replenish your connection by choosing better-feeling thoughts.*

"Follow Your Bliss" Is a
Positive Thought, Is It Not?

As we've touched on previously, much has been written about the power of positive thought, and we are certainly proponents of that. No better guidance has ever been offered to our physical friends than the words "Follow your bliss," for in the steady reaching for bliss, you must surely align with the Energy of your Source. And in that constant alignment, your Well-Being is certain. But when you find yourself engulfed in circumstances that cause you to offer a vibration that is far from that of bliss, then reaching for bliss is an impossible thing, for the *Law of Attraction* does not allow you to make that vibrational jump any more than you could have tuned your radio receiver to 101FM and heard a song that was being played on 630AM.

You Have the Ability to
Direct Your Own Thoughts

You have the ability to direct your own thoughts; you have the option of observing things as they are, or of imagining them as you want them to be—and whichever option you choose, whether you are imagining or observing, is equally powerful. You have the option of remembering something as it actually occurred or imagining it as you would prefer. You have the option of remembering something that pleased you or remembering something that did not please you. You have the option of anticipating something you want or anticipating something you do not want. In every case, your thoughts produce a vibration within you that equals your point of attraction, and then circumstances and events line up to match the vibrations that you have offered.

You have the ability to place your attention wherever you decide, so it is possible to distract yourself from something unwanted and put your attention upon something wanted. But when a vibration within you is one you have practiced a great deal, the tendency is to continue to offer the vibration in the way you have been practicing it—no matter how much you wish it to be different.

It is not a difficult thing to change the pattern of your vibration, especially when you understand that you can do it a little bit at a time. Once you have an understanding of how vibrations work, how they affect your experience, and, most important, what your emotions are telling you about your vibrations, now you can make steady, fast progress toward the achievement of anything that you desire.

If We Were Standing
in Your Physical Shoes

It is not your job to *make* something happen—Universal Forces are in place for all of that. Your work is to simply determine what you want. You cannot cease your constant list of preferences, so your life experience helps you determine, at both conscious and unconscious levels, what you prefer, and how life, from your personal and important perspective, could now be better—and every conscious or unconscious offering (or asking) from you is answered by Source.

When you have lived an experience that helps you understand, in an exaggerated way, the very thing you do not want, you also understand, in an exaggerated way, what you *do* want. But when you are painfully aware of what you do *not* want, you are not in alignment with what you *do* want. When you desire something that you do not believe is possible, you are not in alignment. When there is something that you want and you are feeling unhappy that you do not have it, you are not in alignment; when you see someone who currently has the very thing that you desire and you feel jealous, you are not in alignment.

If we were standing in your physical shoes, our attention would be upon bringing ourselves into alignment with the desires and preferences that we have launched—we would <u>consciously</u> feel our way into alignment.

Your Natural Desires
Cannot Be Held Back

All of your desires, wants, or preferences emanate from you naturally and constantly, for you stand at the Leading Edge of a Universe that makes that so. So, you cannot hold your desires back; the eternal nature of this Universe insists that your desires come forth.

This is the simple basis of this eternally expanding Universe:

- Variety causes contemplation.
- Contemplation produces preference.
- Preference is asking.
- Asking is always answered.

Regarding your creation of your own life experience, there really is only one important question for you to ask: How can I bring myself into vibrational alignment with the desires that my experience has produced?

And the answer is simple: Pay attention to the way you feel, and deliberately choose thoughts—about everything—that feel good to you when you think them.

Chapter 14

Some Things You Knew
Before You Arrived

*I*t is helpful to remember that you are creators who have come into this Leading-Edge time-space-reality to experience the joy of directing Source Energy into the specifics of your physical life experience.

As you made the decision to come into this body, you knew that you were a creator and that the Earth environment would inspire your specific creation. You also knew that whenever you asked, it would be given. And you were thrilled at the prospect of being inspired to attain your own specific desires, understanding that Source would flow through you to achieve the completion of those desires.

You also knew the following:

- By always reaching for the feeling of joy, or Well-Being, you would always be moving toward that which you desire.

- In the process of moving toward your desires, you would experience joy.

- In this Earth-plane environment, you would have sufficient leeway to mold your vibration into a pleasing position for the attraction of a wonderful life experience.

- Since Well-Being is the basis of this wonderful Universe, you would have sufficient opportunity—through a continual offering of thought—to mold your own thoughts into pleasing life experiences.

- Well-Being abounds, so you felt no risk or concern about the contrasting environment into which you were moving.

- Variety would help you choose your specific life.

- Your work was to direct your thoughts, and that in doing so, your life would unfold.

- You are an eternal extension of Source Energy, and that the basis of that which you are is good.

- You would be able to easily allow the Well-Being of your origin, and of your Source, to steadily flow through you.

- You could never get far from your Source, and that you could never completely pinch yourself off from it.

- You would experience immediate emotions to help you understand the direction of your thought, and that your emotions would instantly tell you if you were, in any moment, moving toward or away from what you desired.

- You would know, by the way you were *feeling*, moment by moment, how much you were allowing your connection to your Stream of Well-Being. And so, you came forth into this Earth experience with eager anticipation of a wonderful life.

- And you also knew that there would not be an immediate manifestation of any thought, so that you would have ample opportunity to mold, evaluate, decide, and enjoy the *Creative Process.*

We refer to that time between your offering of a thought and its physical manifestation as "the buffer of time." This is that wonderful time of offering thought, noticing how it feels, adjusting the thought to achieve an even better feeling, and then, in an attitude of absolute expectation, enjoying the gentle, steady unfolding of anything and everything that you have concluded as your desires.

"If I Know So Much, How Come I'm Not Successful?"

There is never a reason for you to be without something that you desire. Nor is there ever a reason for you to experience something that you do not desire—for you hold absolute control of your experiences.

Sometimes our physical friends disagree with that powerful statement, for they often find themselves without something that they desire, or with something that they do not desire. And so, they argue that they must not really be the creator of their own experience, for they would not have done that to themselves; if they were *really* in control, things would be different.

We want you to know that you always hold the power and control of your own life experience. The only reason that you could ever experience something other than what you desire is because you are giving the majority of your attention to something other than what you desire.

"Can I Really Count on the Law of Attraction?"

The <u>Law of Attraction</u> always yields to you the essence of the balance of your thoughts. No exceptions. You get what you think about—

whether you want it or not. And in time, with practice, you will come to remember that the *Law of Attraction* is always consistent. It never tricks you. It never deceives you. It never confuses you, for the *Law of Attraction* responds precisely to the vibration that you are offering. But the confusion, for many, comes because they are offering vibrations that they do not realize they are offering. They know that they hold a desire in a specific direction, and they know that their desire has not yet come to them, but what they often do *not* realize is that they are offering the majority of their thoughts in opposition to their own desire.

Once you understand your own *Emotional Guidance System,* you will never again offer your vibrations in ignorance. And in time, you will achieve such keen awareness of your own valuable emotions that you will know, in every moment, if the thought that you are currently focusing on is taking you toward, or away from, something you desire. You will learn to literally *feel* your way to the things that you desire, on all subjects.

The basis of your world is one of Well-Being. You can allow it or not, but the basis is Well-Being. The Law of Attraction says: That which is like unto itself, is drawn. And so, the essence of whatever you give your attention to is unfolding in your experience. Therefore, there is nothing that you cannot be, do, or have. This is Law.

"But I Can't Get to San Diego from Phoenix!"

So if all of this is true (and it is our absolute promise to you that it is true), then how is it that so many are experiencing so much of what they do not want?

Consider this question: *If I am in Phoenix, Arizona, and it is my desire to be in San Diego, California, how would I go about getting to San Diego?* The answer to this question is easy to hear: No matter what your mode of transportation—by air, by car, or even on foot—if you will face in the direction of San Diego, and continue to move in the direction of San Diego, then you must reach San Diego.

If you head toward San Diego, but then you lose your sense of direction and you head back toward Phoenix, and then you get turned back around again and you head toward San Diego, and then you get confused again and you head back toward Phoenix . . . you could potentially spend the rest of your life experience just moving back and forth, and you could, conceivably, never arrive in San Diego. But because of your knowledge of direction, and with the help of road signs and other travelers, it is not logical that you would remain forever lost in the Arizona desert unable to find your way to San Diego. The 400-mile trip between the two cities is easily understood, and the idea of making the trip is completely believable, and if it were your desire to make the trip, you would find a way to do so.

We want you to understand that the trip between wherever you are, on any subject, and where you desire to be, is as easily attainable as the trip from Phoenix to San Diego—once you understand how to discern where you are along the way.

For example, the thing that makes it seem more difficult to travel from financial insolvency to financial abundance is that you have not been aware when you were turned around and headed in the opposite direction. And, the only reason that your trip has not taken you from no relationship to the perfect, fulfilling, rewarding relationship you desire is that you have not been aware of the power of your thoughts and words that were taking you back to Phoenix. You clearly understand all of the factors involved in transporting yourself from Phoenix to San Diego, but you have not understood the factors involved in transporting yourself from sickness into fabulous health, from the absence of the relationship you have wanted to the fulfillment of this wonderful relationship, or from barely scraping by financially to having the freedom to do the things you really want to do.

Once you understand the clarity that your emotions provide, you will never again not know what you are doing with your current thought. You will always be aware of whether you are, in this moment, moving toward or away from your intended goal or desire. Your awareness of the way you feel will give you the clarity you have been seeking—and you will never be lost in the desert again. Once you have the knowledge that you are mov-ing in the direction of your desires, you may begin to relax a little bit and enjoy the fantastic journey.

Chapter 15

You Are a Perfect Yet Expanding Being, in a Perfect Yet Expanding World, in a Perfect Yet Expanding Universe

It is important that you know these things:

- You are a physical extension of Source Energy.

- The physical world you live in provides a perfect environment in which to create.

- The variety that exists helps you focus your own personal desires or preferences.

- When a desire is focused within you, the summoning of Creative Life Force immediately begins to flow toward your desire—and the Universe expands. And that is good.

- Your conscious realization of the *Creative Process* is not necessary in order for it to continue.

- The Leading-Edge environment that you are physically focused in will continue to stimulate new desires in all who participate.

- Every desire or preference, no matter how large or small it may seem to you, is understood and answered by All-That-Is.

- As every desire from every perceiver is answered, the Universe expands.

- As the Universe expands, the variety expands.

- As the variety expands, your experience expands.

- As your experience expands, your desire expands.

- As your desire expands, the answering of your desire expands.

- And the Universe expands—and that is good. In fact, it is perfect.

- You live in an eternally expanding environment, which constantly causes newly focused desires within you, which Source immediately and always answers.

- With each receiving of that which you are asking for, you achieve a new vantage point from which you spontaneously ask again.

- And so, the expansion of the Universe and your personal expansion will always be as follows:

  — You live in an expanding Universe.

  — You live in an expanding physical world.

  — You are an expanding Being.

— And all of this *is,* whether you consciously
   understand it or not.

— This Universe is eternally expanding, and so are you.

— And that is good.

Consciously Participate in
Your Own Delicious Expansion

We eagerly offer our perspective to you for one reason only: so
that you may *consciously* participate in your own delicious expansion. *Your expansion is a given; the expansion of your time-space-
reality is a given, and the expansion of this Universe is a given. It is just
ever so much more satisfying for you to consciously and deliberately participate in your own expansion.*

❦ ❦ ❦ ❧ ❧ ❧

Chapter 16

You Are Co-creating Within a Magnificently Diverse Universe

*I*f you have the ability to imagine it, or even to think about it, this *Universe has the ability and the resources to deliver it fully unto* *you,* for this Universe is like a well-stocked kitchen with every ingredient imaginable at your disposal. And within every particle of this Universe is that which is wanted and the lack of it. This perspective of abundance, and the lack of it, is the environment in which focus is possible—and focus activates the *Law of Attraction.*

If you do not have the ability to know what you do want, you will not have the ability to know what you do not want. And without the ability to know what you do not want, you could not know what you do want. And so, it is through your exposure to life experience that your natural preferences are born. In fact, these preferences are exuding from you in all moments of every day, at many levels of your Being. Even the cells of your well-tended-to body are having their own experience and are emanating *their* own preferences—and every preference is recognized by Source and immediately answered, with no exceptions.

Unwanted Must Be Allowed,
for Wanted to Be Received

Sometimes our physical friends express their desire for a less diverse Universe. They long for a place where there are not so many unwanted things, a place where more things are exactly as they prefer them to be. And we always explain that you did not come forth into this physical experience wanting to take all of the experiences that exist and whittle them down to a handful of good ideas upon which all of you agree, for that would lead to end-edness, which cannot be. This is an expanding Universe, and all things must be allowed. In other words, for you to understand and experience what you desire, you must understand that which you do not desire, for, in order to be able to choose and focus, both must be present and understood.

You Did Not Come
to Fix a Broken World

As Non-Physical Source Energy expressing through your physical experience, your physical experience is truly the Leading Edge of thought. And as you are fine-tuning your creative experience, you are taking thought beyond that which it has ever been before.

As you enthusiastically made the decision to come into this physical body and create in this way, you understood, from your Non-Physical vantage point, that this physical world was not broken and in need of repair—and you did not come forth to fix it.

You saw this physical world as a creative environment in which you, and everyone else, could express yourselves creatively—you did not come forth to try to get others to stop doing what they are doing and do something else. You came forth understanding the value in the contrast, and the balance in the variety.

Every physical Being on your planet is your partner in co-creation, and if you would accept that and appreciate the diversity of beliefs and desires— all of you would have more expansive, satisfying, and fulfilling experiences.

Do Not Put Those
Unwanted Ingredients in Your Pie

Imagine yourself as a chef in an extremely well-stocked kitchen that contains every imaginable ingredient. Let us say that you have a clear idea of the culinary creation you desire, and you understand how to combine these easily accessible ingredients in order to fulfill your desire. And as you proceed, there are many ingredients that are *not* appropriate for your creation, so you do not utilize them, but you also feel no discomfort about their existence. You simply utilize the ingredients that *will* enhance your creation—and you leave the ingredients that are not appropriate for your creation out of your pie.

Some of the ingredients in this well-stocked kitchen are harmonious with your creation, and some of them are not. But even though adding some of these ingredients to your creation would absolutely ruin your pie, you do not feel the need to push against those ingredients, or to ban them from the kitchen, because you understand that there is no reason for them to end up in your pie unless *you* put them in it. And since you are clear about which ones enhance your creation and which ones do not enhance it, you feel no concern about the great variety of ingredients that exist.

There Is Enough Room for All
Diverse Thoughts and Experiences

From your Non-Physical perspective of the enormous variety of experiences, beliefs, and desires that exist among the people of your world, you felt no need to omit or control some of them. *You understood that there is room enough in this expansive Universe for all manner of thought and experience. You had every intention of being deliberate about your own creative control of your own life experience and your own creations— but you had no intentions of trying to control the creations of others.*

The variety did not frighten you, but instead, inspired you, for you knew that you were each the creator of your own experience, and you understood that your exposure to the contrast would inspire specific directions within you, and that just because others may choose differently, it did not make you right and them wrong, or them right and you wrong. You understood the value of the diversity.

Here Is the Process by Which Your Universe Expands

So from the variety or contrast, your own preferences or desires are born. And in the moment that your preference begins to exist, it begins to draw to itself, through the *Law of Attraction,* the essence of that which matches it—and it then begins an immediate expansion.

And as you pay attention to the way you feel and continue to choose good-feeling thoughts regarding your newly born preference, you stay aligned with it, and now it gently and easily appears in your experience—and you have now created your desire. But, along with this newly achieved physical manifestation of your desire comes an evolved perspective. And so, the vibrational characteristics of you and everything about you have shifted somewhat, and you have moved into a new set of contrasting circumstances that will again inspire new preferences within you—and now, new rockets of desire emanate from you.

And in the moment that this new desire exists, it too begins to vibrationally draw unto itself, and it too expands. So now, as you continue to pay attention to the way you *feel,* and you choose good-feeling thoughts regarding this newly born preference, you remain vibrationally aligned with it. Therefore, it gently and easily appears in your experience. And again, you have created your desire. And again, you have achieved a powerful place of clarity where another new set of contrasting factors surround you—which again will cause a new rocket of desire to be born. . . .

This is how the Universe expands, and this is why you are on the Leading Edge of the expansion. The valuable contrast continues to provide the birthing of endless new desires, and as each desire is born, Source responds to the desire. It is a never-ending, always flowing, pure, positive Energy expansion.

You Will Never Get There,
So Enjoy Your Journey

Once you consciously observe, from your own creative per-spective, how each new achievement leads to another new desire, you will begin to personally understand your part in this expansive Universe. And, in time, you will come to remember that you never get it done because you never cease your awareness of the contrast out of which is always born a new idea or desire. The entire Uni-verse is established in that way. And as you begin to relax into the idea that you are an eternal Being, that your desires will never cease to flow, and that any desire that is born has the power within it to attract (by *Law of Attraction*) all that is necessary for the expansion and fulfillment of itself, then you may remember the immense Well-Being upon which this Universe is established, and, you may then relax into the eternal nature of your own Being. It is then that you will begin to enjoy your journey.

If your goal is to, finally, once and for all, achieve all that you desire, you will find yourself unable to ever fulfill that goal, for the expanding nature of this Universe defies that idea. *You cannot ever get it done because you cannot ever cease to be, and neither can you ever halt your awareness. Yet, out of your awareness will always be born another asking, and each asking always summons another answering.*

Your eternal nature is one of expansion—and in that expansion is the potential for unspeakable joy.

Feel the Balance and Perfection
of Your Environment

So, the contrast causes new desire to be born within you. The new desire radiates from you, and as you offer the vibration of your new desire, that desire is answered. Every time. When you ask, it is given.

Now think about the perfection of this process: *Continuing new ideas for the improvement of your experience emanate from you constantly, and are answered constantly.*

Consider the perfection of this Universal environment: *Every point of Consciousness is improving its state of being in just the same way as you, where every desire is understood and answered, and every perspective is honored and responded to.*

Feel the balance and perfection of your environment: *Every point of Consciousness, even the Consciousness of a cell in your body, can request an improved state of being—and get it.*

Since Every Request Is Granted, There Is No Competition

Each point of view matters; every request is granted; and as this amazing Universe unerringly expands, there is no end to the Universal resources that fulfill these requests. And there is no end to the answers to the never-ending stream of questions—and for that reason, there is no competition.

It is not possible for someone else to receive the resources that were meant for you, and you cannot selfishly squander resources that were intended for someone else. All desires are answered; all requests are granted, and no one is left unanswered, unloved, or unfulfilled. When you stay aligned with your Energy Stream, you always win, and somebody else does not have to lose for you to win. There is always enough.

Sometimes our physical friends have a difficult time remembering this truth because they may experience some shortage in their experience, or observe it in the experience of another. But what they are witnessing is not an evidence of shortage or a lack of resources, but instead the disallowance of the receiving of the resources that have been requested and answered. **Step 1** has occurred: The asking is in place. **Step 2** has occurred: The answering is in place. But **Step 3**, the allowing, has not occurred.

If someone is not receiving what they are asking for, it is not because there is a shortage of resources; it can only be that the person holding the desire is out of alignment with their own request. There is no shortage. There is no lack. There is no competition for resources. There is only the allowing or the disallowing of that which you are asking for.

Chapter 17

Where Are You,
and Where Do You Want to Be?

Have you seen the Global Positioning navigational systems that are available in vehicles today? An antenna on the roof of your vehicle sends a signal to satellites in the sky that identify your current location. Once you enter your desired destination into the keypad, the computer calculates the route between where you are and where you want to go. The monitor informs you of the distance you have to travel and recommends the best route to get there, and once you begin, the system will give you (by spoken word or by text) specific directions to lead you to your new destination.

The navigational system never asks: "Where have you been?" It does not ask: "Why have you been there so long?" Its only mission is to assist you in getting from where you are to where you want to be. Your emotions provide a similar guidance system for you, for their primary function is also to help you travel the distance from where you are to wherever you want to be.

It is extremely important that you know where you are in relationship to where you want to be in order to effectively move *closer* to where you want to be. An understanding of both where you are and where you want to be is essential if you are to make any deliberate decisions about your journey.

You are surrounded by many influences in your physical environment, and often, others ask or insist that you behave differently in order to positively affect their experience. You are deluged with laws, rules, and expectations that are imposed by others, and almost everyone seems to have an opinion about how you should behave. But it is not possible for you to stay on track between where you are and where you want to be if you are using those kinds of outside influences to guide you.

Often you are pulled this way and that in an attempt to please another, only to discover that no matter how hard you try, you cannot consistently move in any pleasing direction, and so, you not only do not please them, but you also do not please yourself. And because you are being pulled in so many different directions, your path to where you want to be usually gets lost in the process.

Your Greatest Gift to Give Is Your Happiness

The greatest gift that you could ever give to another is your own happiness, for when you are in a state of joy, happiness, or appreciation, you are fully connected to the Stream of pure, positive Source Energy that is truly who you are. And when you are in that state of connection, anything or anyone that you are holding as your object of attention benefits from your attention.

No one else needs you to be or do things for them in order for them to be fulfilled—for all of them have the same access to the Stream of Well-Being that you do. Often, others (who do not understand that they have access to the Stream) suffer in their inability to hold themselves in a place of feeling good, and ask you to behave in a way that they believe will make them feel better. But not only do they hold you in a place of discomfort as they try to make you responsible for their joy, they hold themselves in a place of bondage as well. For they cannot control the way any other behaves, and if that control is necessary for their happiness, then they truly are in trouble.

Your Happiness Does Not Depend on What Others Do

Your happiness does not depend on what others do, but only upon your own vibrational balance. And the happiness of others does not depend on you, but only on *their* own vibrational balance, for the way anyone feels, in any moment, is only about their own mix of Energies. The way you feel is simply, clearly, and always the indicator of the vibrational balance between your desires and your vibrational offering, which, from your vantage point, you have launched.

There is nothing in all of the Universe more important for anyone to understand than how the vibration they are offering is matching the vibrations of their desires, and the way you *feel* is your indicator of whether you are allowing your connection to Source or not. Every good feeling; every positive creation; all your abundance, clarity, health, vitality, and Well-Being—and all the things that you consider to be good, are dependent upon the way you are feeling right now and on the relationship that that feeling-vibration has to the vibration of who you really are and what you really desire.

Each Thought Moves You Closer to, or Farther from, San Diego

Just as it is easy for you to contemplate a successful trip from Phoenix to San Diego, it will be easy for you to contemplate a successful trip from financial insecurity to financial security, from sickness to wellness, from confusion to clarity. . . . On your trip from Phoenix to San Diego, there will be no major unknowns, for you understand the distance between the two cities, you know where you are along the way, and you understand what moving in the wrong direction means to your success. Once you understand your own *Emotional Guidance System,* you will never again be confused about where you are in relationship to where you want to be. Also, you will feel, with each thought that you offer, whether you are moving closer to, or further from, your desired outcome.

If you are using any other influence as your source of guidance, you will get lost and go off track, for no others understand, as you do, the distance between where you are and where you want to be. But even though they cannot understand your desires purely, they will still continually add their desires to the mix. And so, only when you pay attention to the way *you feel* can you guide yourself steadily toward your own goals.

Why Does Saying <u>No</u> to It Mean Saying <u>Yes</u> to It?

Your vibrational Universe has the *Law of Attraction* as its basis. That means that your Universe is about inclusion. When you give your attention to something that you desire and you say *yes* to it, you are including it in your vibration. But when you look at something you do not want and you say *no* to it, you are including it in your vibration. When you give no attention to it, you do not include it, but you cannot exclude anything that you are giving your attention to, because your attention to it includes it in your vibration, every time, without exception.

Chapter 18

You Can Gradually Change Your Vibrational Frequency

Just because you make the decision to find a different thought, it does not necessarily mean that you can go directly to that thought right now, for the *Law of Attraction* has something to say about the thoughts you have access to from where you are. *Of course, there is no thought that you cannot eventually have—just as there is no place that you cannot eventually reach from wherever you are—but you cannot instantly jump to a thought that has a vibrational frequency very different from the thoughts you are usually thinking.*

Sometimes one of your friends, who is currently in a much better-feeling place than you are, may encourage you to stop thinking so negatively and choose more positive thoughts. But just because your friend is there in that better-feeling place does not mean that your friend can bring you there—for the *Law of Attraction* will not allow you to find a vibrational frequency that is far from the frequency that you usually sustain. And even though you do want to feel better, you may not feel that you can find the joyful thought that your friend wants you to find. But we want you to understand that you can eventually find that thought, and that once you have deliberately and gradually changed your vibrational frequency, you will be able to sustain that more positive position once you do achieve it.

As you discover that you can always know the vibrational content of your Being, and can therefore always be aware of what your point of attraction is, you will then be in conscious creative control of your own experience. And once you understand that your emotions are giving you specific feedback about your vibrational content, then you can proceed with the deliberate and gradual adjustment of your vibration.

Reach for the Best-Feeling
Thought You Have Access To

Choosing a different thought will always produce a different emotional response. So you could say, "I will deliberately choose my thoughts so that I can feel better." That would be a good decision for you to make. An even better decision, and really, an easier one to make is: "I want to feel good, so I will try to feel good by choosing a thought that *does* feel good."

If it is your decision to "follow your bliss," and you have been focusing on a life situation that is nowhere near bliss, your decision to follow your bliss would be unsuccessful because the *Law of Attraction* cannot deliver a thought that holds such a dramatic vibrational difference. But if your decision is to *reach for the best-feeling thought that you have access to,* that decision can be easily achieved.

The key to moving up the *vibrational emotional scale* is to be consciously aware of, even sensitive to, the way you feel, for if you are not aware of how you feel, you cannot understand which way you are moving on the scale. (You could be turned around and on your way back to Phoenix and not know it.)

But if you take the time to consciously determine the emotion that you are currently experiencing, then any improvement in your feeling means that you are making progress toward your goal, while any intensifying of the negative emotion means that you are going in the wrong direction.

So, a good way to feel your way up this *vibrational emotional scale* is to always be reaching for the feeling of relief that comes when you release a more resistant thought and replace it with a more allowing thought. The Stream of Well-Being is *always* flowing through you, and the more you allow it, the better you feel. The more you resist it, the worse you feel.

❧ ❧ ❧ ❧ ❧ ❧

Chapter 19

Only You Can Know
How You Feel about You

When you expect something, it is on the way. When you believe something, it is on the way. When you fear something, it is on the way.

Your attitude or mood is always pointing toward what is coming, but you are never stuck with your current point of attraction. Just because you have picked up these thoughts, beliefs, attitudes, and moods along your physical trail does not mean that you have to continue attracting in response to them. You have creative control of your own experience. And, by paying attention to your own *Emotional Guidance System,* you can change your point of attraction.

If there are things in your experience that you no longer wish to experience, your belief must change.

If there are things that are not in your experience that you want to bring into your experience, your belief must change.

There is no condition so severe that you cannot reverse it by choosing different thoughts. However, choosing different thoughts requires focus and practice. If you continue to focus as you have been, to think as you have been, and to believe as you have been, then nothing in your experience will change.

Life Is Always in Motion,
So You Cannot Be "Stuck"

Sometimes our physical friends will say, "I'm stuck! I've been in this place for a very long time, and I can't get out of it. I'm stuck!"

And we always explain that it is not possible to stand still or be stuck, because Energy, and therefore life, is always in motion. Things are always changing.

But the reason it may feel to you as if you are stuck is because, while you are continuing to think the same thoughts, things *are* changing—*but they are changing to the same thing over and over.*

If you want things to change to different things, you must think different thoughts. And that simply requires finding unfamiliar ways of approaching familiar subjects.

Others Cannot Understand
Your Desires or Feelings

Others are often eager to guide you. There are endless people—with endless opinions, rules, requirements, and suggestions for how you should live your life, but none of them are able to take into consideration the only thing that matters in achieving your desires: *Others cannot understand the vibrational content of your desires, and they cannot understand the vibrational content of where you are, so they are not in any way equipped to guide you. Even when they have the very best of intentions and want your absolute Well-Being, they do not know. And even though many of them attempt to be unselfish, it is never possible for them to separate their desire for you from their own desire for themselves.*

No One Else Knows What
Is Appropriate for You

When you remember that when anyone asks, it is always given, then can you not feel the perfection of an environment where each specific perspective gets to choose?

Imagine that you will attend an *Abraham-Hicks Art of Allowing Workshop.* You know when and where it will be held, and you have made time in your schedule to attend. So, with relative ease, you make all the decisions that are right for you.

You look down the list of approximately 50 seminars that will be offered during the next year, and you pick a time and location that is most appealing to you. You notice that a seminar will be held in the city where you live, but the date conflicts with something else you had planned to do, so you look for an alternative. You then find a date that matches the time you *do* have open, you look for a seminar within that time frame, and you find one in a city that you have always wanted to visit. So you call Abraham-Hicks Publications and purchase your seat for the seminar.

Since you do not live in the seminar city, you realize that you will need room accommodations and some sort of transportation to the city. So, taking into consideration your specific desires and needs, you make several plans: You decide to travel by air, because of the time factor, and you choose a hotel a few blocks away from the seminar hotel because you are a member of their rewards program and you can get a better rate by doing so. (You also prefer the type of mattresses that particular hotel chain offers.)

Once you arrive at your seminar city, you rent a car from your favorite among the many car-rental agencies. And on your way to the hotel, you stop at a restaurant that perfectly satisfies your cravings, and that fits perfectly into your price range. You have taken very good care of yourself. In fact, you have arranged a perfectly wonderful time.

But what if Abraham-Hicks Publications had decided that they, from their vast experience in offering seminars, were in a better position to make plans for you. So, based on what they have heard from the thousands who have attended their seminars, they have decided that they will make your arrangements.

They assume, based on your address, that you would prefer to attend the seminar in your hometown, so that is the one they sign you up for. But then you explain that you have a scheduling conflict, so they adjust their decision and send you a ticket for the seminar city you prefer.

And, in like manner, as they make their decisions about what is the best airline for you to take, the car-rental agency you rent from, the hotel bed you sleep in, and the food you eat, their choices would fall far short of pleasing you. You are much better equipped to make those decisions for yourself.

When you remember that everyone who asks is given, then how wonderful and appropriate it is for you to make the choices for you—for the Universe operates much more efficiently without a middleman interceding on your behalf. No one else knows what is appropriate for you—but you do. You always know in the moment what is best for you.

Chapter 20

Trying to Hinder Another's Freedom Always Costs You Your Freedom

Yes, when you ask, it is always given, but you must be in vibrational harmony with what you are asking for before you can let it in to your experience. The reason why so many people do not remember or believe that all that they are asking for is being answered is because they are not consciously aware of what they are doing, vibrationally. They are not making the *conscious* connection between their thoughts, the subsequent feelings those thoughts evoke, and the manifestations that are occurring. And without that conscious connection, you cannot know where you are in relationship to that which you desire.

When you know that you want something, and you notice you do not have it, you assume that there is something outside of yourself that is keeping it from you, but that is never true. The only thing that ever prevents your receiving something that you desire is that your habit of thought is different from your desire.

Once you are aware of the power of your thoughts, and of your ability to allow in the things that you desire, you then have creative control of your experience. But if you are predominantly focused upon the *results* of your focused thoughts rather than *feeling* your way within your thoughts, it is easy to lose your way.

Every "Reality" Has Been Focused by Someone into Being

Sometimes people will argue, "But Abraham, I'm only telling you what-is. I'm only facing the reality of the situation." And we say that you were taught to face reality before you knew you were *creating* reality . . . do not face reality unless it is a reality you want to create—for any "reality" only exists because someone has focused it into being.

Someone will say, "But this is a true thing, and therefore it deserves my attention." And we say that you make whatever you give your attention to . . . your *Truth*. And so, it is extremely beneficial for you to focus primarily on the way you feel while giving only scant attention to the manifestations as they are unfolding, for whenever you are giving your primary attention to things as they are, you are hindering the expansion of what-is.

All those statistics that are gathered about your own experiences and about others—are only about how somebody has already flowed Energy. They are not about any hard-and-fast *now* reality.

Within your current society, there are many who gather the statistics of human experience. They spend lifetimes comparing experiences, and categorizing them as appropriate or inappropriate, right or wrong. They weigh the pros and the cons and the pluses and the minuses of topic after topic, but they seldom realize that their vibrational offerings are not serving them. They have no sense of their own power because they are flowing their Energy in opposing directions. Their lives have become more about labeling the behavior or experiences of those with whom they share their planet than about their own creating.

And so, they find themselves in a very uncomfortable position as they come to believe that their happiness or Well-Being depends upon the behavior of others. They point to people, behaviors, or beliefs and call them inappropriate, saying *no* to them, without realizing that they are including into their experience the vibration of the very thing they do not want. And so, without the knowledge of how it is that those unwanted things are making their way into their experience, they become increasingly guarded and fearful.

Unwanted Things Cannot Jump
into Your Experience Uninvited

Freedom from the fear of unwanted experiences will never be achieved by trying to control the behavior or desires of others. Your freedom can only be allowed by adjusting your own vibrational point of attraction.

Without a knowledge of the *Law of Attraction,* and without a conscious awareness of what you are doing with your own vibrational point of attraction, it is understandable why you would attempt to control the circumstances that surround you. But you *cannot* control the many circumstances that surround you. However, once you learn about the *Law of Attraction,* and once you are aware of the way your thoughts feel, you will never again feel fear about unwanted things jumping into your experience. You will understand that nothing can jump into your experience without your invitation. Since there is no assertion in this attraction-based Universe, if you do *not* achieve vibrational harmony with it, it cannot come to you; and unless you *do* achieve vibrational harmony with it, it cannot come to you.

Even the smallest among you, your babies, are offering vibrations that the Universe is matching. And, like you, your little ones are influenced by the vibrations of those who surround them, but nevertheless, they are creating their own reality. Like you, they did not begin the creation of their life in this body once they were in it, but long before their physical birth they set into motion this life experience that they are now living.

The greatest argument we hear from our physical friends who want to understand their relationship with the Non-Physical and how it is that they are here, living and creating, is: "But how is it possible that this little baby who has really learned very little about our physical world could be held responsible for the creation of its own life?" We want you to understand that this little one is very well prepared for its life in your environment because, like you, it was born with an *Emotional Guidance System* to help it find its way.

These babies, like you, came romping joyously into your time-space-reality, eager for the opportunity to continually make new decisions and to align with the Energy of their Source. Do not worry about them, or about anyone. Well-Being is the order of this Universe, no matter how your current vantage point may appear.

Remember, your emotions are telling you everything you need to know about your connection to Source Energy: They are telling you how much Source Energy you are summoning in response to your focused desire; and they are also telling you if you are, in this moment of thought and emotion, in vibrational alignment with your desire.

Was It Your Speed, or Was It the Tree?

If you were driving your vehicle at 100 miles per hour and you hit a tree, you would experience a very big crash. However, if you were to hit the same tree while your vehicle was traveling at just five miles per hour, the outcome would be considerably different. See the speed of your vehicle like the power of your desire. In other words, the more you want something, or the longer you have been focusing upon your desire, the faster the Energy moves. The tree, in our analogy, represents the resistance, or the contradictory thoughts, that may be present.

It is not pleasant to run into trees, and it is also not pleasant to hold powerful desires in the midst of great resistance. Some try to remedy the imbalance by slowing down their vehicle. In other words, they deny their desire, or they try to release it, and sometimes, with great effort, they are able to diffuse the power of their desire to some degree, but by far, the better remedy would be to reduce your level of resistance.

Your desire is the natural result of the contrast in which you are focused. The entire Universe exists to inspire the next new desire. And so, if you are trying to avoid your own desire, you are attempting to move contrary to Universal Forces. And even if you *are* able to suppress a desire here and there, more desires are continually evolving within you, for you have come forth into this body and into this wonderful contrasting environment with the clear intent of focusing the Energy that creates worlds through the powerfully focused lens of *your* perspective. And so, nothing in all of the Universe is more natural than *your* continuing desire.

Behind Every Desire
Is the Desire to Feel Good

There is no desire that anyone holds for any other reason than that they believe they will feel better in the achievement of it. Whether it is a material object, a physical state of being, a relationship, a condition, or a circumstance—at the heart of every desire is the desire to feel good. And so, the standard of success in life is not the things or the money— the standard of success is absolutely the amount of joy you feel.

The basis of life is freedom, and the result of life is expansion—but the purpose of your life is joy. And that is why the main event has never been the manifestation. It has always been the way you feel in the moment. In other words, you intended to come into the physical realm of contrast to define what is wanted, to connect with the Energy that creates worlds, and to flow it toward your objects of attention—not because the objects of attention are important, but because the act of flowing Energy is essential to life.

In Your Appreciation,
You Offer No Resistance

Remember, you are an extension of Source Energy, and when you are allowing your full connection to your Source, you feel good, and to the degree that you disallow your connection, you feel less good. You are pure, positive Energy. You are love. You expect good things. You respect and love yourself. You respect and love others—and you are a natural born appreciator.

Appreciation and self-love are the most important aspects you could ever nurture. *Appreciation of others and the appreciation of yourself are the closest vibrational matches to Source Energy of anything we have ever witnessed anywhere in this Universe.*

Whenever you are focused upon something you appreciate, since that current choice of thought is so similar to who you really are as Source Energy, there is no contradiction in your Energy. You are, in your moment of appreciation, offering no resistance to who you are, so your resulting emotional indication is one of love, joy, or the feeling of appreciation. You feel very good.

But if you criticize someone or even find fault with yourself, your resulting feeling would not feel good, because the vibration of this thought of criticism is so very different from that of your Source. In other words, because you have chosen a thought that does not match who you really are, you can, in this moment, feel the discord of your choice through your emotions.

If your grandmother, who adores and appreciates you, tells you how wonderful you are, the reason those words feel so good is because they cause you to focus in a way that connects you with who you really are. But if a teacher or an acquaintance chastises you for some action you have offered, you feel bad because you have now been influenced to a thought that does not match who you really are.

Your emotions let you know, in every moment, whether you are allowing your connection to who you are or not. When you allow your connection, you thrive. When you do not allow your connection, you do not thrive.

You Must Be Selfish Enough to Align with Well-Being

Now, occasionally, someone will accuse us of teaching selfishness. And we agree. Indeed, we do teach selfishness, for if you are not selfish enough to deliberately align with the Energy of your Source, you have nothing to give anyway.

Some worry, "If I selfishly achieve what I want, wouldn't I be unfairly taking it from others?" But that concern is based on the misconception that there is a limit of available abundance. They worry that if they take too much of the pie, others will be left with nothing, while, in reality, *the pie expands in proportion to the vibrational requests of all of you.*

You never say, "I feel guilty about the abundance of good health that I have been living, so I have decided that I will be sick for the next couple years in order to allow someone who has been sick the opportunity to use my portion of wellness for himself." For you understand that by your being well, you are in no way depriving another of the experience of wellness.

There are some who fear that a selfish person may deliberately intend harm to another, but it is not possible for someone who is connected to Source Energy to wish harm upon another—for those vibrations are not compatible.

Some say, "I saw a picture of a mass murderer, and he looked gleeful. He showed no remorse at all. He said he enjoyed what he did." But you have no way of accurately accessing what he is feeling. You experience your own emotions because of the relationship between your desire and your current state of thought about the subject, but you have no way of accurately feeling *his* emotions. It is our absolute promise to you that no one connected to Source Energy would ever cause harm to another. They lash out in their defensiveness, or in their disconnectedness, but never from their state of connection. You must understand that the ultimate act of selfishness is to connect with Self. And when you do that, you are pure, positive Energy focused in this physical body.

If everyone on your planet were connected to their own Source Energy, there would be no assaults, for there would be no jealousy, insecurity, or uncomfortable feelings of competition. If everyone understood the power of their own Being, they would not seek to control others. Any feelings of insecurity and hatred are born from your disconnection with who you are. Your (selfish) connection with Well-Being would bring only Well-Being.

And, most important, we want you to understand that it is not necessary for everyone else (or *anyone* else, for that matter) to understand what you are learning here in order for *you* to live a wonderful experience. Once you remember who you are, and once you deliberately reach for thoughts that hold you in vibrational alignment with who you are, your world will also fall into alignment—and Well-Being will show itself to you in all areas of your life experience.

If You Are Not Expecting It,
You Are Not Allowing It

Remember, each emotion indicates how much Energy you are summoning because of your desire, and how much of that summoned Energy you are allowing because of the predominant thoughts and beliefs that you currently hold relative to that desire. If you are feeling strong emotion, whether positive or negative, that means that your desire is powerfully focused, and you are summoning a great deal of Source Energy toward your desire. When your strong emotions feel bad—like depression, fear, or anger—that means you are offering resistance to your desire. When your strong emotions feel good—like passion, enthusiasm, expectation, or love—that means you are offering no resistance to your desire, so the Source Energy that you have summoned through your desire is not being challenged vibrationally by you—and you are currently allowing the unfolding of your desire.

So it seems obvious that the perfect creative situation is to really, really want something that you truly believe is possible. And when that combination of desire and belief is present within you, things will quickly and easily unfold in your experience. But when you want something that you do *not* believe is possible, when you hold a desire for something that you do *not* expect— although a strong enough desire can override a weaker belief—it does not unfold easily, for you are not allowing it into your current experience.

The Feeling of a Pure
Desire Feels Good to You

Unfortunately, many people think that the uncomfortable feeling of wanting something they do not expect to experience is what the feeling of *desire* is; they no longer recognize the feeling of pure desire as that fresh, eager, feeling of expectancy that they knew when they were younger. The feeling of pure desire is always delicious, as it represents the vibrations that are stretched out before you into your unseen future, preparing the way for the *Law of Attraction* to match things up on your behalf.

The value in recognizing your emotions and then *consciously* working to offer thoughts in order to deliberately produce better-feeling emotions is truly what *Deliberate Creation* is. It is also what the *Art of Allowing* is all about.

Why Would You Want
to Be Over There?

Sometimes a person will say, "I'm not happy over here where I'm standing. I would much rather be over there—over there where my body is not sick, or over there where I'm not overweight, or over there where I have more money or a better relationship."

And we ask, *Why would you like to be over there?*

Often the reply is, "Because I'm not happy over here where I'm standing."

We then explain that it is important to talk about what is believed to be "over there" and to try to find the *feeling-place* of what's "over there." For as long as someone is talking about, and *feeling* what's "over here," it is not possible for them to get "over there."

If you have been accustomed to thinking and speaking about where you are currently standing, it is not an easy thing to suddenly shift your vibrations and to now begin thinking and feeling something that is very different. In fact, the *Law of Attraction* says that you do not have access to thoughts and feelings that are very far from where you have recently been vibrating, but with some effort, you could find other thoughts. With a determination to feel better, you could change the subject and therefore find other thoughts with better-feeling vibrations—but vibrational shifting is usually a gradual process.

In fact, a continual attempt, in defiance of the *Law of Attraction,* of trying to jump vibrational ranges is a major factor in the feelings of discouragement that eventually cause people to conclude that they really do not have control of their own life experiences.

⌘ ⌘ ⌘ ⌘ ⌘ ⌘

Chapter 21

You Are Only 17 Seconds Away from 68 Seconds to Fulfillment

With only a few seconds of focusing your attention on a subject, you activate the vibration of that subject within you, and immediately the *Law of Attraction* begins to respond to that activation. The longer you keep your attention focused on something, the easier it becomes for you to continue to focus upon it because you are attracting, through the *Law of Attraction*, other thoughts or vibrations that are the essence of the thought you began with.

Within 17 seconds of focusing on something, a matching vibration becomes activated. And now, as that focus becomes stronger and the vibration becomes clearer, the *Law of Attraction* will bring to you more thoughts that match. At this point, the vibration will not have much attraction power, but if you maintain your focus longer, the power of the vibration will become further-reaching. And if you manage to stay purely focused upon any thought for as little as 68 seconds, the vibration is powerful enough that its manifestation begins.

When you repeatedly return to a pure thought, maintaining it for at least 68 seconds, in a short period of time (hours in some cases or a few days in others), that thought becomes a dominant thought. And once you achieve a dominant thought, you will experience matching manifestations until you change it.

Remember that:

- The thoughts you think equal your point of attraction.

- You get what you think about, whether you want it or not.

- Your thoughts equal vibration, and that vibration is then answered by the *Law of Attraction.*

- As your vibration expands and becomes more powerful, it eventually becomes powerful enough for manifestation to occur.

- In other words, what you think (and therefore feel), and what manifests in your experience, is always a vibrational match.

Your Uncontrolled Thoughts Are Not to Be Feared

Once the *Law of Attraction* is understood and accepted (which usually does not take long since there is not a shred of evidence anywhere in your environment to refute it), many people become initially uncomfortable with their own thoughts. Once they understand the power of the *Law of Attraction,* and they begin to examine the content of their own mind, they sometimes worry about the potential of what they may now be attracting through their uncontrolled thoughts. But there is no reason to worry about your thoughts, for they are not like a loaded gun that may wreak powerful and instantaneous destruction. For although the *Law of Attraction* is powerful, the basis of your experience is that of Well-Being.

And even though your thoughts are magnetic and expand with your attention, you have plenty of time—as soon as you become aware of any negative feelings—to begin to choose other less resistant thoughts and thereby choose a more desired outcome.

Remember, you can allow it or resist it in varying degrees, but the Stream of Well-Being always flows. So, even a small effort made toward choosing a better-feeling thought will net you obvious results. And once you have taken that step and you do find that better-feeling thought, you have given yourself the conscious freedom to go from wherever you are, on any topic, to anywhere you want to be. *Once you deliberately choose a thought and consciously feel the improvement in the way you feel, you have successfully utilized your own guidance system, and you can now be on your way to the freedom that you desire and deserve—for there is nothing that you cannot be, do, or have.*

Chapter 22

The Different Degrees of Your Emotional Guidance Scale

You might say that different emotions have different vibrational frequencies, but a more accurate way of saying it would be: Your emotions are *indicators* of your vibrational frequency. When you remember that your emotions indicate your degree of alignment with Source Energy and that the better you feel, the more you are allowing your alignment with the things you desire, then it is easier to understand how to respond to your emotions.

Absolute alignment with your own Source Energy means that you know the following:

- You are free.
- You are powerful.
- You are good.
- You are love.
- You have value.
- You have purpose.
- All is well.

At any time that you are thinking thoughts that cause you to know your true nature, you are in alignment with who you really are, for this is the state of absolute alignment. And the way those thoughts *feel* is the ultimate emotion of connection. When you think in terms of a fuel gauge on a vehicle, this state of alignment would be the same as a full tank.

In other words, imagine a gauge or scale with gradations or degrees, which indicate the position of the (fullest) allowance of your connection with your Source Energy all the way to your (emptiest) most resistant disallowance of your alignment with your Source Energy.

A scale of your emotions would look something like this:

1. Joy/Knowledge/Empowerment/Freedom/Love/Appreciation
2. Passion
3. Enthusiasm/Eagerness/Happiness
4. Positive Expectation/Belief
5. Optimism
6. Hopefulness
7. Contentment
8. Boredom
9. Pessimism
10. Frustration/Irritation/Impatience
11. "Overwhelment"
12. Disappointment
13. Doubt
14. Worry
15. Blame
16. Discouragement
17. Anger
18. Revenge
19. Hatred/Rage
20. Jealousy
21. Insecurity/Guilt/Unworthiness
22. Fear/Grief/Depression/Despair/Powerlessness

Since the same words are often used to mean different things, and different words are often used to mean the same things, these word labels for your emotions are not absolutely accurate for every person who feels the emotion. In fact, giving word labels to the emotions could cause confusion and distract you from the real purpose of your *Emotional Guidance Scale*.

The thing that matters most is that you consciously reach for a feeling that is improved. The word for the feeling is not important.

An Example of Consciously Moving Up Your *Emotional Guidance Scale*

So, something has happened in your experience that makes you feel terrible. Nothing sounds good, nothing feels good, it seems as if you are suffocating, and each thought is equally painful. The best word to describe your nearly constant state of emotion is one of *depression.*

If you could throw yourself into taking some action, you might feel better; if you could put what is bothering you out of your mind altogether and focus upon your work, you could feel better. There are many thoughts that you could entertain that could free you from your depression. However, vibrationally, you do not have access to most of them right now. But if your intention is to find a thought, any thought, that feels better, and you are consciously aware of how that thought feels, you can begin to move up the *Emotional Guidance Scale* immediately. It is really a process of thinking a thought, any thought, and then consciously evaluating whether the new thought gives you any feeling of relief from where you were before that thought. So, you think and feel and think and feel, with one intention only: to feel even the slightest bit of relief.

Let us say that someone has said something that made you angry, or someone did not keep her word. And as you focus upon this angry topic, you notice that you do feel some relief from your depression. In other words, in the midst of this angry thought, you are no longer having any trouble breathing. The feeling of claustrophobia has lifted, and you do feel slightly better.

Now, here is the crucial step in effectively utilizing your *Emotional Guidance System:* Stop, and consciously acknowledge that your chosen thought of anger *does* feel better than the suffocating depression that it replaced. And in the *conscious* recognition of your improved vibration, your feeling of powerlessness softens and you are now on you way up your *Emotional Guidance Scale,* back into full connection with who you really are.

Why Would Anyone Want to Discourage My Better-Feeling Anger?

Often, from a very resistant vibration such as depression or fear, you will have already, instinctively, even unconsciously, discovered the pain-relieving thought of anger. But there are so many who have convinced you that your anger is inappropriate—but of course, they are not inside of you, so they cannot feel the improvement that the angry thought really is—that they often counsel you against your anger . . . only to leave you back in your former state of depression. But when you *consciously* know that you have *chosen* an angry thought and that it has brought you relief, then you can consciously know that you can move from the angry thought to a less resistant one such as frustration, and then up the *Emotional Guidance Scale* you go—right back into your full alignment.

Why Your Slightest Improvement Is of Such Great Value

When you are consciously aware of where you are, and you also know where you would like to be, and you have a means of understanding whether or not you are pointed in the direction of where you want to be . . . then nothing can keep you there. The seeming lack of control of your life experience is mostly because you do not realize in which direction you are headed. Without a conscious realization of your own emotions and what they mean, you often move away from where you really want to be.

There are many words that are used to describe emotions, but there are really only two emotions: One feels good, and one feels bad. And every incremental place along the emotional scale only indicates degrees of the allowance of the powerful, pure, positive Source Energy. The fullest state of connection, which feels like joy, love, appreciation, freedom, or knowledge, is really speaking to your own feeling of self-empowerment. And the fullest state of disconnection, which feels like despair, grief, fear, or depression, is really speaking to your own feeling of disempowerment.

There is tremendous value when you are able to *deliberately* cause even the slightest improvement in the way you feel, for even in that small emotional improvement, you may have regained a measure of control. And even though you may not have fully exercised your control to bring yourself entirely back into full connection with your full power, you no longer feel powerless. And so, your trek back up the emotional scale is now not only possible, but it is relatively easy.

Only *You* Know If Choosing Anger Is Appropriate for You

If a severely depressed person could consciously discover the relief of an angry thought, and, more important, could consciously recognize that he has *deliberately chosen* the angry thought, he would immediately regain a sense of his own power, and his depression would lift. Now, of course, it is important that he does not remain in his place of anger. But, from that angry place, he now has access to the relieving thoughts of frustration.

There are many who do not yet understand the vibrational content of emotions (or even what an emotion is or its reason for being) who counsel with great forcefulness against the projection of anger. For most people do not enjoy being in the presence of someone who is angry, and most would selfishly prefer that the angry person return to their former state of powerless depression, because their depression is usually turned inward, while their anger is often thrust outward toward whoever is nearby.

Someone outside of you does not know if your chosen thought of anger is an improvement for you; only you know—by the relief that you feel— the appropriateness of any thought. Until you decide that you are going to guide yourself by the way you feel, you can make no steady progress toward your own desires.

"I'm Doing My Best to Make the Best of It"

Those who are watching you might feel better if they understood that you have no intention of remaining in your state of anger. If they knew that your greater plan is to move through your anger, and then through frustration through overwhelment to optimism to belief and onward to your knowing that all is well, they might be more patient with where you are right now.

There are many people who just naturally move from the powerless feeling of depression or fear into anger as a sort of self-surviving mechanism, but when they are met with so much disapproval from family members, friends, and counselors with respect to the inappropriateness of their anger, they return to the feeling of powerlessness, only to repeat the cycle again and again: from depression to anger, to depression to anger, to depression to anger. . . .

The key to regaining your wonderful feeling of personal empowerment and control is to decide, right now, no matter how good or how bad you are feeling, that you are going to do your best to make the best of it. Reach for the best-feeling thought that you have access to right now, and as you do that again and again, in a short period of time you will find yourself in a very good-feeling place. That is just the way it works!

"If I Can Get There Emotionally, I Can Get Anywhere"

"Right now I am going to find the best-feeling thought that I can. I am going to reach for more relief, more relief, more relief." Remember:

- Rage gives you a feeling of relief from depression, grief, despair, fear, guilt, or powerlessness.

- Revenge gives you a feeling of relief from rage.

- Anger gives you a feeling of relief from revenge.

- Blame gives you a feeling of relief from anger.

- Overwhelment gives you a feeling of relief from blame.

- Irritation gives you a feeling of relief from overwhelment.

- Pessimism gives you a feeling of relief from irritation.

- Hopefulness gives you a feeling of relief from pessimism.

- Optimism gives you a feeling of relief from hopefulness.

- Positive Expectation gives you a feeling of relief from optimism.

- Joy gives you a feeling of relief from positive expectation.

In time, and with practice, you will become very adept at understanding what your *Emotional Guidance System* is telling you. Once you make a determined decision to continually reach for the relief that an improved emotion brings, you will find yourself feeling good most of the time, and allowing into your experience all the things you desire.

Attention to how you are feeling is necessary in order to understand everything that is happening to you. How you feel—and the feeling of relief that you discover as you reach for better-feeling thoughts—is your only true measurement of what you are attracting into your experience.

"But What about Those Who Desire Not to Desire?"

We would describe the sensation of *desire* as the delicious awareness of new possibilities. Desire is a fresh, free feeling of anticipating wonderful expansion. The feeling of *desire* is truly the feeling of life flowing through you. But many people, while they are using the word *desire,* feel something quite different. Desire, for them, often feels like yearning, for while they are focused upon something that they want to experience or have, they are equally aware of its absence. And so, while they are using *words of desire,* they are offering a *vibration of lack.* They come to think that the feeling of *desire* is like wanting something that they do not have. But there is no feeling of lack in pure desire.

So, if you will keep in mind that whenever you ask, it is always given—then each of your desires will now be pure non-resisted desire.

Many people desire things that they are not currently living fully, and in some cases they have desired them for a long period of time. And so, they think about the thing they desire, and then they think about not having it. In time, they come to believe that the way they feel (as they think about what they want, and realize they do not have it, but cannot figure out how to get it) is the way desire feels. But they are not in the state of pure desire; they are in the state of resisted desire. Often their vibration is more about the absence or lack of what they want than it is about what they want.

Without even realizing what they are doing, they are holding themselves vibrationally apart from their own desires, so in time they come to believe that this sluggish, unfulfilled feeling of not getting what they want is really what *desire* feels like.

There have been some who have said to us, "Abraham, I've been taught that it's not appropriate for me to have any desires. I've been taught that the state of desire will keep me from being the spiritual Being that I'm supposed to be, and that my state of happiness depends upon my ability to release all desires." We reply, *But is not your state of happiness, or your state of spirituality, a desire?*

We are not here to guide you toward, or away from, any desire. It is our work to help you understand that you are the creator of your own experience and that your desires will naturally be born from your experience in this environment, in this body. It is our desire to assist you in coming into perfect alignment with Source so that you can then achieve the creation of your desires.

We understand why some would suggest that if you would release your desire, you would feel better, because the negative emotion that you are feeling is due to the vibrational difference between your current vibration and the vibration of your desire. But releasing desire is the hard way to go about bringing yourself into alignment, because the entire Universe is poised to help you give birth to yet another new desire. So, a much easier way to come into alignment with your Source, and therefore to feel better, is to work on releasing your resistance.

Does Your Desire Feel Like the Next Logical Step?

Your ability to imagine will help the next logical steps come to you faster. You can work the bugs out of it in your imagination; you do not have to build little things and bigger things—you can do it all in your mind. We are not talking about the next logical *action* step. We are talking about using your imagination until your big dream feels so familiar that the manifestation is the next logical step.

For example, a mother and her adult daughter were contemplating purchasing a lovely house in a beautiful area and creating a wonderful bed-and-breakfast facility. The daughter said to her mother, "If only we could find a way to make this happen, it would make me happy for the rest of my life. If this could happen, it would make up for all of those things that I wanted that didn't come to pass."

We explained that the vibration of her desire was not yet in the pure place that it needed to be in order to allow this experience to manifest. *When your desire feels so big that it feels unreachable, it is not on the verge of manifestation. When your desire feels to you like it is the next logical step, then it is on the verge of manifestation.*

Once You Feel in Control,
You Will Enjoy It All

You can tell by the way you *feel* whether your vibration is in the place where you are allowing Universal Forces to deliver your desire to you now . . . or not. With practice, you will know whether you are on the brink of a manifestation or whether it is still in the becoming stages, but most important, *once you are in control of the way you feel, you will enjoy it all:*

- You will enjoy your exposure to the variety and contrast that helps you identify your desire, and you will enjoy the sensation of your own desire, which is being launched from your own valuable perspective and is flowing from you.

- You will enjoy the sensation of your conscious awareness when you are not a vibrational match to your own desire, and you will enjoy the sensation of deliberately bringing yourself back into vibrational alignment with your desire.

- You will feel relief as doubts slip away, and as the secure feelings of Well-Being replace them.

- You will enjoy sensing things that are about to happen, you will enjoy seeing things beginning to fall into place, and you will adore witnessing the manifestations of your desires.

- You will revel in the conscious awareness that you have deliberately molded your desires into being in as real a way as if you had created a statue with the clay in your own hands.

- You will adore the sensations you feel as you align, again and again, with the fruits of your own experience.

The entire Universe exists to produce new life-giving desire within you, and when you go with the flow of your own desires, you will feel truly alive—and you will truly live.

PART II

Processes to Help You Achieve
What You Now Remember

Introducing 22 Proven Processes That Will Improve Your Point of Attraction

So now that you have made it this far into the book, you have been reminded of many things that you have always known: You now remember that you are an extension of Source Energy and that you have come into your physical body, into this Leading-Edge time-space-reality, for the purpose of joyously taking thought beyond that which it has been before.

You now remember that you have a guidance system within you that helps you to know, in every moment, how much of your connection to that which is your Source you are right now allowing.

You now remember that the better you feel, the more you are in alignment with who you really are; and the worse you feel, the more you are disallowing that important connection.

You now remember that there is nothing that you cannot be, do, or have; and you remember that if your dominant intention is to feel good and that if you try to make the best of where you are, you must reach your natural state of joy.

You now remember that you are free (in fact, you are so free that you could choose bondage), and that everything that comes to you is in response to the thoughts you are thinking.

You now remember that whether you are thinking about your past, present, or future, you are offering a vibration that equals your point of attraction.

You now remember that the *Law of Attraction* is always fair, and there is no injustice—for whatever is coming to you is doing so in response to the vibrations that you are offering due to the thoughts you are thinking.

And, most important, you now remember that Well-Being is the basis of your world, and that unless you are doing something that is disallowing it, then Well-Being is your experience. You may allow it or resist it, but only a Stream of wellness, abundance, clarity, and all good things that you desire . . . flows.

And you now remember that there is no dark switch; there is no Source of "evil" or Source of sickness or lack. *You may allow or you may resist Well-Being—but everything that happens to you is all your doing.*

Is There Something I Want to Improve?

If your current life is pleasing to you in every way, then you may have no reason to read further. However, if there is something about your life that you wish to improve—perhaps something missing that you would like to include or something unwanted that you would like to release—the following processes will be of immense value to you.

Your habit of resistant thought is the only thing that ever keeps you from allowing the things you desire. And although you certainly did not intentionally develop these resistant patterns of thought, you did pick them up along your physical trail, bit by bit and experience by experience. But one thing is very clear: *If you do not do something that causes a different vibrational offering, then nothing in your experience can change.*

The processes on the following pages have been designed to help you gradually release any patterns of resistance. And, in the same way that you did not develop your resistant patterns all at once, you will not release them all at once—but you *will* release them. Process by process, game by game (we use the word *game* interchangeably with *process*), and day by day, you will gradually but steadily return to being a person who allows your own natural Well-Being to flow to you.

Those who observe you will be amazed at the things they begin to see happening in your experience and at the joy that you will obviously be radiating. And you will explain, with the confidence and certainty that you were born with, "I have found a way to allow the Well-Being to flow that is natural to me. I have learned to practice the *Art of Allowing*."

A Suggestion for Utilizing These Processes

So, it is with tremendous enthusiasm and powerful expectation that we offer the processes that will follow shortly. When you have time, we encourage you to read through each process without actually performing the action that is suggested. As you read through the processes, if they hold any immediate value for you, you will feel a strong impulse to perform them. You might earmark those that you feel enthusiasm toward. Then, when you have the time to perform the processes, begin with the one for which you felt the most enthusiasm. This is the best place for you to start.

Actually, you could choose any process at random, perform it, and receive noticeable benefits from it, for every process in this book will assist you in releasing resistance and raising your vibration. However, the power of your desire and the degree of your current resistance does make certain processes of greater value to you right now than others.

As you read through these processes, and the examples of applications that are provided, you may recognize that something similar is happening in your own life, so you may benefit from applying the same process. However, because your own life offers a broad spectrum of experiences as well as a broad spectrum of emotions, there are no hard-and-fast rules about which specific process is best for you to apply to which specific experience right now.

Let Us Remove the
Trees from Our Path

Some of the processes will assist you in focusing your desire more clearly, causing your point of attraction to be stronger. But if, for whatever reason, you are in the midst of offering a great deal of resistance, then a process that would cause you to summon even more Energy could actually be counterproductive to you.

Earlier we gave you the example of driving your vehicle at 100 miles per hour and hitting a tree, which is a much bigger problem than driving your vehicle at 5 miles per hour and hitting a tree. Now, in our analogy, the speed of your vehicle equals the Creative Energy that you are summoning because of your desire, and the tree equals your contradictory thoughts, or resistance. Often, people conclude that the only option that makes sense is to slow the vehicle down—but we are teachers who encourage removing the trees from your path.

The processes we present in this book are designed to help you remove the resistance from your path, for there is nothing more delicious than moving at the speed of life that you are accustomed to—with no trees in the way.

Let Your Emotions Be Your Guide

You are, without exception, experiencing emotional responses to your life experience, and these emotions are your key to knowing which processes would be best for you to utilize right now. Generally speaking, the better you feel, the more the lower-numbered processes will be of benefit for you; and the worse you feel, the more the higher-numbered processes will be of benefit.

The most important thing for you to acknowledge before you apply any of these processes is how you are feeling right now—and how you would like to feel. At the beginning of each process, we have indicated an emotional range that we suggest for each one. Any of the processes that fall within the emotional range that you believe you are feeling right now is a perfect place to begin.

Let Us Begin by
Improving the Way We Feel

Some of the processes are oriented toward specific life experiences, such as increasing your financial or physical Well-Being, but the majority of these processes can be successfully applied to any situation.

It is our absolute promise to you that your life will improve with the application of these processes, for you cannot apply the process without improving the way you feel. And you cannot improve the way you feel without releasing resistance and thereby improving your point of attraction. And when you improve your point of attraction, the *Law of Attraction* must bring you circumstances, events, relationships, experiences, sensations, and powerful evidence of your shift in vibration. It is Law!

Some of these processes will become your favorites. Some you will want to utilize every day, some you may never use, some you may use at first and then no longer find necessary, and some you will resurrect when special circumstances arise.

It is our desire that you comfortably begin to utilize these processes, for it is our knowing that they will positively change your life experience. From our perspective, they have been designed for the powerful reason of helping you realign with the Energy that is really You. And in that process, you will return to your natural joy. Oh, and yes, there will be the added side benefit of helping you achieve anything you have ever desired.

Have You Put a Happy Face on It?

Your emotions are essential to your conscious control of your own experience. And, of course, they are essential to your maintenance of a happy life experience.

In the same way that you would not deaden your fingertips to desensitize them to heat, or put a "Happy Face" sticker on the dashboard of your vehicle to cover your fuel gauge indicator because you do not like seeing that you are out of fuel, you would not want to mask your own feelings, pretending to feel different from how you really feel. For pretending in this way does nothing to change your vibrational point of attraction. The only way you can do so is to change your vibrational offering, and when you do change your vibrational offering, the way you feel changes, too.

Focusing Energy to Change
Your Vibrational Offering

When you remember an incident from a past experience, you are focusing Energy. When you are imagining something that may occur in your future, you are focusing Energy, and, of course, when you are observing something in your *now,* you are focusing Energy. It makes no difference whether you are focusing on the past, present, or future, you are still focusing Energy—and your point of attention or focus is causing you to offer a *vibration* that is your point of attraction.

When you spend time pondering, remembering, or imagining something, a vibration is activated within you. If you return to that thought, you again activate the vibration. The more often you revisit the thought, the more familiar the vibration becomes, and the easier it is for you to activate it, until eventually it becomes a dominant vibrational pattern within you. And as it plays a larger role in your vibrational pattern, things that match it begin to show up in your experience.

And so, there are two surefire ways to understand what your vibrational offering is: Notice what is happening in your experience (for what you are focused upon and what is manifesting are always a vibrational match), and notice how you feel (because your emotions are giving you constant feedback about your vibrational offering and your point of attraction).

You Must Be Consciously Aware to Be a Deliberate Creator

We think it is a wonderful thing when you begin to make the correlation between what you have been thinking and feeling, and what is manifesting. For in that conscious awareness, you are then able to deliberately modify your thoughts in order to attract something that is even more pleasing. But the most satisfying aspect of *Deliberate Creation* comes from being sensitive to the way the thoughts you are thinking feel, for then it is possible to modify a bad-feeling thought to one that feels better, and to thereby improve your point of attraction before something unwanted manifests. *It is far easier—before an unwanted physical manifestation appears—to deliberately change the direction of your thought to something that feels better.*

You will come to understand that *Deliberate Creation* is about deliberately guiding your thoughts in good-feeling directions. You will feel the satisfaction of deliberately choosing a good-feeling thought, and then you will enjoy observing the good-feeling manifestation that must follow. There is even some satisfaction to be found in recognizing the not-so-good-feeling thought and then observing the not-so-good-manifestation that must follow, for now your conscious awareness of the powerful *Law of Attraction* will give you the feeling of control. Without making the correlation between your thoughts and feelings and the manifestations that are occurring, you have no conscious control of what happens in your experience.

There Is Always Another Uncontrollable Circumstance When Trying to Control Others

Most people offer the majority of their thought vibrations in response to something they are observing. When they observe something wonderful, they feel wonderful; when they observe something awful, they feel awful, but they believe they have no control over how they feel because they realize that they cannot control the circumstances that they have observed.

Many people spend the majority of their lives attempting to control circumstances because they believe that in the controlling of the circumstance, they will feel better. But no matter how much control they gain over the actions of others, it is never enough— because there is always another uncontrollable circumstance.

You have no creative power within the lives of others, for they are offering their own vibrations, which equal *their* own point of attraction, just as you are offering your own vibrations, which equal *your* own point of attraction.

Deliberate Creation Is about
Choosing Better-Feeling Thoughts

Many say, "Once that condition changes, I'll feel better. When I have more money or move into a better house or find a better job or a better mate, then I'll feel better." We do not disagree that it does feel better to observe something that is pleasing than something that is not, but that is going about it in a very backwards way.

Deliberate Creation is not about the condition changing and then your finding a better feeling in response to the changed condition. *Deliberate Creation* is about choosing a thought that feels good when you choose it, which then causes the condition to change. For example, unconditional love is really about wanting so much to remain in connection with your Source of love that you deliberately choose thoughts that allow your connection, no matter what manifestations may be happening nearby. And when you are able to control your point of attraction by deliberately choosing better-feeling thoughts, the conditions that surround you have to change. The *Law of Attraction* says that they must.

You Can Only Attract Thoughts
Within Your Vibrational Range

Some say, "All this stuff about *Deliberate Creation* sounds simple enough, but why am I having so much difficulty doing it? Why do I have such a hard time controlling my thoughts? It feels like my thoughts are in charge! It feels like my thoughts are thinking themselves!"

Well, remember that the *Law of Attraction* is a powerful Law, and that it is not possible for you to find and hold a thought if your current *vibrational set-point* is very different from that thought. You only have access to thoughts whose vibrations are somewhere in your current vibrational range.

Have you ever had the experience of enjoying a piece of music, then later hearing the same music, but this time not enjoying it at all? At one listening, you were smiling, maybe even moving to the music, but at another listening, you found the piece irritating and annoying. What you are noticing is your vibrational alignment with the music. In other words, at your time of closer alignment with who you really are, the music blends with your good feeling. But when you are not in alignment with who you really are, the music only points out to you the difference between the vibration of Well-Being, which is who you really are, and your resistant vibration of this moment.

There are those times when friends can prod or tease you into a better-feeling thought, but at other times their prodding or teasing just makes you feel worse. Any success they may have had in helping you feel better has been, for the most part, about how far out of alignment you already were, because while it is easy to make small vibrational jumps, it is difficult, or even impossible, to make large ones.

The Purpose of These Processes
Is to Release Your Resistance

You will find, in the pages that follow, processes that are being offered to assist you in gradually improving your vibrational point of attraction. Your current vibrational state of being is one that varies from person to person and from time to time, so you will know— only by the way you feel as you experience the process—whether it is the appropriate process for you right now.

Through observing, remembering, pondering, and discussing, you have practiced thoughts that have become more powerful thoughts or beliefs, which now dominate your point of attraction. And each thought you consider or focus upon causes you to feel an emotional response. And so, over time, you have come to feel certain ways about certain things. We call that your *Emotional Set-Point.*

The following processes are numbered 1 through 22. The closer you are, right now, to vibrational alignment with your own Source of Well-Being, the more effective the lower-numbered techniques will be in helping you to fully realign. The further you are, right now, from your vibrational alignment with Source, the higher the number of the process will have to be in order to bring you back into alignment.

Now you may be one who is usually so close to alignment with your own Source of Well-Being that you will rarely utilize one of these processes that is past the number of Process #12. But there may be some special circumstances that could cause your vibration to dip further out of your usual range of connection, and if so, then you may benefit from one of the higher-numbered processes— but that would be an exception for you.

Deliberately Creating Change in Your Current Emotional Set-Point

On the other hand, you may be one who cannot remember the last time you felt good about anything. Through the circumstances of your life that you have been observing, you may have developed a *set-point* that holds you consistently out of range of your con- nection to Well-Being, so you may discover no relief at all with the first five or six processes. And you may find only slight relief if you even begin with the last processes we have offered here. But the most important thing we want you to realize is that it does not mat- ter how good you feel or how fast you feel it—the only thing that matters is that you *consciously* discover some relief, no matter how slight it is, and that you understand that your relief has come in response to some *deliberate* effort that you have offered. For when you are able to find relief, then you have regained creative control of your own experience, and then you are on your way to wherever you desire to go.

Remember, the purpose of each process is to raise your vibra- tional frequency. Another way of saying that is: *The purpose of each process is to release your resistance,* or *The purpose of the process is to find the relief from resistance,* or *The purpose of this process is an improved feeling,* or *The purpose of this process is to improve my Emotional Set-Point.*

If, after a few minutes with a process, you do not feel as good or better than when you began, simply discontinue it and choose another with a higher number.

Lighten Up Now, and
Have Fun with All This

We use the words *process, technique,* or *game* interchangeably because, while these are powerful processes that will assist you in achieving anything that you desire, if you will take a playful approach to them, you will hold far less resistance than if you see them as tools to fix something that is broken. *The key to the success that you will find in these processes actually hinges upon your ability to release resistance, and the more playful you are, the less resistance you hold.*

A deliberate utilization of these processes will help you move your *Emotional Set-Point,* and therefore change your point of attraction. You will begin to observe immediate improvement—even on your first day of the application of these games. And with more practice, you will improve your point of attraction on every subject of your life.

You Are, in This Moment,
the Creator of Your Reality

You are the creator of your own experience whether you know that you are or not. Your life experience is unfolding in precise response to the vibrations that radiate as a result of your thoughts, whether you know that it is or not.

The processes that we offer here will help you transform yourself from one who may be creating your own reality unwittingly or by default, to someone who is the deliberate creator of your own reality. Your utilization of these processes is going to give you precise control of every aspect of your own life experience.

It is with tremendous love and enthusiasm that we offer these life-changing processes to you. There is great love here . . . for you.

Process #1
The Rampage of Appreciation

When to Use This Process

- When you want to parlay a good mood into an even better one

- When you want to enhance your relationship with someone or something

- When you want to deliberately maintain your current good-feeling set-point

- When you want to maintain or even improve your current good feeling

- When you want to deliberately focus upon something that is beneficial to your set-point

- When you are driving, walking, or standing in line, and you want to do something that is creatively productive

- When there is something in your line of sight that could potentially take you to a place of negative emotion, and you want to maintain control of your own vibration

- When your own thoughts, or the words of someone you are with, start off in a potentially negative direction, and you want to control the direction of the subject matter

- When you are aware that you are experiencing negative emotion and you want to change the way you feel

Current *Emotional Set-Point* Range

This *Rampage of Appreciation Process* will be of the most value to you when your *Emotional Set-Point* is ranging somewhere between:

(1) Joy/Knowledge/Empowerment/Freedom/Love/Appreciation
and
(5) Optimism

(If you are not sure what your current *Emotional Set-Point* is, turn back to Chapter 22 and scan the 22 categories on the *Emotional Guidance Scale.*)

So, let us say that you are feeling Positive Expectation. Since *Positive Expectation* is ranked at (4), and (4) falls between the (1) and (5) suggested current *Emotional Set-Point Range* for the *Rampage of Appreciation,* this process would be one of the most valuable ones for you to use right now.

This *Rampage of Appreciation* game can be played anywhere and at any time because it is a game that is easily played simply by directing pleasant thoughts in your mind. If you were to write your thoughts on paper, it would enhance this process, but it is not necessary.

Begin by looking around your immediate environment and gently noticing something that pleases you. Try to hold your attention on this pleasing object as you consider how wonderful, beautiful, or useful it is. And as you focus upon it longer, your positive feelings about it will increase.

Now, notice your improved feeling, and be appreciative of the way you feel. Then, once your good feeling is noticeably stronger than when you began, look around your environment and choose another pleasing object for your positive attention.

Make it your objective to choose objects of attention that easily evoke your appreciation, for this is not a process of finding something troubling and fixing it; this is a process of practicing the higher vibrations. The longer you focus upon things that feel good to you, the easier it is for you to maintain those vibrational frequencies that feel good. And the more you maintain these good-feeling frequencies, the more the *Law of Attraction* will deliver to you other thoughts, experiences, people, and things that match your practiced vibration.

Since it is your primary intention, as you move through your day, to find things to appreciate, you are practicing a vibration of less resistance, and you are making your connection to your own Source Energy stronger.

Because the vibration of appreciation is the most powerful connection between the physical you and the Non-Physical You, this process will also put you in a position to receive even clearer guidance from your Inner Being.

The more you practice appreciation, the less resistance you will have in your own vibrational frequencies. And the less resistance you have, the better your life will be. Also, by practicing this *Rampage of Appreciation,* you will become accustomed to the feeling of higher vibrations, so that if you ever revert to an old pattern of conversation that causes resistance in your vibration, you will notice it, early on, before the vibration gets too strong.

The more you find something to appreciate, the better it feels; the better it feels, the more you want to do it; the more you do it, the better it feels; the better it feels . . . the more you want to do it. The *Law of Attraction* assists with the powerful momentum of these positive thoughts and feelings until, with very little time and effort, you will find your heart singing in your joyous alignment with who you really are.

And in this wonderful-feeling vibration where no resistance exists, you will be in an exaggerated state of *allowing;* you will be in the vibrational state where the things that you desire can flow easily into your experience. The better it gets, the better it gets!

If your vibration is in a close enough proximity to these higher vibrations when you begin the game, and you find yourself easily and quickly soaring into the better-feeling places—then continue your *Rampage of Appreciation* for as long as you have the time, and for as long as it feels good.

If you attempt this game and you do not feel good, if you do not feel the momentum picking up as you focus upon one happy thought after another—that is, if the process annoys you in any way—then discontinue it and choose a process with a higher number.

Even if you understand nothing about the *Law of Attraction,* even if you understand nothing about your connection to your own Source Energy, practicing this process would cause you to practice the *Art of Allowing* without even knowing it—and all things that you have identified as objects of your desire would have to begin flowing into your experience. When you are in the mode of appreciation, there is no resistance within your vibration. And your own achievement of resistance is the only thing that ever holds you apart from anything that you desire.

In the *Rampage of Appreciation,* you actually set your vibrational frequency to one of allowing what you have asked for into your experience. You have been asking, in every day of your experience, and Source has answered, without exception. And now, in your mode of *Appreciation,* you are in the practice of receiving. You are now engaging in the last step in the process of *Creation* (you are letting it in).

At first, it would be a good idea to deliberately set aside 10 or 15 minutes a day to specifically do this process. After a few days of enjoying the benefit of deliberately achieving and maintaining a raised vibration, you will find yourself doing it many times during every day, a few seconds here and a few seconds there, in a variety of situations, just because it feels so pleasing.

For example, while standing in line at the post office, you may think:

This is a very nice building.
It's great that they keep it so clean.
I like how friendly that postal worker is.
I appreciate the way that that mother is interacting with her child.
That's a good-looking jacket.
My day is really going well.

While driving to work, you may think:

I love my car.
This new freeway is wonderful.
Even though it's raining, I'm making very good time.
I love how reliable my vehicle is.
I'm grateful for my job.

You could focus more specifically on any of your objects of appreciation and find even more reasons to feel appreciation. For example:

This is a very nice building . . .

There's so much more parking here than at the old post office.
There are more counters here, and the line moves much faster
than before.
The big windows make this room feel much airier.

This new freeway is wonderful . . .

There are no traffic lights to slow me down.
I can travel so much faster than before.
This drive offers such a beautiful view.

Once you become oriented toward looking for things to appreciate, you will find that your day will be *filled* with such things. Your thoughts and feelings of appreciation will flow from you naturally. And often, while in the midst of a genuine feeling of appreciation for someone or something, you will feel ripples of goose bumps— those sensations are confirming your alignment with your Source.

Abraham, Speak to Us More about the <u>*Rampage of Appreciation*</u>

Every time you appreciate something, every time you praise something, every time you feel good about something, you are telling the Universe: "More of this, please." You need never make another verbal statement of this intent, and if you are mostly in a state of appreciation, all good things will flow to you.

We are often asked, *Isn't <u>love</u> a better word than <u>appreciation</u>? Isn't <u>love</u> more descriptive of the Non-Physical Energy?* And we say that *love* and *appreciation* are really the same vibration. Some use the word *gratitude*, or a feeling of *thankfulness*, but all of these words are descriptive of Well-Being.

A desire to appreciate is a very good first step, and then as you find more things that you would like to say "Thank you" about, it quickly gains momentum. And as you want to feel appreciation, you *attract* something to appreciate. And as you appreciate it, then you attract something else to appreciate, until, in time, you are experiencing a *Rampage of Appreciation.*

You Cannot Control How Others Feel

As you move through your day, you may see unhappy people who are ornery, disappointed, or in pain; and as they direct their negative emotion toward you, you may find it very difficult to feel appreciation toward them. And then you may blame yourself for not being strong enough to appreciate them in spite of their negative offerings toward you. Well, we would never suggest that you should be able to look right at something you do not want and feel good about it. Instead, look for things that cause you to feel good when you find them, and then the *Law of Attraction* will bring you more things like those.

Whenever you are looking for things to appreciate, you have control of your own vibrational offering and your own point of attraction, but when you are responding to the way others seem to feel about you, you have no control. However, when you are more interested in how *you* feel than how they feel about you, you do have control of your experience. You do not know who ran over their dog today or who divorced them or who took money out of their bank account. You do not how they are living, so you cannot understand why they react to you in the way they do—and you cannot control it.

Once you have made a decision that nothing is more important than that you feel good, and you have decided that you are going to consciously look for some things to appreciate today, the object of your attention has now become the feeling of appreciation. You have now established a circuit between you and that object of appreciation that the Law of Attraction will begin working on immediately, so you will start seeing more things to appreciate right away.

You Cannot Feel Defensive While Feeling Appreciative

If you do not understand that the only thing that affects your experience is how you are flowing Energy; if you think it is about chance, luck, coincidence, statistics, or the law of averages, then when you see on the news that there is a killer on the loose, shooting wildly from his car into your neighborhood, you feel vulnerable because you think that your happiness or your Well-Being is dependent upon his behavior. But if your Well-Being is dependent upon his behavior and you cannot control him, you do not even know where he is, you cannot get enough police officers to take care of him . . . then your vulnerability soars.

We want you to feel the value of connecting with Non-Physical Energy, and *appreciation* is the easiest and fastest way. When your desire to connect with the Non-Physical Energy is sufficient enough, you will find dozens of ways, in every hour, to flow your appreciation.

You have to come to remember that it makes no difference whatsoever how anybody is flowing back at you, otherwise you are going to be defensive—and you cannot be defensive and appreciative at the same time. When you concentrate on appreciating, then appreciation comes right back. But you are really not looking for appreciation to come *to* you; you want the feeling of it flowing *through* you.

As you move through your day and you become aware of something that you do *not* want, your desire about what you *do* want comes into clearer focus. And now, since you have been practicing the *Rampage of Appreciation,* you can easily refocus your awareness of what you do not want into your awareness of what you do want. Now you are the hands-on creator that you have come forth to be.

Life is not about tomorrow, it is about right now. Life is about how you are currently molding the Energy!

Process #2
The Magical Creation Box

When to Use This Process

- When you are in the mood for a pleasing activity that will focus the Energy that creates worlds into specific directions of your personal preferences

- When you want to give the Universal Manager even more specific information about the details of things that please you

Current *Emotional Set-Point* Range

This *Magical Creation Box Process* will be of the most value to you when your *Emotional Set-Point* is ranging somewhere between:

(1) Joy/Knowledge/Empowerment/Freedom/Love/Appreciation
and
(5) Optimism

(If you are not sure what your current *Emotional Set-Point* is, turn back to Chapter 22 and scan the 22 categories on the *Emotional Guidance Scale*.)

If the way you are feeling falls somewhere between (1) Joy and (5) Optimism, then this *Creation Box Process* would be a good one for you to utilize right now.

To begin the *Creation Box* process, find a nice-looking box, one that is pleasing to you when you see it. On the lid, in a conspicuous place that you will easily notice, write the words: *Whatever is contained in this box—IS!*

Next, gather magazines, catalogs, and brochures, and leisurely look through them for whatever you would like to include in your experience. Then clip out pictures of anything that exemplifies any desires that you hold: pictures of furniture, clothing, landscaping, buildings, travel destinations, vehicles; images of physical characteristics; photos of people interacting with one another . . . if it feels appealing to you in any way, clip it, and drop it into your *Creation Box*. And say, as you drop it in, "Whatever is contained in this box—IS!"

When you are away from your box, continue to gather more pictures, and then drop them in when you return home. If you witness something you would like to experience, write a description of it, and drop that into your box.

The more things you find for your box, the more the Universe will deliver to you other ideas that match them. And the more ideas you drop into your box, the more your desire will be focused. And the more your desire is focused, the more alive you will feel—for this Energy flowing through you is what life is.

If you have little or no resistance—in other words, if you have no doubt that you can achieve these things, the experience will feel invigorating to you. The more you clip, the better you will feel, and you will begin to see evidence of these things moving closer and closer into your experience. Doors will begin to open to make it possible for many of these things to easily come in right now.

The process will help you focus your desires, and so, you will consciously amplify **Step 1** (Ask)—and now, in your absence of resistance, things will begin to happen quickly.

If you are usually a good-feeling person who has not established strong habits of feeling unhappy about not having the things you have put into your box, you will experience the immediate positive result of feeling more focused and more excited about life, and the things you have put into your *Creation Box* will begin to manifest in your experience right away. In other words, for someone who has not been practicing thoughts of resistance, this process will be all that you will ever need to create a wonderful life: You ask; Source answers; you let it in. *You ask, and it is given.*

If you are enjoying this process, it is serving you in a powerful way; it is helping you focus upon the things you desire; you are practicing the attainment of a consistent vibration that matches your desires; and you are experiencing *Deliberate Creation.* And, most important, your good-feeling emotion is telling you that you are in the receiving mode right now. Your attention to this process is helping you maintain the vibrational frequency that is required for you to allow what you are asking for into your experience—you are practicing the *Art of Allowing.*

Abraham, Speak to Us More about the <u>Magical Creation Box</u>

Imagine that you are sitting in your chair, and next to your chair is a box, a pretty good-sized box. And you know that you are a creator, and that this box is your creation; it is your world, so to speak. And you are like a giant, sitting here on this big chair, and you have the ability to reach out anywhere in this physical Universe and pluck whatever you want and drop it into that box.

So you bring a beautiful house, and you put it in a city that pleases you. And you bring a means of income for you, and maybe a means of income for your mate. You bring all the things you like to do—the beautiful things that you find here and there, feelings of elation and feelings of sensuality, and all of these things that you want, and you drop these things into your *Creation Box.*

You could play this game as a mental game only, but it is so much more fun if you actually get a box and drop in things that represent your desires. You will begin to notice that when you put something in your *Creation Box* that does not have a pattern of resistance, the Universe will bring it to you right away. The things you drop into the box where you do have patterns of resistance will take more time in coming.

When Visualizing, You Have Complete Creative Control

This process may feel whimsical to you, but it is a powerful process, for it will enhance your ability to visualize. Most people offer most of their vibrational offerings in response to what they are observing, but there is no creative control in that. Your creative control comes only in *deliberately* offering thought—and when you are visualizing, you have complete control.

Esther was playing the *Creation Box* game as she and Jerry were flying home from New York City to San Antonio one day. And as she was packing and getting ready for the airport, she was *mentally* dropping things in her box—for example, a beautiful sky; a beautiful, clear day (she loves it when they take off from LaGuardia Airport and she can see all the landmarks that she has come to know and recognize). *Such a beautiful place, so many bridges and all that shimmering water, and all those majestic buildings.* She thought about happy flight attendants, joyful passengers around her, and lots of fun on the trip. And then she thought, *I hope this United Nations meeting doesn't have the freeways all gridlocked.* And then Esther said, "Now that's an odd thing for me to bring to my box; I don't want that in my box."

As you deliberately put things into your *Creation Box,* you will be more aware of when you are thinking about something that you would not want to experience. Your relationship with this *Creation Box* will help you recognize the power your thoughts hold.

Another example: Jerry and Esther had been looking for an Oriental rug for their home. One day while on an airplane, Esther was tearing pages out of magazines of all sorts of different things for her *Creation Box,* and she tore out a page that had a picture of a beautiful rug. When they arrived home, they had several boxes of mail to organize, and as Esther reached into a box, she took out a postcard from a new rug company in San Antonio—and on the postcard was the very same rug. And she squealed, "Look how fast this works!" That picture had not been in her box 24 hours before a fast and easy means to achieve it was delivered.

We want you to feel the fun and joy of the process. Often, when you get something that you have been wanting, your feeling of elation is very short-lived, but this game will give you the opportunity to savor the things that you desire longer. And then, the thrill of the manifestation, even though short, will be all the sweeter.

Once you begin this process, you will just be knocked over by the effectiveness and efficiency of the enormous Non-Physical staff that responds to your vibrational requests. When you ask, it is given, and as you play with this *Creation Box,* you will learn to let it in.

⋙ ⋙ ⋙ ⋘ ⋘ ⋘

Process #3
The Creative Workshop

When to Use This Process

- When you want to focus upon what is most important to you personally

- When you want to be in more deliberate control of the primary areas of your own life

- When you want to improve your state of *allowing* so that even more wonderful things can flow into your experience

- When you want to practice a positive point of attraction until it becomes a dominant point of attraction

Current *Emotional Set-Point* Range

This *Creative Workshop Process* will be of the most value to you when your *Emotional Set-Point* is ranging somewhere between:

(1) Joy/Knowledge/Empowerment/Freedom/Love/Appreciation
and
(5) Optimism

(If you are not sure what your current *Emotional Set-Point* is, turn back to Chapter 22 and scan the 22 categories on the *Emotional Guidance Scale*.)

Like most of the other processes offered here, this one is most effective when you perform the action in writing, but it can also be valuable to play the game in your mind while driving or walking, or anytime you are alone and have a few minutes where it is not likely that you will be disturbed.

Begin this *Creative Workshop Process* with four pieces of paper, and at the top of each sheet write one of the following headings, or categories: *My Body. My Home. My Relationships. My Work.*

Now, focus on the first topic *(My Body)* and on your first page, write: *This is what I desire regarding my body.* Do not work hard on this list. If you cannot think of anything, move on to the next category. Write a short list of things that easily come to your mind that you desire, right now, about your body. For example:

I want to return to my ideal body weight.
I want to get a great haircut.
I want to find some wonderful new clothes.
I want to feel strong and fit.

Now focus on each statement of desire that you have written about your body, and write the reasons *why* you want each of those things. For example:

I want to return to my ideal body weight . . .

. . . because I feel best when I'm at that weight.
. . . because I'll be able to wear some of my favorite clothes.
. . . because it will be fun to shop for a new wardrobe.

I want to get a great haircut . . .

. . . because I want to look good.
. . . because a great haircut is much easier to manage.
. . . because when my hair is cut well, it takes less time to look good.

I want to find some wonderful new clothes . . .

. . . because new clothes always make me feel good.
. . . because I like looking good.
. . . because I like people responding to me in a positive way.
. . . because they always give me a fresh outlook.

I want to feel strong and fit . . .

. . . because I love the feeling of stamina.
. . . because I love having the energy to do all of the things I want to do.
. . . because it just feels good to feel good!

This *Creative Workshop Process* will assist you in focusing upon the areas that are the most immediate and important to your life experience. When you identify the four basic subjects of your life, a focusing of Energy occurs. When you make more specific statements of desire, you activate the Energy around those subjects even more. And when you think about *why* you want those things, you can usually be softening your resistance around the subject while you are adding even more clarity and power to the thoughts. *Why* you want something defines the essence of *what* you want . . . the Universe always delivers to you the vibrational essence of your desire.

When you think about *why* you want something, you usually soften resistance, but when you think about *when* it will come to you or *how* it will come or *who* will help it to come, you often add resistance, especially if you do not already know the answers to those questions.

Now complete the other three categories: *My Home. My Relationships. My Work.*

Write a short list of things that easily come to your mind that you desire, right now, about your home. For example:

I want to find some really great furniture.
I want to get more organized.
I want sliding shelves in the cupboards where I keep my pans.
I want beautiful tile in my bathroom.

And now, write the reasons *why* you want these things.

I want to find some really great furniture . . .

> *. . . because it's so much fun to make changes.*
> *. . . because I love entertaining, and I want my home to feel good.*
> *. . . because it will be easier to get organized.*
> *. . . because furniture adds so much to a home.*

I want to get more organized . . .

> *. . . because I feel better when things are neat.*
> *. . . because I work better in an uncluttered environment.*
> *. . . because we all get along better when things are in order.*
> *. . . because I can accomplish so much more.*

I want sliding shelves in the cupboards where I keep my pans . . .

> *. . . because it will be much easier to find what I need.*
> *. . . because I'll feel like cooking more often.*
> *. . . because it will be more convenient to put the pans away when I'm done with them.*
> *. . . because it will make the kitchen feel so much better.*

I want beautiful tile in my bathroom . . .

. . . because it will make the room more vibrant.
. . . because it will add value to my home.
. . . because it will be easier to keep clean.
. . . because this tile will make me feel good just to look at it.

Write a short list of things that come to your mind easily that you desire, right now, about your relationship (choose the relationship that feels most significant to you right now).

I want to spend more time together.
I want to have more fun together.
I want to eat out together more often.
I want to relax more and play more often.

I want to spend more time together . . .

. . . because I'm at my very best when we're together.
. . . because there's no one I'd rather be with.
. . . because we have so many things that are fun to talk about.
. . . because I love this person so much.

I want to have more fun together . . .

. . . because that's the first thing we loved about each other.
. . . because I love laughing.
. . . because I love finding even more things to do that are fun.
. . . because having fun feels so good.

I want to eat out together more often . . .

. . . because it reminds me of when we first met.
. . . because I love the luxury of someone else cooking.

*. . . because I love relaxing in a nice place and focusing
    on my partner.*
. . . because there are so many wonderful things to eat.

I want to relax more and play more often . . .

. . . because we're both playful by nature.
. . . because I love the free feeling of just being together to relax.
. . . because our best ideas come under these conditions.
. . . because it enhances our relationship.

Write a short list of things that come to your mind easily that
you desire, right now, about your work.

I want to make more money.
I want to feel excited about what I'm doing.
I want to enjoy the people I work with.
I want to feel a stronger sense of purpose.

I want to make more money . . .

. . . because I want to buy a new car.
. . . because I feel proud of what I'm accomplishing.
*. . . because there are so many fun places to go and interesting
    things to do.*
. . . because it will feel good to pay off some bills.

I want to feel excited about what I'm doing . . .

*. . . because work is a big part of my life, and being happy
    there is important.*
. . . because it feels good to be really interested in what I'm doing.
. . . because the day moves quickly when I feel invigorated.
. . . because it feels good to feel good.

I want to enjoy the people I work with . . .

. . . because they're a big part of my life.
. . . because we can be of great value to each other.
. . . because every interaction has wonderful potential.
. . . because I like to uplift others.

I want to feel a stronger sense of purpose . . .

. . . because I want to make a difference.
. . . because I love getting ahold of an idea and running with it.
. . . because I love the feeling of wanting to go to work.
. . . because I love the experience of getting a great new idea.

This process will help you get your juices flowing toward focusing Energy on the four main topics of your personal experience. We would encourage playing this game once a week for a month or so, and then once a month thereafter.

Do not try to write *everything* you want regarding each of the four topics. Just write the things that are most immediate in your mind.

This relaxed and simple process will cause an increased activation of the things that matter most to you, and you will immediately begin to see evidence of increased activity in circumstances and events that are associated with these topics.

Abraham, Speak to Us More about the <u>Creative Workshop Process</u>

Like a magnet, you are attracting thoughts, people, events, lifestyles—everything that you are living. And so, as you see things as they are, you attract more of the same. But as you see things as you would like them to be, you attract them as you would like them to be. This is why the better it gets, the better it gets; or the worse it gets, the worse it gets—people tend to look mostly at what-is.

The Creative Workshop Process will help you choose what sort of magnet you will be. And so, no longer will you be subject to what others believe, want, or see, for you will be the powerful *Deliberate Creator* of you and your experience.

Welcome, Little One, to Planet Earth

If we were speaking to you on your first day of physical life experience, we would have said to you: *Welcome, Little One, to Planet Earth. There is nothing that you cannot be, do, or have. You are a magnificent creator, and you are here by your powerful and deliberate desire to be here. You have specifically applied the wondrous law of Deliberate Creation, and by your ability to do that, you are here.*

Go forth and attract life experience to help you decide what you want. And once you have decided, give thought only to that. Most of your time will be spent collecting data that will help you decide what it is you want, but your real work is to decide what you want and then focus upon it, for it is through focusing upon what you want that you will attract it. That is the process of creating.

But we are *not* talking to you on the first day of your life experience. You have been here for a while, and most of you see yourselves not only through your own eyes—in fact, not even primarily through your own eyes—but you see yourselves mostly through the eyes of others. And so, many of you are not now currently in the state of being that you want to be.

The *Creative Workshop Process* is one where you can achieve the state of being that is your choosing so that you consciously access the power of the Universe and begin attracting the subject of your desire rather than the subject of what you feel is your reality. From our perspective, there is a great difference between that which now exists—that which you call your reality—and that which your reality really is.

Even as you may be sitting there in a body that is not healthy, or in a body that is not the size or shape or vitality that you choose, in a lifestyle that may not be pleasing you, driving a vehicle that perhaps embarrasses you, or interacting with others who may not bring you pleasure, we want to assist you in understanding that while this may seem to be your state of being, it need not be.

What we are offering here is the process by which you may spend a little bit of time, every day, *intentionally* attracting into your experience good health, vitality, prosperity, and positive interactions with others—all the things that make up your vision of what the perfect life experience for you would be.

Another Example of a Creative Workshop

We encourage you to go to your workshop every day, but only for a short period of time. Fifteen or twenty minutes is enough. It is good if it is a place where you can sit and write, although it can be done in your mind at any place where you are not distracted. But it is not a place where you will enter an altered state of consciousness; it is not a meditative state. This is a place where you will go, clearly giving thought to what you want, so much so that it stirs positive emotion within you. Go to your workshop with an uplifted, lighthearted feeling. If you are not happy, it is not a good time for your *Creative Workshop.*

Your work here in this workshop is to assimilate data that you have been collecting from your real-life experience, and to bring the data together in a picture that satisfies and pleases you. During your day, no matter what you are doing—as you are going to your job, working around your home, interacting with your family and friends—collect the data on things you like that you may later bring into your workshop.

You may see someone who has a joyful personality. Collect that data, and bring it into your workshop later. You may see someone driving a vehicle that you would like; collect that data. You may see an occupation that pleases you . . . whatever it is that you are seeing that pleases you, remember it, even write it down, and then when you go into your workshop, you can begin the assimilation of the data. And as you do so, you will prepare a picture of self that you will begin attracting into your experience.

Here is a broader example of your *Creative Workshop:*

> *I like being here, for I recognize the value and power of this time. I feel very good as I am here. And as I see myself, I see myself as a sort of total package, one that I know is of my own creating, and certainly one of my choosing. I'm full of Energy, tireless, really, moving through life experience with no resistance. I see myself gliding about in this picture of self, moving in and out of my car, in and out of buildings, in and out of rooms, in and out of conversations, and in and out of life experiences. I am flowing effortlessly, comfortably, and happily.*
>
> *I see myself attracting only those who are in harmony with my current intent. And I'm becoming more aware of what I desire. When I get into my vehicle and I'm moving to a place, I see myself arriving at that place healthy, refreshed, and on time, and prepared for whatever it is that I'm about to do there. I see myself dressed to perfection in just the manner I choose.*
>
> *And it's nice to know that it does not matter what others are doing, or what others are thinking about what I'm doing. What is important is that I'm pleased with me. And as I see myself in this picture of self, I certainly am.*
>
> *I recognize that I'm unlimited in all facets of my life. I have an unlimited bank account. I am experiencing no financial limitations. I'm making all my decisions based upon whether I want the experience or not, not based upon whether I can afford it. I know that I'm a magnet attracting whatever level of prosperity, health, or relationships I choose.*
>
> *I choose absolute and continuing abundance, for I understand that there is no limit to the wealth in the Universe, and that by my attracting abundance to me, I'm not limiting another. There's enough for everyone. It's not necessarily about putting a big stash away. For whatever I want or need, I can easily bring into my experience. There's an unlimited supply of money and prosperity of all kinds available to me.*

I see myself surrounded by others who, like me, desire growth, who are drawn to me by my willingness to allow them to be, do, or have whatever they're wanting. I see myself interacting with others—talking, laughing, and enjoying that which is perfect in them while they're enjoying that which is perfect in me. We're appreciating each other. No one is criticizing or noticing unwanted things.

I see myself in perfect health, in absolute prosperity, appreciating this physical life experience, which I wanted so very much as I decided to be this physical Being.

It's glorious to be here, making decisions with my physical brain but accessing the power of the Universe through the power of the <u>Law of Attraction</u>. And it's from this marvelous state of being that I now attract more of the same. It's good. It's fun. I like it very much.

And now, my work for this day is done. I will leave my <u>Creative Workshop</u> and I'll set out, for the remainder of this day, looking for more things that I like. My work is done.

As you enter your workshop already feeling good, and then you bring to your workshop specific aspects of life experience that please you, and as you envision these things in greater detail, your life outside of your workshop will begin to reflect the images that you have created within your *Creative Workshop*. This is a powerful tool that will help you create the perfect life for yourself.

⊸ ⊸ ⊸ ⊸ ⊸ ⊸

Process #4
Virtual Reality

When to Use This Process

- When you are feeling good, and you want to practice a vibration of *allowing*

- When you find yourself remembering a pleasant experience, and you want to extend the feeling longer and even move it to a better-feeling place

- When you have extra time, and you wish to spend it in a pleasant way

Current *Emotional Set-Point* Range

This *Virtual Reality Process* will be of the most value to you when your *Emotional Set-Point* is ranging somewhere between:

(1) Joy/Knowledge/Empowerment/Freedom/Love/Appreciation
and
(8) Boredom

(If you are not sure what your current *Emotional Set-Point* is, turn back to Chapter 22 and scan the 22 categories on the *Emotional Guidance Scale.*)

Remember, you live in a Vibrational Universe, and all things are managed by the *Law of Attraction.* And you get what you think about, whether you want it or not, because whenever you achieve vibrational harmony with something because you are giving it your attention, the vibrational essence of it will, in some way, begin to show up in your life experience.

So, you could say that the Universe responds to your vibrational offering, to your point of attraction, to the thoughts you think, and to the way you feel. The Universe is not responding to what *has* been manifested in your experience, but instead, to the vibration that you are *now* offering. The Universe makes no distinction between your actually having a million dollars and your giving thought to having a million dollars. *Your point of attraction is about your thoughts, not about your manifestations.*

This *Virtual Reality Process* is not one where you try to fix something that is broken. It is one where you deliberately activate a scene in your own mind that causes you to offer a vibration matching the scene you have activated—and as you practice visualizing pleasant scenes in your mind, these good-feeling vibrations can then become your new set-point.

Most are presenting the majority of their vibrational offering in response to things, people, and conditions that they are observing. And so, the lives of most people continue to unfold very much as they have been, with no significant improvement from day to day. This is because there is not much thought being offered that is much different from what has already been experienced. However, the game of *Virtual Reality* will change that, because an application of this process, on any subject of your choice, will cause your vibration to move far beyond where you are currently standing. Since the Universe responds to your vibration—and not to what you are living right now, amazing things can now begin to flow into your experience even though they have never done so before.

The thing that we see that most commonly trips you up is that in the contrast—which is necessary and valuable to help you give birth to a rocket of desire—often there is an activation of many kinds of jumbled Energy. Usually, in order for you to know that you want something, you have to pretty well have chewed on details or events that have helped you know what you do not want. In other words, when do you speak most clearly about wanting to be well? Usually when you are less than well, correct? When does your strongest desire for more money really kick into high gear? Most likely when there is not enough money. When you are confused, that is when you want more clarity, right? When you are over-whelmed, isn't that when you want more serenity? And when you are bored, isn't that when you want more stimulation?

Remember, the *Creative Workshop Process* comprises three steps: (1) Ask (that is easy, you do it all the time). (2) Answer the asking (that is not your work—Source Energy does that). (3) Allow (be in the receiving mode of what you are asking for).

It is important that you realize that **Steps 1** and **3** are different. When you are focused upon, or praying for, something you really want or need, often you are not a vibrational match to the thing you want. Instead, you are a match to the absence of it.

When the bills all come at once, there is not enough money to pay them, and you feel frightened and fearful and say, "I *need* more money," or you try to use more positive words such as "I *want* more money," you are doing **Step 1**. You are setting forth your desire. But you are not in **Step 3**, so you are holding yourself apart from what you are asking for.

You are continually asking. You cannot stop asking; contrast is evoking the desire from you. Your real work is to find a way to be in the receiving mode. It is similar to wanting to receive a satellite or radio signal. To do so, you have to set your receiver on the same wavelength as the transmitter or you are going to get static; you are not going to get a clear signal. In like manner, you recognize the alignment of your (transmitted and received) signals by feeling the alignment of your emotions. In other words, when you are out there in that ragged place where you are feeling frazzled and frustrated or angry and hurt, you are out of alignment.

We want you to relax and not be so hard on yourself when you find yourself in a place of negative emotion. Negative emotion is a good thing in that it is letting you know that some tweaking is required in order for you to be in harmony with who you are.

If you are really out of sync; in other words, if you can really feel that you are not in a good-feeling place, then a more soothing process that we would recommend would be that of *Meditation*. Because when you quiet your mind, you stop thought, and when you stop thought, your vibration automatically rises.

Of course, if you can find something to focus upon, something that you can easily appreciate, then the *Rampage of Appreciation Process* would be an even better one because you can do it under all conditions no matter where you are. But this process of *Virtual Reality* will help you in two specific ways: You will become accustomed to the way non-resistance feels, so you will recognize when you have moved into resistant thought at an earlier stage when it is easier to move back out again. And, in every moment that you are in your state of non-resistance, the *Law of Attraction* will be responding to you in a positive way.

Abraham, Speak to Us More about the <u>Virtual Reality Process</u>

Virtual Reality is a process where you get to choose everything about this moment in time, just like a director in a movie would do. To begin this process, you would first decide: *Where does this scene take place?* Choose a location that feels really good to you. It could be a place that you may have visited, heard about, seen in a movie, or even imagined.

Is it indoors or outdoors? What time of day is it? Is it morning, afternoon, or evening? Is the sun just coming up or going down? Is it broad daylight? What does the air feel like? What is the temperature? How are you dressed? Who else is there? Choose something that feels good to you.

It does not matter if you are alone or with someone else, but it *is* important that if you choose to bring someone else into your *Virtual Reality* that it feels good to have them there.

What kind of mood are you in? Are you laughing? Are you sitting and quietly contemplating? Once you have set the scene, you can imagine what you might say to each other.

The purpose of this *Virtual Reality Process* is to cause you to activate vibrations within you that put you in the place of allowing your Well-Being. So you would not create a *Virtual Reality* where you build your new house with a leaky roof and then bring repair people into your *Virtual Reality* to fix the leaky roof. You would not put up ugly wallpaper and then bring someone in to replace it. In your *Virtual Reality,* you can make it be precisely the way you want it to be.

Do not use this process to try to improve a specific existing situation, because in your attempt to fix something, you will bring the existing vibration into your Virtual Reality, and in doing so, you will lose the power of the <u>Virtual Reality Process</u>.

Nothing Is More Important Than Feeling Good

There is no reason that Well-Being is not pouring into your experience in precise detail in response to all of the things that you have identified that you want, other than the fact that you are in a bad mood, or are angry or worried about something.

This exercise of *Virtual Reality* will help you train yourself to feel better more of the time. And, like working a muscle, the more you do it, the better it works for you.

Esther once practiced this game of *Virtual Reality* while she was driving the big bus she and Jerry travel in. She discovered that it worked best for her to get into the scene quickly, bring herself to a place of really feeling good, and then get out. If she stayed too long, she would get too practical and try to reform people or fix things. But when she would just decide where the good-feeling place was going to be by picking something that made her heart sing . . . deciding who else was going to be there, identifying what kind of mood they would be in, and then just speaking a few words of dia-logue—and getting out—it felt wonderful.

We would encourage you to play this game when you are driv-ing, standing in a line, or lying in your bed, or you could even just set some time aside to do it. As you create these scenarios that make you feel good, you activate a vibration that *does* feel good, and then the *Law of Attraction* matches that vibration. *There is nothing more important than that you feel good—and there is nothing better than cre-ating images that cause you to feel good.*

When Esther, as she was driving, would think about what the air felt like, sometimes she would give it just a little humidity; some-times it would be so dry that it would feel good as it blew across her body; sometimes it would be 90 degrees with no humidity at all. She thought of every pleasant combination of temperature, humidity, and time of day that she could think of.

And then she would bring lovely friends to come and play with her. And they would have all kinds of wonderful experiences. She got so good at *Virtual Reality* that she wanted to stay longer, because when she played this game, she could control everything about everything.

Every Thought That Feels Bad *Is* Bad

The Universe does not know (or give attention to) why your vibration is what it is in any moment. In other words, the doctors could have diagnosed you as being disease-ridden yesterday, and today you could be driving down the highway (like Esther did), in some sort of fantasy *Virtual Reality.* In that moment, there would be no representation of any disease within your body. And if you could maintain that vibration more than you maintain your aware-ness of the disease, it could not remain in your body. It is only there because, somehow, without knowing it, you have chosen thoughts that are a vibrational match to the essence of the disease.

Every thought that you have chosen that is a vibrational match to disease . . . feels bad when you think it. It feels like anger, frustration, resentment, blame, guilt, or fear. . . . Those thoughts are not good for you, and you can tell they are not good for you because they feel bad when you think them. In the same way that touching and feeling a hot stove hurts, feeling negative emotion hurts.

Something that you lived a long time ago that is not active in your vibration, or something that you lived yesterday that you are not thinking about right now, does not have any vibrational weight in your point of attraction—none whatsoever. So you do not have to rid yourself of all negative thoughts.

Sometimes, as you are interacting with others, you will hear, see, or smell something that triggers a vibration within you that does not feel very good as it is activated. And that is the time for you to say, "Oh, my guidance system is working. I can feel that there's something activated within me that's not serving me very well. Because, in the activation of this vibration, there's some resistance within me that is now disallowing the Well-Being that would be there otherwise."

So *that* is the time to choose a thought that feels better. And if you have practiced *Virtual Reality*, then it will be very easy for you to reach for a thought that feels better. But if you have not been practicing, then when you are in the middle of a negative thought, you do not have anywhere positive to go. So you just have to wait until that thought peters out.

Another Example of a *Virtual Reality Process*

The more you practice the process of *Virtual Reality*, the more you will be practicing the vibration of no resistance; the more you practice the vibration of no resistance, the better you will feel, and, of course, the things that you want will now easily begin to flow into your experience as well. For example, imagine the following scenario:

Place: A lovely, white sandy beach.
"It's wintertime, but the weather is delightful. It's 70 degrees with scattered clouds, and the air feels wonderful on my skin.

"I have no shoes on, so I'm enjoying the feeling of the cool, clean sand under my feet. My clothes are loose fitting and very comfortable, and I feel very good in my body. And I am lazily walking down the beach, feeling strong, happy, and secure.

"My five-year-old granddaughter is with me, and she is loving this glorious day, as I am. She's glad to be with me, but she does not seem to need me to entertain her; and I'm enjoying watching her happy, self-empowered activity as she runs, digs in the sand, and enjoys this lovely beach. I'm very glad that we've come to this place. It was a very good choice.

"My granddaughter runs up to me, holding a shell that she's discovered, and with a gleeful sweet voice and bright sparkling eyes, she says, 'Grandma, I'm so happy we're here. Thank you for bringing us here.' And I tell her, 'You are most welcome, sweet girl. I love being here with you.'"

Now this is a good time to get out.

Worrisome or Thrilling, Your Visualizations Are Matched

In Tucson, a dear friend gave Esther a windshield repair kit. And Esther thought, *I wonder how it works.* She read the instructions, and thought, *This is a wonderful thing.* And every time she picked it up, she thought, *What an ingenious thing this is.*

So she and Jerry were on the road, and in about ten minutes, a truck swiftly passed them, causing a rock to ricochet off the windshield of their motorcoach. Almost immediately, Esther got to experience the need for windshield repair that she had been visualizing.

No matter whether you worry or rejoice in your *Virtual Reality,* you set up a vibration that the *Law of Attraction* matches.

Someone said to us, "Abraham, I have a hard time visualizing. When I think about going to *Virtual Reality,* it's just sort of a blank place for me. I don't know how to do this."

And we said, *Can you remember events that have happened? If you can remember, then you can do <u>Virtual Reality</u>, because none of that is right here, right now; and as you are remembering, you are re-creating it from something.*

So, visualizing, or *Virtual Reality,* is no different. It is conjuring, but with the singular intention of pleasing yourself as you do so.

As you practice this process and stimulate your imagination more, you will not only find the process to be a delightful, good-feeling way to spend some time, you will discover that your dominant vibration on a myriad of subjects is changing, and your life experience will now begin to reflect these wonderful improvements.

～ ～ ～ ～ ～ ～

Process #5
The Prosperity Game

When to Use This Process

- When you want to expand your ability to imagine

- When you want to add more clarity or specificity to your desire

- When you want to enhance the flow of money into your experience

- When you want to enhance the flow of abundance with respect to a variety of things

Current *Emotional Set-Point* Range

This *Prosperity Game* will be of the most value to you when your *Emotional Set-Point* is ranging somewhere between:

(1) Joy/Knowledge/Empowerment/Freedom/Love/Appreciation
and
(16) Discouragement

(If you are not sure what your current *Emotional Set-Point* is, turn back to Chapter 22 and scan the 22 categories on the *Emotional Guidance Scale*.)

In this process, you will begin by establishing an imaginary checking account. In other words, there will be no actual bank involved, but you will make deposit entries and check withdrawals just as if it were an actual account. You could use an old checkbook system that is no longer in use, an accounting program in your computer, or you could even manufacture a complete system by using a notebook as your checkbook register and blank pieces of paper for your deposit slips and checks. It is of value to make this process feel as real to you as possible.

On the first day, deposit $1,000. And spend it. In other words, make a $1,000 deposit entry into your checkbook register, then write out checks to spend those dollars. You could spend your money all in one place, using one check, or you could spend it for several different things, using several different checks. The point of the game is to have fun thinking about what you would like to purchase, and to enjoy the process of actually writing out the checks.

Be descriptive on the memo portion of the check. For example: *For a beautiful writing pen* or *Great running shoes* or *Membership at Gordon's Health Spa*. You can spend it all today, or save some of it for another day. However, we encourage you to do your best to spend it today, because tomorrow you will be making another wonderful deposit.

On the second day, deposit $2,000.

On the third day, deposit $3,000.

On the fourth day, deposit $4,000.

When you reach day 50, deposit $50,000. When you reach day 300, deposit $300,000. If you play this game every day for one year, you will have deposited and spent more than $66 million.

You will be benefiting by increasing your ability to imagine. In other words, you will discover, as you play the game for a few weeks, that it will begin to take real concentration to spend that much money. And so, your ability to imagine will expand tremendously.

Most of our physical friends really do not exercise their imagination very much. Most people offer their vibrations almost exclusively in response to what they are observing, but by playing this game, you will find yourself reaching for new ideas, and in time, you will feel the expansion of your own desire and expectation. In doing so, you will benefit by shifting your point of attraction.

You see, the Universe is responding to your vibrational offering, not to your current state of being. So, if you are giving your attention only to your current state of being, then your future evolves much the same. But if you are giving focused attention to these wonderful expanding ideas that this game evokes from you, the Universe now responds to the vibrations of those thoughts.

The Universe makes no distinction between the vibration you offer in response to what you are living and the vibration that you offer in response to what you are imagining, so this <u>*Prosperity Game Process*</u> *is a powerful tool for shifting your vibrational point of attraction.*

You can play the game for a short time, or you can play it for an entire year or more. Whatever you choose is appropriate. It may feel awkward in the beginning, but the longer you play the game, the more expansive your imagination will become. And as your imagination expands and you focus on the spirit of fun and expansion, your point of attraction will shift.

By writing the checks, using your imagination, writing the memos, focusing as you write, and feeling no resistance as you write the checks because there is no fear of overspending, you will achieve what is necessary in the achievement of anything: You will have made a statement of desire while you are in the state of non-resistance, or better said, in the state of *allowing*.

So, not only will you have the benefit of an expanded imagination, but your point of attraction will shift, and your life experience will then shift as well. Not only will your financial situation improve, but all manner of things that you have focused upon with pleasure will begin to flow into your experience.

You can start the game or stop it, and you can play it in any way you like. There are no rules; there is nothing that you should or should not do. In other words, pick it up and play with it. Spend as much as you want. But the important thing is: *Do your best to exercise your imagination.*

If you were a sculptor on your first day of sculpting, you would not take your big clump of clay and throw it down on the table and say, "Oh, it didn't turn out right." You would mold it. You would get better at it. You would get more clay. You would get different-colored clay. You would find a way to continue to evolve in your creative endeavor. And yet, when it comes to the creation that you mold with the clay of the Energy that creates worlds, most of you make no conscious effort to direct your thought. In other words, it is as if somebody else took the clay and threw it down there, and now you spend your life just talking about how it looks.

"Well, *that* didn't turn out very good. My parents should have done something different about that," or "The economy should be doing something different than that," or "There is injustice or unfairness," or "I don't like the way somebody else dealt with that." And we say, *Get your hands in your own clay! Summon the Energy through the power of your desire, and mold it through the power of your imagination.*

A friend said to us recently, "Abraham, I don't think you care if my lover ever comes to me. I think you want me to get so good at imagining him that I don't notice that he's not here." And we said, *That is exactly right, because when you are imagining that he is here, then, in your joy, in that moment, you vibrate in a place where you summon and allow GOD Force—Life Force—to flow through you. And there is nothing more wonderful than that.*

And then we said, *Oh, and by the way, when you get there, he cannot not come. But as long as your desire for him to come is more about your awareness that he has not come, not only can he not come, but the misery that you are feeling in that moment is because you are choosing a vibration that does not allow the Energy that your desire is summoning.*

Joyously playing this *Prosperity Game* will not only improve your financial state of being, but every aspect of your life will improve as well. It will not only help you activate more vibrations around things that you want, but it will assist you in focusing, more of the time, in a way that allows the things that you want to flow into your experience.

Playing this game will cause you to offer a more expansive, expectant vibration. And it is our promise to you that manifestations will begin to arrive in response to your changed vibration.

Process #6
The Process of Meditation

When to Use This Process

- When you want relief from resistance

- When you want an easier way of immediately raising your vibration

- When you want to raise your general level of vibration

- When you want to feel an awareness of your *Inner Being*

Current *Emotional Set-Point* Range

This process of *Meditation* will be of the most value to you when your *Emotional Set-Point* is ranging somewhere between:

(1) Joy/Knowledge/Empowerment/Freedom/Love/Appreciation
and
(22) Fear/Grief/Depression/Despair/Powerlessness

(If you are not sure what your current *Emotional Set-Point* is, turn back to Chapter 22 and scan the 22 categories on the *Emotional Guidance Scale*.)

Any thought that you continue to think is called a *belief*. And many of your beliefs serve you extremely well: thoughts that harmonize with the knowledge of your Source, and thoughts that match the desires that you hold . . . but some of your beliefs do *not* serve you well: Thoughts about your own inadequacy or your unworthiness are examples of those kinds of thoughts.

Now, with an understanding of the Laws of the Universe and some willingness to deliberately choose thoughts, you can, in time, replace all hindering beliefs with life-giving beliefs, but here is a process that can give you the immediate benefit of changing your beliefs in a much shorter time. We call this the process of *Meditation*.

We playfully tell our physical friends that the reason we teach the process of *Meditation* is because it is easier for most of you to clear your minds, having no thought, than it is for you to think pure, positive thoughts. For when you quiet your mind, you offer no thought; and when you do so, you offer no resistance; and when you have activated no resistant thought, the vibration of your Being is high and fast and pure.

Imagine a cork bobbing on a body of water. (That represents the place of high, pure, fast vibration that is actually natural to you.) Now, imagine holding the cork down under the water. (That is what resistance is like.) And now, imagine letting go of the cork—and see it rise back up to the surface of the water.

Like the cork, naturally floating on the water's surface, it is natural for you to experience the high, fast, pure vibration, free of the hindering resistance. And, like the cork, if you are not doing something that holds you down under the water, you will bob right back up to the surface where you belong. In other words, you do not have to *work* at being in the high vibration that is natural to you, because it *is* natural to you. But you do have to stop holding the thoughts that cause you to lower your vibration. It is a matter of no longer giving your attention to things that do not allow your cork to float or do not allow you to vibrate in harmony with who you really are. If you are not focused upon unwanted things that are the opposite of your own pure desire, you will activate no vibration of resistance—and you will experience your natural state of thriving and Well-Being.

A decision is the focusing of the vibration of desire, and the decision point happens when the desire is powerful enough. The only discipline that we would like you to exercise is to make a decision that nothing is more important than that you feel good, and that you are going to find thoughts that feel better. Your cork floating is the only thing that is worthy of discipline.

You could say that the process of *Meditation* is a shortcut to changing your beliefs, for in the absence of thought, there is no resistance within you; and your cork, so to speak, bobs naturally back up to the surface.

Now, to begin the process of *Meditation,* sit in a quiet space where you are not likely to be interrupted. Wear comfortable clothing. It does not matter if you sit in a chair or on the floor, or even lie on your bed (unless you tend to fall asleep when doing so). The important thing is that your body be comfortable.

Now, close your eyes, relax, and breathe. Slowly draw air into your lungs, and then enjoy the comfortable release of that air (your personal comfort here is very important).

As your mind wanders, gently release any thought, or at least do not encourage it by pondering it further—and refocus upon your breathing.

You are, by nature, one who wants to focus, so in the beginning, this process of *Meditation* will feel unnatural, and you will find your mind wanting to return to things you have been focusing on previously. When that happens, relax, breathe again, and try to release the thought.

You will find it easier to quiet your mind if you will choose small thoughts that do not have the potential for expanding into something interesting: You could focus upon your own breathing. You could mentally count your breaths, in and out. You could listen to the dripping of a faucet. . . . In choosing the soft, gentle thought, you will leave behind all thoughts of resistance—and your vibration (like the cork) will naturally rise.

This is not a process where you work on your desires, but instead, this is one of quieting your mind. As you do so, any resistance will subside, and your state of vibration will rise to its natural, pure state.

As you quiet your mind, you may feel a sense of physical detachment. For example, you may feel no real difference between your toe and your nose. Sometimes you will feel the sensation of twitches and itches beneath your skin. And often, once you have released resistance and are soaring in your natural pure, high vibrations—you will feel an involuntary movement in your body. It may sway slightly from side to side or forward and backward, or your head may roll gently from side to side. Or, you may simply feel the sensation of movement or of a yawn. But any or all of these sensations or movements are indicators of your achievement of a state of *Meditation.*

Your point of attraction will now have changed, and your state of *allowing* will be in place. Things that you have been asking for—all of which have been given—are now flowing gently into your experience. And as you come out of your state of meditation, this state of *allowing* will continue until you focus upon something that changes your vibrational frequency. But with enough practice, those higher frequencies will become so familiar to you that you will be able to reclaim them whenever you choose.

Over time, if you meditate regularly, you will become quite sensitive to the way the higher frequencies feel within your body. In other words, whenever you focus on anything that causes a dip in your vibration, you will now be more likely to recognize it at the early, subtle stages before the dip is too significant—and you will be able to easily change your resistant thought in order to maintain your balance.

Abraham, Speak to Us More about <u>Meditation</u>

Many teachers, and we are among them, teach *Meditation* as a very good process for raising vibration. An effective *Meditation* would be one that distracts you from any physical awareness that causes resistance within your vibration, for when you turn your attention away from what holds your vibration in a lower place, your vibration will naturally rise. It is like a withdrawal of Consciousness, but while you are still awake. When you are asleep, you withdraw Consciousness, too, but when you slumber you are not consciously aware of what it feels like to be in that higher vibration. When you are awake and in a state of meditation, you can then *consciously* recognize what it feels like to be in that higher vibration. And in time, you will gain a new sensitivity to your vibration so that you will immediately know whenever you are focusing on something that is causing resistance.

Sometimes people say, "Abraham, is it normal for all hell to break loose in someone's life when they begin the *Meditation Process?*" And we say *yes,* because you are bringing yourself to a place of heightened sensitivity so that your formerly achieved patterns of lower vibration are now less comfortable to you.

Some Other Ways to Raise Your Vibration

Now, there are other ways of raising your vibrations than *Meditation,* such as listening to music that makes your heart sing, jogging in a beautiful place, petting your cat, walking your dog, and so on. These are just some of the many pleasant activities that cause a release of resistance and a rise in vibration. Often you are in your highest state of connection to Source Energy while you are driving your vehicle. That is the reason why there are relatively so few traffic accidents. The rhythm of the road, the distraction from what has been bothering you, and the idea of going someplace new often causes you to leave behind thoughts of things that have been bothering you.

Your goal is to release any thought that causes resistance so that you are then in a place of pure, positive thought. It is not a problem if you cannot completely quiet your mind—unless your mind is chattering about negative things. If you are softly thinking about pleasant things during *Meditation,* it can be of value.

For example, after spending time with a family they adore, Jerry and Esther enjoyed many pleasant hours of thought and conversation about that wonderful day. Anytime they wanted a good-feeling moment, they had only to remember something about that day—something one of them said, something one of the children did, the beautiful weather, the delicious food, the invigorating walk through the woods. . . .

In other words, it is quite easy to find something that is pure, positive Energy. Thinking about your pets can be a good source of positive thought because animals are so unconditional in their love. *Just find any thought that feels good when you think it, and practice it until you begin to set that tone within you. And then, other good-feeling thoughts will follow.*

Another Example of the *Meditation Process*

So, here is the process that, if we were in your physical shoes, we would utilize: Every day, for 10 or 15 minutes, and not for much more time than that, we would sit quietly by ourselves in some pleasant place where we would not be interrupted—maybe under a tree, maybe in our vehicle, maybe in the bathroom or garden . . . . We would do our best to shut down our physical senses. In other words, we would draw the curtains if the light was too bright; we would close our eyes; we would choose a quiet place.

We would be aware of breathing air into our lungs, and we would be conscious of breathing out. We would concentrate on long breaths in and long breaths out. We would breathe air in, and when we thought it was all our lungs would comfortably hold, we would softly bring still more air in. And then, at a place of full expansion of our lungs, we would take a long, slow, delicious moment to let the air out. Our intention would be nothing more than being in this moment and being consciously aware of our breathing, nothing to do other than breathe—not fixing breakfast, not combing hair, not wondering how someone is doing, not thinking about yesterday, not worrying about tomorrow, not focusing on anything in this moment except air in and air out.

This is a state of *allowing* where, for just a few moments, you stop running the show. You stop trying to make anything happen. This is the time when you are saying to your Source Energy, to your *Inner Being,* to your GOD (or whatever you want to call it): *Here I am, in a state of allowing. I'm allowing Source Energy to flow purely through me.*

Fifteen minutes of effort will change your life because it will allow the Energy that is natural to you to flow. You will feel better in the moment, and you will feel more energized when you come out of it.

Can 15 Minutes Make That Much Difference?

A big benefit that you will notice right away is that things you have been wanting will begin showing up. Now, why is this? "After all," you might say, "Abraham, I didn't sit and intend. I didn't sit and set goals. I didn't sit and clarify what I want. I didn't tell the Universe what I wanted. Why does 15 minutes of just being, set those kinds of things in motion?" Because you have already been asking, and now, during your time of *Meditation,* you have stopped the resistance that has been holding it away. Because of your practiced *Meditation,* you are now *allowing* your desires to flow into your experience.

You cannot be part of this physical environment without endless desires being born within you. And as these desires are being born within you, the Universe is answering them. And now, because of 15 minutes of *allowing,* whether you were petting the cat, practicing your breathing, listening to a waterfall or soothing music, or were on a *Rampage of Appreciation,* for that time of *allowing* you established a vibration that no longer caused resistance to the things that you have been asking for.

"Well, Abraham, if I've been really negative for 50 years, is it going to take me 50 years to turn it around?" *No, 15 minutes ought to do it.*

"In 15 minutes I can undo all of the disallowing that I've learned to do?" *In 15 minutes you can allow—you do not have to undo anything.*

"Well, what if I've really developed major habits of negativity? Is 15 minutes going to change that?" *Probably not. But the next time you go to one of those negative thoughts, you are going to be more aware of it. Your guidance system is going to be stimulated so that you will be aware—probably for the first time in your life—of what you are doing with your Non-Physical Energy.*

That is so important, because everything that happens to you and everything that happens to everyone you know, occurs because of the Energy that you are summoning and allowing or not allowing. Everything is about that relationship with Energy. Everyone you know, who is having every experience that you know, is having it because of the focused desire that their life has brought to them and the state of *allowing* or resistance that they're in at any moment.

What Could I Accomplish in 30 Days?

Do you know that you could have every deadly disease known to man (and some they have not even figured out yet) in your body right now, and tomorrow they could all be gone if from one day to the next you learned how to allow the Energy to flow? We are really not encouraging those kinds of quantum leaps; they're a little uncomfortable. What we are really encouraging is that every day, you be selfish enough to say, "Nothing is more important than that I feel good. And I'm going to find ways to do so today. I'm going to begin my day by meditating and bringing myself into alignment with my Source Energy. And as I move through the day, I'm going to look for opportunities to appreciate, so that all day long I'll bring myself back into Source Energy. If there's an opportunity to praise, I'm going to praise. If there's an opportunity to criticize, I'm going to keep my mouth shut and try to meditate. If I feel like criticizing, I'll say, 'Here kitty, kitty,' and I'll pet my cat till that feeling goes away."

Within 30 days of mild effort, you can go from being one of the most resistant people on the planet to one of the *least* resistant people on the planet. And then those who are watching you will be amazed by the number of manifestations that begin to occur in your physical experience.

We sort of see you from an aerial view, and it is like you are standing on one side of a closed door, and on the other side are all the things you have been wanting, just leaning up against the door, waiting for you to open it. They have been there from the first moment you asked for them: your lovers, your perfect bodies, your ideal jobs, all the money that you could ever imagine, all the things that you have ever wanted! Things little and things big, things that you would call extraordinary and significant and things that you would call not very significant—*everything that you have ever identified that you have ever wanted will be lined up right outside your door.*

And in the moment that you open the door, all things wanted will flow to you. And then we will hold a seminar on "How to Deal with Manifestations of All This Stuff That Is Flowing In."

❧ ❧ ❧ ☙ ☙ ☙

Process #7
Evaluating Dreams

When to Use This Process

- When you want to understand why you are having a particular dream

- When you want to understand what your vibrational point of attraction is, and what you are in the process of creating even before it manifests into your real-life experience

Current *Emotional Set-Point* Range

This process of *Evaluating Dreams* will be of the most value to you when your *Emotional Set-Point* is ranging somewhere between:

(1) Joy/Knowledge/Empowerment/Freedom/Love/Appreciation
and
(22) Fear/Grief/Depression/Despair/Powerlessness

(If you are not sure what your current *Emotional Set-Point* is, turn back to Chapter 22 and scan the 22 categories on the *Emotional Guidance Scale*.)

What you think about and what manifests in your life experience is always a vibrational match, and, in the same way, what you think about and what manifests in your dream state is always a vibrational match.

Your dominant thoughts always match your manifestations, and so, once you understand the absolute correlations between your thoughts, how you feel, and what is manifesting in your experience, you can then accurately predict everything that will come into your life.

It is nice when you are aware of your thoughts and therefore aware of what you are creating before it manifests, but it is also of value, after something has manifested, to then acknowledge the thoughts that led up to it. In other words, you can make the conscious association between your thoughts, feelings, and manifestations *before* the manifestation occurs or *after* the manifestation occurs. Both are helpful.

When you dream about something, it is always a match to the thoughts that you have been thinking. And so, since each of your dreams is, in fact, your creation, it is not possible for you to dream about anything that you have not created through your thoughts. The fact that it has now manifested in your dream state means that you have given it a significant amount of thought.

The essence of the way you feel about the things you think about most will eventually manifest in your real-life experience— but it takes even *less* time and attention for it to manifest in your dream state. And for that reason, your dreams can be of immense value in helping you understand what you are in the process of creating in your awake state. If you are in the process of creating something that you do *not* want, it would be easier to change the direction of your thoughts *before* it manifests than waiting to change your thoughts *after* it manifests.

The process for *Evaluating Dreams* is as follows: As you go to bed, consciously acknowledge that your dreams accurately reflect your thoughts. Say to yourself, *It is my intention to rest well and to awaken refreshed. And if there is anything important for me to recall from my dream state, I will recall it when I awaken.*

Then, as you awaken, before you get up, lie there for a few minutes and ask yourself, *Do I remember anything from my dream state?* Although you may be able to recall different aspects of your dream state throughout the day, usually the best chance of recalling your dreams is when you first awaken. And as you begin to recall one of your dreams, relax and try to remember how you *felt* during the dream sequence, for recalling your emotions will give you even more important information than recalling the details of your dream.

You must give significant attention to any subject for it to become powerful enough to manifest in your experience. And quite a bit of attention must also be given to a subject before it will begin to show up in your dream state. For that reason, your more meaningful dreams are always accompanied by strong emotion. The emotion may feel good or bad—but it will always be strong enough so that you will recognize the feeling.

"How did I feel as that was happening?" If you have awakened from a very good-feeling dream, you can be confident that your dominant thoughts surrounding that subject are pointed toward manifestations that you *do* want. When you awaken from a bad-feeling dream, know that your dominant thoughts are in the process of attracting something that you do *not* want; however, no matter where you stand in terms of what is manifesting in your experience, you can always make a new decision and change the manifestation to something that is even more pleasing.

It is truly more fulfilling to consciously create increasingly satisfying scenarios in your life experience than it is for you to create by default things that you really do not want—and then try to turn those around to things that you do want. For once something does manifest, then you have all that observing-of-the-unwanted-thing to deal with as well as the habit of thought that brought it about to begin with.

As soon as you begin to understand that your dreams are wonderful reflections of how you really feel and what you are creating, then you can begin to deliberately change your thoughts in order to positively affect your dreams. And as soon as you receive the positive dream, you will know that you are on the path of a more positive real-life manifestation.

If you awaken from a bad dream, do not worry; instead, feel appreciation for your awareness that you have been giving attention to something you do not want. In the same way you appreciate the sensors in your skin that alert you to the fact that you are approaching something that is very hot, appreciate that your emotions have made you aware that your thoughts are approaching something unwanted.

Now, you do not create while you are dreaming. Your dream is a manifestation of what you have been thinking during your awake state. However, once you are awake and you are now thinking about, or discussing, your dream, those thoughts do affect your future creations.

It is helpful to keep a written record of your dreams, but it is not necessary to be extremely elaborate in the recording of the details. Record the general setting where the dream took place, the basic people who appeared in the dream, what you were doing in the dream, what others were doing in the dream, and, most significantly, how you *felt* within the dream.

You may discover more than one emotion within the dream, but the emotions will not be very different from each other. For example, you would not feel both ecstatic and angry in the same dream because the vibrational frequency of those two emotions is too extreme to show up in the same dream. So, once you have identified how the dream felt, if you want to do something about changing or enhancing that emotion, you may want to move on to Process #22: *Moving Up the Emotional Scale.*

Abraham, Speak to Us More about *Evaluating Dreams*

Dreams can give you a wonderful insight into your current vibrational state of being. Your recall of a dream is your physical translation of blocks of Non-Physical thought that you have inter-acted with in your dream state. When you sleep, you reemerge back into the Energy of the Non-Physical, and you have conversations (not conversations in words, but vibrational ones). Then, as you are awakening, you translate that block of thought back into its phys-ical equivalent.

Sometimes when you have wanted something for a long while but you do not see any way for it to really happen, you will expe-rience a dream where it *does* happen. And then, in the pleasant rec-ollection of the dream, you soften your vibration of resistance—and then your desire can be fulfilled.

Many years ago, Jerry and Esther were mutually involved in a business enterprise, but they were not romantically involved. They felt appreciation for one another, but there was not a romantic feel-ing because neither of them would allow themselves to have that. Each of them, due to circumstances and beliefs, had not even tip-toed into that arena of thought relative to one another.

One night, Esther dreamed that Jerry (she saw him clearly) kneeled by her bedside and kissed her on the cheek, very much like the fairy tales that she had heard as a child. And when he touched her on the face with his lips, an extraordinary feeling began surg-ing through her—a feeling of exhilaration, a feeling that all was well, a feeling beyond description. It was a feeling that she had never experienced, asleep or otherwise. And when she awakened, she could not stop thinking about that dream, and she could never again think of Jerry in the way she did before her dream. This dream left a feeling in her that she had not known before. It was so deli-cious that she tried to dream it again and again. And if she was not able to dream it, then she would just try to remember it. She wanted to recapture the feeling of that dream. And that vibration was the catalyst that brought them together.

Esther had been thinking things like *I want to live happily ever after. I want a partner who appreciates me. I want a joyful life experi-ence.* As Esther had been thinking those things, even though she was living the lack of much of it, her *Inner Being,* hearing her want-ing, offered her something visual and sensual, something tangible enough so that she could not forget it—and something potent enough that it kept calling her. And as she flowed Energy toward it—oh, what a productive segment of time that was!

Dreams As Sneak Previews of Your Future

Now if you have things you want, but they are not the things that you have any touchstones about in your own life . . . for instance, you may want to be well, but you have never been well; or you might want to be prosperous, but you have never been prosperous; or you want a loving mate, but you have never had a loving mate . . . talk to your *Inner Being* about *what* you want and *why* you want it. And let your *Inner Being* offer to you, in your dream state, images that you can flow Energy toward, which will cause your vibrational state to be as you want it to be. And then the *Law of Attraction* will bring it to you.

Your dreams are manifestations of your vibrational point of attraction, so you can evaluate your dreams to determine what you are really doing with your vibration. Your dreams are sort of a sneak preview of that which is to come, so if you evaluate the content of your dream, you can often determine what your point of attraction is, and then if you do not wish to live out the dream you have been dreaming, you can do something about changing it.

As a result of what the influence surrounding you has been encouraging you to think, you may be flowing Energy toward financial disaster, you may be flowing Energy toward a body that will not function well, and so on. As such, your *Inner Being,* which is aware that you are projecting sickness into your future, may offer you a dream showing you where you are going. And so, you awaken and you say, *Ah, I don't want that!* And then you say, *What is it I do want? And why do I want it?* And then you start flowing your Energy productively toward what you *do* want, transmuting your Energy and thereby changing your future experience.

Process #8
The Book of Positive Aspects

When to Use This Process

- When positive emotion floods through you in response to a positive thought you are focusing upon, and you wish to ride the positive, good-feeling wave longer

- When you are aware that a subject that requires your consistent attention does not feel good, and you want to improve your vibration on that topic

- When most subjects that you focus upon feel good to you, but there are a few uncomfortable holdouts that you want to mold into a better-feeling place

Current *Emotional Set-Point* Range

This *Book of Positive Aspects* will be of the most value to you when your *Emotional Set-Point* is ranging somewhere between:

(1) Joy/Knowledge/Empowerment/Freedom/Love/Appreciation
and
(10) Frustration/Irritation/Impatience

(If you are not sure what your current *Emotional Set-Point* is, turn back to Chapter 22 and scan the *Emotional Guidance Scale*.)

To begin the process of the *Book of Positive Aspects,* purchase a notebook that feels good when you hold it in your hands. Choose a pleasing color, with a line width that matches your writing style, with paper that allows your favorite pen to glide along comfortably, and which opens comfortably and lies flat.

Because of the action that will be involved in this process, not only is an improved degree of focus certain, but with the focus will come an increase in both your clarity and in your feeling of being alive.

Now, on the cover of your notebook write: *My Book of Positive Aspects.*

It would be beneficial to set aside at least 20 minutes for this process on your first day, but after that, you could continue in smaller increments of time. However, you may discover the benefits of this process to be so rewarding, and the good feelings within the process so satisfying, that you may want to spend even more time at it.

Next, at the top of the first page of your notebook, write the name or a brief description of someone or something that you always feel good about. It could be the name of your lovable cat, your best friend, or the person you are in love with. It could be the name of your favorite city or restaurant. And as you focus upon the name or title that you have written, ask yourself these questions: *What do I like about you? Why do I love you so much? What are your positive aspects?*

Then, gently and easily, begin writing down the thoughts that come to you in response to your questions. Do not try to force these ideas, but let them flow easily through you onto your paper. Write as long as the thoughts flow, and then read what you have written and enjoy your own words.

Now, turn to the next page and write another name or title of someone or something that you feel good about, and then repeat the process until your 20 minutes has passed.

You may discover, even during the first sitting, that you will have managed to activate within yourself such a powerful vibration of appreciation and Well-Being that ideas of other names or titles for your *Book of Positive Aspects* will continue to flow to you; and when they do, take the time, if you can, to enter those titles at the top of other pages in your book. If you feel you have the time to ask the questions: *What do I like about you, why do I love you so much, and what are your positive aspects?* then do so at that time; if not, wait until tomorrow, when you will begin the process again.

The more positive aspects you search for, the more you are going to find; and the more positive aspects you find, the more you will search for more. In the process, you will activate within yourself a high vibration of Well-Being (which matches who you really are). And you will feel wonderful. And even better: This vibration will become so practiced that it will become your dominant vibration, and all aspects of your experience will now begin to reflect this higher vibration.

As soon as your notebook is filled, you will probably find yourself eager to purchase another and another, for there is a true power of focus in the experience of writing, and there is a true power of connecting to your own Source Energy in the experience of writing things that feel good when you write them.

The benefits of this process will be many: You will feel wonderful during the process. Your point of attraction will continue to improve, no matter how good it is now. Your relationship with each subject that you write about will become richer and more satisfying—and the *Law of Attraction* will deliver even more wonderful people, places, experiences, and things for you to enjoy.

Abraham, Speak to Us More about the
Book of Positive Aspects

Imagine a beautiful city. Not a big city, but a perfect city. The traffic flows nicely. There are beautiful points of interest. Living and working in this city is a wonderful experience. As you think about this city as we have described it to you, you may be thinking, *I could live there happily ever after.* Oh, but there's one little thing we forgot to mention: *There is a very deep pothole on Sixth Avenue.*

Now, if you were to focus on the positive aspects of this city, it is our expectation that if you were to live in this city, you would live happily ever after. Most people have not been introduced to their life by someone who was pointing out the positive aspects of it; instead, most have been introduced more often by someone saying, *Watch out for the pothole on Sixth Avenue!* And so, because of the negative orientation that surrounds them, most are consumed by the pothole.

Let us say that someone has been declared terminally ill; her doctor has given her a death sentence. And yet, the majority of her body, over 99 percent of it, is as this magical city—it is functioning well. All the arteries of traffic are working very well. It is just that because of the attention the doctor has given it, she is now giving her full attention to the "pothole"—until it will eventually consume her city.

Remove Your Attention
from the City's Potholes

"As I focus upon what I want, I feel good. If I focus upon lack of what I want, I will feel bad."

So let's take it a little further. Can you focus upon more than one thing at a time? You cannot. Can you feel more than one way at a time? Can you feel good and bad at the same time? You cannot. And so, is it not logical—for it certainly falls within the guidelines of the *Law of Attraction*—that if you are focusing upon what you *do* want, you cannot, at the same time, be focusing upon what you *do not* want? *And, if, when you focus upon what you want, you will feel good; and, if, when you feel good, you would be in the positive mode of attraction, then would not your most important work be to look for the positive aspects of all things, to look for the parts of all things that are uplifting to you—and to get your attention off of the potholes?*

Sometimes, when first learning about *Deliberate Creation*, our physical friends will worry. They are afraid that every negative thought they think is going to reach out into the cosmos and bring some monster into their experience. We want to ease your fear by reminding you that you are living the balance of your thought, so it requires quite a bit of thought about something before it will manifest in your experience. But as a people who have lived in a society that is predominantly oriented toward criticism and to what is wrong, always wanting to face the facts, you have become those, even in your individual thoughts, who predominantly worry, rather than predominantly know that all is well.

We want to encourage you to give more of your attention to what makes you feel good—not something so radical that you must control every thought—*just make a decision that you will look for what you want to see.* It is not a difficult decision to make, but it can make a big difference in what you bring into your experience.

Give Attention to What Feels Good

Something that is reality seems like it deserves your attention. "It's true, after all, it's true. Shouldn't I document it? Shouldn't I count it? Shouldn't I make the statistics of it? Shouldn't I tell others about it? Shouldn't I warn my children about it?"

Shouldn't we beat the drum of these things that we do not want, because they are reality, and therefore make them more reality? And, we ask, why would you do that? Why not look out into the database of creation and selectively sift the realities that you want to replicate, and beat those drums? And your answer is never a good enough one. It is: "We do it because it's reality. We do it because somebody else did it."

If we were standing in your physical shoes, we would not let the reality of something be our basis for attention; we would let the feeling-vibration of it be our basis. So we would start saying to anyone who was interested in knowing what we were about, "If it feels good, I give it my full attention; if it doesn't, I don't look at it at all."

And you know what they'll say to you? "You should face reality!" So answer back, "I do—I do it all the time. I've just become a more selective sifter of the reality that I face. Because I've begun to discover that whatever reality I'm facing; whatever reality I'm talking about, thinking about, remembering, regurgitating; whatever reality I'm making statistics of; whatever reality I'm holding for very long in my vibration, becomes my own reality. And I've become particular about the realities that I replicate in my experience because I've discovered that I can create reality. I can create reality! I can create reality—and I can choose the reality that I'm creating."

Oh, we love saying that to you. You are creators, and you can create anything that you want, but there's a better way of saying it: *You can and will create anything that you are giving your attention to.*

Wherever You Go, You Will Be There, Too

Jerry and Esther had been giving workshops at a hotel in Austin, Texas, which seemed to regularly forget that they were coming. Even though contracts had been signed and Esther had called on the day of arrival to confirm, when they got there, the sweet girl behind the desk always acted surprised. And then there was always a scurry to get things ready for their workshop. Esther said to us, "Maybe we should find another hotel!" And we said, that is one way of going about it—*but it is our expectation that wherever you go, you will take yourself with you, for you take your vibrational habits and patterns with you everywhere you go.*

So we told them to buy a notebook, and across the front of it, in bold letters, write: *My Book of Positive Aspects.* And then turn to the first page and write: *Positive Aspects of Southpark Hotel in Austin.* So Esther began to write: "It is a beautiful facility. It is well situated, very easy access to the interstate, and easy to give directions to. The parking lot is adequate and convenient. Our room is always very clean. There are many sizes of rooms, so we can accommodate whatever size group will be attending. . . ."

And as she made these entries, she found herself wondering why she had ever considered finding a new hotel. In other words, her attention to the positive aspects put her in such a mode of feeling good about this hotel that (it is our knowing) she cannot attract anything that is not good from that hotel. In other words, she took her attention—by virtue of her deliberate writing in this book—off of the pothole.

Is It Inspiration, or Is It Motivation?

You can look at this in two different ways: *If I do such and such, these good things will happen,* or *If I don't do such and such, these bad things will happen.* The first *inspires* you to action from a positive place. The second *motivates* you to action from a negative place.

Your *Book of Positive Aspects* will put you more and more in the position of attracting—by virtue of your inspired positive feeling—whatever you desire.

Process #9
Scripting

When to Use This Process

- When you are feeling good and want to add specifics to what you are creating in your life experience

- When you want the thrill of identifying and writing down things you would like to experience, and then seeing the Universe deliver to you the details you described

- When you want to consciously experience the power of your specifically focused thought

Current *Emotional Set-Point* Range

This *Scripting Process* will be of the most value to you when your *Emotional Set-Point* is ranging somewhere between:

(2) Passion

and

(6) Hopefulness

(If you are not sure what your current *Emotional Set-Point* is, turn back to Chapter 22 and scan the categories on the *Emotional Guidance Scale*.)

Esther turned on the television one evening and found herself immediately captivated by a movie that was well under way by the time she found it. In this movie, a seemingly unsuccessful scriptwriter was just discovering that his typewriter seemed to be magical. Each day, after he had described the scenes and written the words that the actors would speak, these same things would then come to pass in his own experience. And so, if a situation was not going the way he wanted it to, he went to his typewriter and wrote an improved version, and that scenario would then play out in his life experience.

As Esther watched the movie, we said to her, "That is really the way it always works. As you focus clearly upon things you desire, and hold no contradictory vibration that causes resistance—whatever you desire must be. For when you ask, it is always given, every time, with no exceptions." If something that you desire is not coming, it can only be that you are not allowing it to come because of the thoughts that you practice that are contrary to your own desire. Nothing else prohibits you from realizing every dream.

So, this is how the *Scripting Process* works: Pretend that you are a writer and that whatever you write will be performed exactly as you write it. Your only job is to describe, in detail, everything, exactly as you want it to be.

As you are having fun playing this game, and are not taking it too seriously, any of your hindering beliefs are less likely to be activated. In other words, by pretending that your typewriter, word processor, computer, or notebook is magical, and that whatever you write can be realized, you accomplish the two things that are necessary in the achievement of anything: You focus the lens of your desire, and you offer no resistance.

This process will help you be more specific about your desires, and, with that greater clarity about exactly what you *do* desire, you will feel the power of this specific focus. The longer you concentrate on a subject, and the more detail you give to it, the faster the

Energy moves. And, with practice, you can actually feel the momentum of your desire; you can feel the Universal Forces converging. Often, you will be able to know when you are upon the brink of a breakthrough or a manifestation just by virtue of the way you feel.

Because of the whimsical approach of this game, you are less likely to bring to your point of focus thoughts of doubt or disbelief. As you stay light and playful, you will be able to maintain a specific focus in the absence of resistance, and again, you will have achieved the perfect balance for the creation of anything.

If you play the game often, and enjoy it when you play it, you will begin to see amazing evidence of the power of the game. Things that you have written will begin to occur in your experience as if you are directing a play upon a stage. And when someone you are interacting with says words to you that you have *scripted,* you will be delighted as you recognize the power of your own intent.

You are the vibrational writers of the script of your life—and everyone else in the Universe is playing the part that you have assigned to them. You can literally script any life that you desire, and the Universe will deliver to you the people, places, and events just as you decide them to be. For you are the creator of your own experience—you have only to decide it and allow it to be.

Abraham, Speak to Us
More about <u>Scripting</u>

Scripting is one of those processes that we offer to assist you in telling the Universe the way you want it to be. If you are already in vibrational harmony with your desire, you know it, because your desire is already a physical reality. But if there is something that you want that has not yet come to fruition, then *Scripting* is a good way to speed it up. *Scripting* will help you break your habit of talking about things as they are, and will help you begin talking about how you would like things to be. *Scripting* will help you offer your vibration deliberately.

Script the Plot You'd Like to Live

We would begin by identifying ourselves as the central character, then we would identify the other main characters in the scenario, and then we would write the plot. (It is most effective if you write it, especially in the beginning, because writing is your most powerful point of focus. But you do not have to keep writing it over and over again.)

One day a woman was practicing one of her scripts with us, and she said, "I see two people walking down the beach." We teased her by asking, "Well, are you one of them?" The point we were making was that the whole point of writing the script is to begin to *feel* life experiences in the way you would like to live them.

The purpose of this process is to practice the feeling of the life you would like to live. The Universe does not know or care if what you are vibrating is in response to something that you are living, or in response to something that you are imagining—in either case, the Universe will deliver it to you.

If you regurgitate your script often enough, you begin to accept it as reality, and when you are accepting it in the way you accept reality—the Universe believes it and responds in the same way.

꙳ ꙳ ꙳ ꙳ ꙳ ꙳

Process #10
The Place Mat Process

When to Use This Process:

- When you want to more effectively utilize your Universal Manager

- When you want to create your own reality more through the flowing of Energy

- When you want to create your own reality less through the offering of your own action

- When you feel you have too much to do

- When you want more time to do more things that bring you pleasure

Current *Emotional Set-Point* Range

This *Place Mat Process* will be of the most value to you when your *Emotional Set-Point* is ranging somewhere between:

(2) Passion

and

(11) Overwhelment

(If you are not sure what your current *Emotional Set-Point* is, turn back to Chapter 22 and scan the 22 categories on the *Emotional Guidance Scale*.)

As Jerry and Esther's life evolved, and as their ideas and projects expanded, Esther began carrying a notebook that contained her list of things she needed to do. The list had evolved to several pages, and was comically called "Things to Do Today." Well, ten people could not have accomplished this list in only one day.

With each new entry to her list, Esther felt heavier and less free. Because of her desire to be of value, and because of her willing nature, she had created a huge sense of responsibility, and her feeling of freedom was being crushed by the weight of it.

Sitting in a restaurant and waiting for their meal to be delivered to the table, Esther pored through the pages of her list. Occasionally she would cross off something already accomplished, and immediately, with each omission, she would think of three more items to add to the list. As a sense of hopelessness washed through her, she asked us, "Abraham, what should I do?"

Take this large paper place mat, we explained, *and we will guide you. Draw a line down the center of your place mat, and as a heading on the left side of the line, write: <u>Things I Will Do Today.</u> As a heading on the right side of the line, write: <u>Things I Would Like the Universe to Do.</u>*

Now, looking over your long <u>Things to Do Today</u> list, select only those things that you absolutely intend to do this day. Things you feel you must do. Things you really want to do. Select only those things that, no matter what, you intend to do today, and enter them on the left side of your

Place Mat beneath the heading: <u>Things I Will Do Today</u>. And now, enter all other tasks on the Universe's side of your place mat.

Esther looked over the list and chose a handful of things that she really *did* need to do on this day, and she entered them on her side of her place mat. And then she began transferring her long list of remaining important tasks to the Universe's side of the place mat. One by one she transferred her tasks to the right side of the line, and as each task was transferred, she felt lighter.

We explained to Esther that in order to achieve anything, she has only two things to accomplish: She must identify her object of desire, and then she must get out of the way of letting it happen. In other words, ask, and then find a way of achieving a vibration that allows it—because it is always given, whenever you ask.

As Esther had been poring over her long list of responsible tasks, she was certainly amplifying the *asking* part of the equation, but her confusion and feelings of overwhelment were certain emotional indicators that she was not in the vibrational state of *allowing* in what she had been asking for.

During the process of transferring these items to the Universe's side of the place mat, her resistance began to soften, and her vibration began to lift. And while she did not realize it in that moment, her point of attraction had shifted, and she had begun, immediately, to allow the realization of her desires.

What Esther experienced in the next few days left her feeling amazed. Not only was she able to easily accomplish her own short and manageable list, but the items on the Universe's side of the place mat were accomplished, too—but without requiring Esther's time, attention, or action. People she had been unable to reach by telephone called her. Employees on her staff felt inspired to assist in some way, and they would accomplish something that was on Esther's list and then report it to her after it was done, without Esther's attention or request. Time seemed to stretch to allow more to be accomplished, and her timing with people and places and traffic improved dramatically.

The *Place Mat Process* caused Esther to focus her desires more specifically and, for the first time, to release her resistance regarding the same. For when you ask, it is always given—but you do have to let it in.

Abraham, Speak to Us More about the _Place Mat Process_

Very often, whenever Esther and Jerry are having lunch, Esther gets a big piece of paper from her purse, and then they draw a line right down the middle of the paper. On the left side they write, _Things to Do Today: Jerry and Esther._ And on the right side of the paper they write, _Things to Do: Universe._ On _their_ side of the page, they write the things they plan to take action on that day. On the other side, they write what they would like the Universe to act upon.

Esther has always been a big maker of lists. She often has about ten days' work on her _Things to Do Today_ list. And very often the list has served as an excuse to become overwhelmed. In other words, with so many things to do that she cannot possibly accomplish, the _Things to Do Today_ list has sort of dragged her down. But what she is discovering now is that she only puts on her list what she really intends to do. And in that way, there is very little resistance, even with respect to the things she is going to do. And anything else that she wants to do, whether it is today, a year from today, or ten years from today, she writes on the right side of the list—and allows the Universe to deal with it.

As they left a restaurant one day, Jerry said, "Do you want to take that place mat with you?" And Esther replied, "This is the best part, there's no follow-up." She left the list on the table; she left it there for the Universe to deal with. There is no follow-up, you see, not anything for her to drag around and hound herself about. And so, these are the sorts of things that you are doing there when you understand that there is this constant steady Stream of Well-Being flowing to you.

In the moment that you say "I prefer" or "I like" or "I appreciate" or "I want," the heavens part for you, and the Non-Physical Energies, in that instant, begin orchestrating the manifestation of your desire. In that instant! Faster than you can speak it, the Energy begins to flow, and circumstances and events, in an orchestration that we cannot begin to describe, begin to fall into place in order to give you exactly what you want. And if it were not for your resistance, things would happen really fast.

Are You Clear about What You Want?

You do not have to keep telling the Universe what you want; you only have to tell the Universe once. But the advantage of continuing to talk about it is that *you* get clearer about it. Usually you cannot clearly articulate everything you want with your first statement, so the more you talk about it, the more you fine-tune it. But as you say "I want it," the Universe begins manifesting it, and then when you say, "I would like it to be this way," the Universe modifies that. You say, "And a little bit of this would be nice," and the Universe . . . you see what we are getting at? And once you are clear about what you want; once you have zeroed in on it and you know what you want—it is on its way to you. It is done. The manifestation of it will probably follow later, however, because most often, there is enough resistance that you will not receive it instantly.

<center>~~~ ~~~ ~~~ ~~~ ~~~ ~~~</center>

Process #11
Segment Intending

When to Use This Process

- When you want your influence to dominate during a particular segment of your day

- When you recognize the potential of something not going quite right, and you want to make sure it goes the way you want

- When time or money is especially important to you, and you want to make the most of it

Current *Emotional Set-Point* Range

This *Segment Intending Process* will be of the most value to you when your *Emotional Set-Point* is ranging somewhere between:

(4) Positive Expectation/Belief
and
(11) Overwhelment

(*If you are not sure what your current Emotional Set-Point is, turn back to Chapter 22 and scan the 22 categories on the Emotional Guidance Scale.*)

It is easier to begin with a fresh, less powerful thought, and then focus upon it and cause it to expand, than to try to change an already expanded powerful thought. In other words, it is easier to create an improved future experience than it is to change a current existing experience.

If you are experiencing a physical condition that has your attention, you are, through your attention to your current condition, projecting it on into your future experience. But, by focusing on a *different* future experience, you are now activating that *different* experience, and as you project that changed experience into your future, you leave your current experience behind.

That is the power of the process of *Segment Intending.* It is the process whereby you define the vibrational characteristics of the time segment you are moving into. It is a way of pre-paving your vibrational path, so to speak, for easier and more enjoyable travel.

If you are in a bad mood, meaning that there is considerable resistance in your vibrational frequency, then, because you do not have access to very different thoughts from where you currently are, you usually project that same vibrational expectation into the segment that you are moving into. For that reason, we encourage the application of *Segment Intending* when you are already feeling good. If you are feeling bad in this moment, try one of the other processes in order to improve your current mood and point of attraction. And then once you are feeling better, you could return to this powerful *Segment Intending* process.

This process will help you be more deliberate about focusing your thoughts. It will help you become more aware of where your thoughts currently are, and it will help you be able to more deliberately choose the thoughts that you offer. In time, it will feel very natural to you to stop for a moment upon entering a new segment and direct your own intent or expectation.

You enter a new segment anytime your intentions change: If you are washing dishes and the telephone rings, you enter a new segment. When you get into your vehicle, you enter a new segment. When another person walks into the room, you enter a new segment.

If you will take the time to get your thought of expectation started even before you are inside your new segment, you will be able to set the tone of the segment more specifically than if you walk into the segment and begin to observe it as it already is.

For example, you are cooking dinner and are enjoying the rhythm and flow you have established. Everything is on schedule, and you expect everything to turn out just right.

The telephone rings. (You enter into a new segment.) You set forth the intention not to answer the telephone. You set forth the intention that your answering device can take the call, and you set forth the intention that you will return the call later when you have time.

So, the rhythm and flow of your meal preparation is not disrupted; your segment changed slightly, but you maintained your balance, and all is well.

Or, the telephone rings. (You enter a new segment.) You remember that you have been expecting an important call, and you do not want to miss it. You set your intentions for the segment to be efficient and brief, and to gather the information quickly and politely. And because of the positive flow you already have going, your positive expectation dovetails into that perfectly, so you have prepared the conversation, even before you pick up the telephone, to comply with your good-feeling intentions.

You are actually pre-paving your future experiences constantly without even knowing you are doing so. You are continually projecting your expectations into your future experiences, and this *Segment Intending* process helps you to *consciously* consider what you are projecting—and it gives you control of your future segments.

You can pre-pave future experiences that are immediate, or experiences that are in your more distant future, and once you have an opportunity to see how your deliberate thought positively impacts your experiences, you will want to do it even more. And like all processes, the more you apply it, the more skilled you become and the more fun it is, and the more effective your results will be.

If the new segment includes something that you have never enjoyed doing, *Segment Intending* is not the best process to apply. Of course, it is better than no deliberate intention at all, but when you have an opportunity, it would be of value to apply one of the more heavy-duty processes (Processes #13 to #22) to this subject.

For example, you are going to visit your mother-in-law, who, you believe, has never liked you, or you are on your way to work in a two-person office with someone who annoys you in many ways. . . .

Whenever you are setting forth your intentions about how you want to feel and how you would like the segment to unfold, it is always beneficial if, when you find yourself struggling for a positive scenario, that you do not continue the process. Change the subject in your own mind; think about something pleasant, and apply another process later.

Abraham, Speak to Us More about *Segment Intending*

You are living in a wonderful physical time. You are living in a highly technological society where you have access to stimulation of thought from all around your world. You benefit from all this, for it provides you an opportunity for much growth, but you also experience some disadvantages from the stimulation of thought—and the disadvantage comes forth in the form of confusion. For while your ability to focus upon a more narrow subject brings forth clarity, your ability to focus upon many things at once brings confusion.

You are receptive Beings. Your thought processes are very fast. And as you are considering any one subject, you have the ability, by the power of the *Law of Attraction,* to bring forth more and more clarity upon that subject until you can accomplish anything regarding it. But because of the availability of so much stimulation of thought, very few of you remain focused upon anything long enough to take it forward very far. *Most of you are so distracted by so much thought that you do not have an opportunity to develop any one thought to any great degree.*

Here Is the Key to Your Deliberate Creation

The point of the *Segment Intending Process* is to clearly *identify* what you want so that you can deliberately begin to set forth the *attraction* of that which you want.

Here is the key to your *Deliberate Creation:* See yourself as a magnet, attracting unto you the way you feel at any point in time. When you feel clear and in control, you will attract circumstances of clarity. When you feel happy, you will attract circumstances of happiness. When you feel healthy, you will attract circumstances of health. When you feel prosperous, you will attract circumstances of prosperity. When you feel loved, you will attract circumstances of love. The way you feel is actually your point of attraction.

And so, the value of the *Segment Intending Process* is to encourage you to pause many times during the day to say, "This is what I want from this period of my life experience. I want it and I expect it." And as you set forth those powerful words, you become what we call a *Selective Sifter.* You attract into your experience what you want.

However, the reason why segments are so effective is because although there are many things you want to consider, when you try to consider them all at the same time, you become overwhelmed and confused. The value of your intending, segment by segment, is that you do not try to chew on so much at any one time. You say, "What is it that I want now?"

If you want many things all at the same time, it adds confusion. But when you only focus upon the specifics of what you want in any particular moment, you bring clarity and power to your creation—and therefore, speed. And that is the point of <u>Segment Intending</u>*: to stop, as you are enter-ing a new segment, and to identify what it is you most want so that you may give your attention to (and therefore draw, power unto) that.*

Some of you are focused during *some* segments of your day's experience. But there are very few of you who are focused *much* of your day. And so, an identification of segments—*and an intent to identify what is most important within those segments*—will put you in the position of being a deliberate, magnetic attractor, or creator, in *each* of your segments throughout your day.

Not only will you find that you are more productive, but you will find that you are happier, for as you are deliberately intending, and then allowing and receiving, you will find great contentment. You are growth-seeking Beings, and as you are moving forward, you are at your happiest. When you are having a feeling of stagnation, you are not at your happiest.

An Example of a *Segment Intending* Day

We would like to guide you through an example of a day where you may be deliberately intending as you are recognizing that you are moving into new segments. Let us say that you have decided to apply this process before going to bed at the end of the day, and you recognize that entering into the sleep state will be a new seg-ment of life experience. And so, as you are lying there on the pil-low, getting ready to sleep, set forth the intent of a restful slumber. Set forth the intention of refreshing your physical apparatus, and imagine yourself awakening the next day feeling refreshed.

As you open your eyes in the morning, recognize that you have now entered into a new segment of life experience, and that from the time you remain in bed until the time you remove your-self from it is a segment. Set forth your intent for that time: "While I'm lying here, I'm intending to have a clear picture of this day. I'm intending to become exhilarated and excited about this day." And then, as you are lying there, you will begin to feel that refreshment and exuberance about the upcoming day.

As you get out of bed, you have now entered into a new segment of life experience. This may be the segment that you are preparing yourself for that day. And so, as you are brushing your teeth or taking your bath or doing whatever it is you do in this segment, let your intent be to do it efficiently, to enjoy yourself, to have it be an uplifting time that prepares you for the day.

As you are preparing breakfast, let your intent be to do it efficiently, and to select that which is most nutritiously balanced for your physical apparatus at this point in time. Let your intent be that you will be replenished or refreshed by it, that you will enjoy it. And as you set forth this intention, you will notice that as you are eating, you are feeling more rejuvenated, more replenished, and more refreshed. And you will enjoy the food more than if you had not set forth that intent to do so.

As the telephone rings, recognize that you are now about to enter a new segment. And as you pick up the phone, identify who it is, and then clearly set forth your intent before you begin speaking. As you get into your vehicle, or as you are traveling to your place of work or wherever it is you are going, let your intent be to travel from one place to another in safety, to feel invigorated and happy as you are moving forth, to be aware of what the other drivers are intending or not intending so that you may move through traffic in a sort of flow, safely and efficiently.

When you get out of your vehicle, you have now entered into another new segment. And so, pause for a moment and imagine yourself walking from where you are to where you are intending to go, seeing yourself feeling good as you walk, intending that you will move efficiently and safely from point to point, intending to feel the vitality of your apparatus, intending to feel the clarity of your thinking mechanism, and setting forth your vision, or your intention, for the next segment in which you are about to enter. Imagine greeting the secretary, the employees, or the employer. Imagine seeing yourself as one who uplifts others, having a smile ready, recognizing that everyone you meet is not deliberate in their intending, but knowing that by *your* deliberate intending, *you* will be in control of *your* life experience, and you will not be swept up by their confusion, their intent, or their influence.

Of course, your segments will not be just as we have offered. And they will not be the same from day to day. In the beginning, you will find that you are not so quick to identify your segments as you will be after you have done it for a while. For some, you may find it more efficient and effective to carry a small notebook and physically stop and identify the segment while you write a list of your intentions in your notebook, for as you are writing, you will find yourself at your strongest point of clarity and at your strongest point of focus. And so, in the beginning of this deliberate *Segment Intending,* you may find the notebook a very great and valuable asset.

As you are moving through such a day, you will feel the power and the momentum of your intentions building; you will find yourself feeling gloriously invincible; you will feel as if there is nothing that you cannot be, do, or have as you are seeing yourself again and again in creative control of your own life experience.

⌘ ⌘ ⌘   ⌘ ⌘ ⌘

Process #12
Wouldn't It Be Nice If . . . ?

When to Use This Process

- When you find yourself leaning toward the negative, and therefore offering resistance, and you want to turn it around to something more positive

- When you are already feeling good, and you want to focus more specifically on certain areas of your life to make them even better

- When you want to gently guide a negative, or potentially negative, conversation to a more positive place for your benefit or to gently guide someone else

Current *Emotional Set-Point* Range

This *Wouldn't It Be Nice If . . . ? Process* will be of the most value to you when your *Emotional Set-Point* is ranging somewhere between:

(4) Positive Expectation/Belief

and

(16) Discouragement

(If you are not sure what your current *Emotional Set-Point* is, turn back to Chapter 22 and scan the 22 categories on the *Emotional Guidance Scale*.)

When you say, "I want this thing to happen that hasn't happened yet," you are not only activating the vibration of your desire, but you are also activating a vibration of the absence of your desire—so nothing changes for you. And often, even when you do not speak the second part of the sentence and you say only, "I want this to happen," there is an unspoken vibration within you that continues to hold you in a state of not allowing your desire.

But when you say, "Wouldn't it be nice if this desire would come to me?" you achieve a different sort of expectation that is much less resistant in nature.

Your question to yourself naturally elicits from you a more positive, expectant response. And so, this simple but powerful game will cause a raising of your vibration and an improvement in your point of attraction because it naturally orients you toward the things that you want. The *Wouldn't It Be Nice If . . . ? Process* will help you let in the things that you have been asking for, on all subjects.

Wouldn't it be nice if we had the best time we have ever had with these friends?

Wouldn't it be nice if the traffic is light and we have a wonderful trip?

Wouldn't it be nice if I had a really productive day at work?

Or, the subject may be to find a wonderful new relationship. For instance:

Wouldn't it be nice if I find the most spectacular partner who adores me in the same way that I adore him?

Wouldn't it be nice if I find someone, and we waltz off into the sunset together?

Wouldn't it be nice if there's somebody out there who's looking for somebody just like me?

The reason the *Wouldn't It Be Nice If . . . ?* game is so important and so powerful is because when you say "Wouldn't it be nice if . . . ?" you are choosing something that you want, and you're being soft and easy about it. In other words, it is not the end of the world. It is a much softer vibration.

For example, let us say you want to reduce your body weight. Here is a *Wouldn't It Be Nice If . . . ?* example for you:

Wouldn't it be nice if I stumbled onto something that really worked for me?

Wouldn't it be nice if my metabolism began to cooperate with me a little more?

Wouldn't it be nice if the desires that I've been holding for a long time sort of came to a peak, like a guiding light?

Wouldn't it be nice if I could meet someone who's just run across something that really worked for them, which would light a fire in me?

Wouldn't it be nice if I could reclaim the body weight I had when I was such and such an age?

Wouldn't it be nice if I looked like I did in this picture?

Your logic would tell you, "Hey, I've been at this for a long time. If I knew how to do it, or if I was good at it, I'd have already gotten it done." So you are contradicting your own desire. And so, you would hold yourself in *that* vibration. However, when you are playing *Wouldn't It Be Nice If . . . ?,* much of that vibration is diffused.

Wouldn't it be nice if my physical body came into alignment with my dream?

Wouldn't it be nice if I discovered this to be much easier than it's ever been before?

Wouldn't it be nice if I came into Energy alignment, and everything around me came into vibrational harmony with that?

Wouldn't it be nice if the cells of my body cooperate with the mental picture that I'm holding?

Wouldn't it be nice if I could feel ease about my body?

Wouldn't it be nice if my physical body began responding differently to food?

Wouldn't it be nice if I began feeling a greater inspiration to exercise?

Wouldn't it be nice if the food-burning characteristics of my body kicked into high gear, and this process turned into an easy, almost effortless scenario?

Wouldn't it be nice if my ideas about food came into alignment so that I find myself taking such pleasure from foods that are really in vibrational harmony with what my body wants and needs?

By softly playing this game, what happens is that you hold yourself in this place of alignment. The other thing you could do is get off that subject altogether and never think about it again. But that is a difficult thing to do, because your body sort of goes everywhere you go. In other words, it is hard to get that off your mind. So, since it is hard to get it off your mind, you almost have to force yourself to choose pleasant *Wouldn't It Be Nice If . . . ?* thoughts.

One more thing: Do not expect instant results. Know that it is coming into being in its perfect time. In other words, you have been encouraging, through your thought and behavior, a cellular community, a large part of which you are about to extinguish. And so, there is some cellular cooperation that is going to take place, and all cells are willing to cooperate. They are not sacrificing; they are not holding little cellular funerals in advance. There is no mourning going on, as in, "Ah, she's going to kill 25 percent of us."

What is happening is that there is a sort of collective alignment. Your cells are getting ready, you see. And in that preparation and in that readiness, all kinds of things are beginning to come into alignment; things that you could not orchestrate even if you tried. Your body knows what to do. Your body has come into active agreement and alignment with all of this.

So, as you play the gentle *Wouldn't It Be Nice If . . . ?* game, leave the rest of your physical apparatus to the cellular knowing, which means that it is not your job to be the food police, it is not your job to be the exercise police, any more than it is your job to decide what cell has to go.

Whatever the subject of your desire, there is an orchestration that is being taken care of in response to the *Wouldn't It Be Nice If . . . ?* game that you are playing. So whenever you play this game and you trust that everything else will come into alignment—it will.

❧ ❧ ❧ ❧ ❧ ❧

Process #13
Which Thought Feels Better?

When to Use This Process

- When you want to be consciously aware of how you really feel about something right now

- When you are faced with a decision, and you want to go in the best direction possible

- When you want to determine your current *Emotional Set-Point*

- When you want to become consciously aware of your *Emotional Guidance System*

Current *Emotional Set-Point* Range

This process of *Which Thought Feels Better?* will be of the most value to you when your *Emotional Set-Point* is ranging somewhere between:

(4) Positive Expectation/Belief
and
(17) Anger

(If you are not sure what your current *Emotional Set-Point* is, turn back to Chapter 22 and scan the 22 categories on the *Emotional Guidance Scale.*)

Every subject is really two subjects: something that you desire, and the absence of something that you desire. If you do not understand that these are very different vibrational frequencies, then you may believe that you are focused on something that you desire, when you may, in fact, be focused in the opposite direction.

Some believe that they're focused upon the subject of a healthy body, when instead, they're focused on the fear of a sick body. Some believe that they're thinking about improving their financial situation, when instead, they're focused on not having enough money.

But because the *subject* is money or health, they believe that anytime they are focused upon the *subject,* they are thinking about what they want. And often that is not the case. Often people say, "I've wanted this for as long as I can remember. Why hasn't it happened yet?" Because they were not aware that every subject is really two subjects: what is wanted and the lack of it . . . For example, they thought that because they were talking about money, they were talking about what they wanted, when instead, they were focused on the opposite of what they wanted. Only when you are sensitive to the way you *feel* do you really know what your vibrational content is. But with some practice, you will become very adept at always knowing exactly where you are focused.

The *Which Thought Feels Better? Process* will help you consciously identify the vibrational frequency of your current thought. The game is most effectively played when you are alone because no one else can really know or understand which thoughts feel best to you. Often, when you are interacting with others, you may be confused about whether the thought actually feels better to *you,* or whether you are offering it because you think it is the choice someone else would want you to make.

It is important to leave everyone else's ideas, desires, opinions, and beliefs aside while you identify, for yourself, how you feel.

When Would You Play This Game?

There are limitless possibilities of thoughts that you might think on limitless subjects, but your own life experience, and the contrast that you are living, will help you identify the subjects on which you may want to focus.

This game is especially helpful when something has occurred in your own experience that causes a noticeable amount of negative emotion.

Understanding that negative emotion is an indicator of resistance, and further understanding that this resistance is the only thing that holds you apart from the things you really want, you may have decided to do something about releasing some resistance on this newly energized subject.

A *"Which Thought Feels Better?"* Game Example

This process works best if you can sit for a few minutes and write your thoughts on paper. In time, when you have played the game sufficiently, you will find success with it just by rolling the thoughts across your mind, but writing them down onto paper causes a much more powerful point of focus, which makes it easier for you to *feel* the direction of your chosen thought.

To begin: First, write a brief statement of how you *feel* about the subject right now. You could describe what has happened, but what is most important is that you describe how you feel.

Next, write another statement that *amplifies* exactly how you feel. This helps you more easily recognize any improvement as you move through the process.

For example, you have just had an argument with your daughter because she makes no effort to help around the house. She does not even take care of her personal things, and her own room is a terrible mess. She seems to hold no regard for the effort you are making to maintain an orderly environment. Not only does she not try to help, but it seems that she deliberately tries to hinder you. So you write:

She [or write your daughter's name] *is deliberately trying to make my life difficult.*

She doesn't care about me at all.

She doesn't even come close to doing her share of the work.

Once you have made a few statements that indicate how you really feel right now, make this statement to yourself: *I'm going to reach for some thoughts about this subject that feel a little better.* Now, once you have written each thought, evaluate whether it feels better, the same, or worse than when you initially began. So you write:

She never listens to me. (same)
I want her to be more responsible. (same)
I shouldn't have to pick up after her. (same)
I should have taught her better. (worse)
I wish her father would support me more. (worse)
A clean house is important to me. (slightly better)
I know she has a lot on her mind. (better)
I remember what it's like to be a teenager. (better)
I remember when she was a sweet little girl. (better)
I wish she were still that sweet little girl. (worse)
I don't know what to do about this. (worse)
Well, I don't have to figure it all out today. (better)
There are so many things about her that I adore. (better)
I know there is more to life than a clean house. (better)
It should be okay that I want a clean house. (worse)
It's all right that I want my house to be clean. (better)
It's fine that she doesn't care about that now. (better)

Remember, there are no right and wrong answers here, and no one else can really know which of your thoughts bring better or worse feelings to you. The value of this process is that you will become aware of how your thoughts feel—and you will become more adept at choosing better-feeling thoughts.

Many would ask, "But what good would it be to feel better about my daughter's sloppy habits? My thoughts won't change her behavior."

We want to say to you that your thoughts change the behavior of everyone and everything who has anything to do with you. For your thoughts absolutely equal your point of attraction, and the better you feel, the more that everything and everyone around you improves. In the moment that you find an improved feeling, conditions and circumstances change to match your feeling.

The *Which Thought Feels Better?* game will help you begin to realize the power that your own thoughts have to influence everything around you.

Abraham, Speak to Us More about the Process of <u>Which Thought Feels Better?</u>

"Will I ever stop reaching for something better?" No. And when you take the limitations of time or dollars out of the equation, and you trust that the Universe will conspire to satisfy every idea you can conjure up, then you let your ideas rip. But as long as you feel limitations, then you keep trying to rein them in and rein them in and rein them in.

Perhaps you may say, "Well, our current circumstances really don't allow us the money to do all this stuff that we want to do. We want to remodel our kitchen, and our decisions about not going into great debt about it are very clear decisions that we don't want to violate. So what do we do with these exploding ideas?" *And we say, does every one of them have to manifest right now? Or can you begin to take pleasure from the idea itself?*

Can you say, "Well, if not right now, then soon, we will do this and this and this"? And so, you can begin to take pleasure from the growing of the idea, but when you put yourself on a schedule where there is a deadline, then very often the shortage of time or money looms up and contradicts the Energy, making you miserable. It also makes you wish that you had never broached the idea to begin with. But then you can say, "Hmm, there's a lifetime of kitchens before us, and, for now, we are most pleased with the manifestation of this, and what ideas we are conjuring for the future!" Then, one day, you might move into a new home, shocked that it already has all of the things within it that you have been conjuring. And it will come when you have enough money; you have enough time. In other words, the Universe will line it up in response to the ideas that you are giving birth to and freely letting flow.

There Is No Right or Wrong in This

A good way to approach all this is: If the desire feels good to you, everything is going great. If the desire is uncomfortable, it means that you have a desire that is raging out there ahead of your belief, but then you can soothe that by saying, "We don't have to do it right this red-hot minute. We'll just hold this as a future idea. We're not going to shut the idea down because we know it's a good one. It's not a perfect match for where we are right now, but someday that will be a part of it. For now, this is quite satisfying."

Which thought feels better? To have it right now and to go into debt, or to say, "Oh, this is something that we have to look forward to . . . "?

Jerry and Esther go through this all the time because Esther wants everything, and she wants it right now. And there is no earthly reason why she should *not* have it right now—except that she is married to a savorer. He is not afraid that he will run out of money; he is afraid that he will run out of ideas. In other words, he does not want to eat up the ideas too fast. He wants to milk each one for everything he can get out of it. And Esther just wants to skip across the top. Esther eats the point of the pie first, while Jerry saves it till the last bite. But Esther worries that by the time she gets to the last bite, she will not want it anymore—so she eats it first.

So, both Esther and Jerry find their own way. There is no right or wrong formula there. We would say to Jerry that he will never run out of ideas, so he can skip across the top of them if he wants. And then he would say to us, "But I love getting my *doing* into the evolvement of it; the more intimately involved I am in my creations, the more satisfaction I'm receiving from them." So we say, *Then that is the right way for you. There is no right or wrong in this. Which feels better?*

Which thought feels better? To go into debt or to wait until later? *To wait until later.* Which thought feels better? To say that you have settled for less, or to say that this is part of your future experience? *To say that this is part of my future experience.* Which thought feels better? To be mad at yourself that your kitchen is not as modern as it can be, or to acknowledge that it is a perfect kitchen for now, and that it will always be growing—just like you will always be growing? Which thought feels better?

Which feels better, to appreciate or to condemn? Which feels better, to applaud what you have done, or to feel critical that you did not do enough?

Think about it: *Which thought feels better?*

<hr>

Process #14
The Process of
Clearing Clutter for Clarity

When to Use This Process

- When you are feeling stress due to your disorganization

- When you feel you are spending too much time looking for items

- When you find yourself avoiding your home because you feel better elsewhere

- When you feel that there is not enough time to do all you need to do

Current *Emotional Set-Point* Range

This *Clearing Clutter for Clarity Process* will be of the most value to you when your *Emotional Set-Point* is ranging somewhere between:

(4) Positive Expectation/Belief
and
(17) Anger

(*If you are not sure what your current Emotional Set-Point is, go back to Chapter 22 and the Emotional Guidance Scale.*)

A cluttered environment can cause a cluttered point of attraction. If you are surrounded by unfinished work, unanswered letters, incomplete projects, unpaid bills, unattended-to tasks; unsorted piles of paperwork; and stray magazines, catalogs, and all manner of miscellaneous items—they can negatively affect your life experience.

Because everything carries its own vibration, and because you develop a vibrational relationship with everything in your life, your personal belongings do have an impact on the way you feel and on your point of attraction.

There are two major hindrances to clearing away clutter: First, you may remember throwing something away, only to discover, soon after, that you really did need it after all. So now you are reluctant to throw *anything* away. And second, you realize that to really do a good job of getting organized would take far more time than you have to give to the project, for every time you have ever attempted to get organized, you have become bogged down in the sorting process and have ended up leaving an even bigger mess than when you began.

The *Clearing Clutter for Clarity Process* eliminates those hindrances because it is a sorting procedure that can be done extremely quickly without the possibility of discarding valuable things that you may need later on.

To begin the process: Obtain several sturdy cardboard boxes with lids. (Banker's boxes work well for this.) It is best if they are the same size and color. That way they will stack neatly and look attractive. We would suggest that you begin with a minimum of 20 boxes, but you may want to obtain more as you discover the productive power of this process. (Also, procure a package of alphabetized index cards and a handheld voice recorder.)

First, assemble the boxes and put five or six of them in the middle of the room that you wish to organize. Next, number each box with its own unique number, from 1 to 20, and so on. Now, look around the room, focus upon an item, and ask yourself, "Is this item important to my immediate experience?" If the answer is yes, leave it where it is. If the answer is no, put it in one of the boxes. Then pick up another item and continue the process as you focus upon each item in the room.

A great advantage of this process is that you will not be doing a great deal of sorting right now. This really is a process whereby you simply remove the clutter from your environment.

As you put the item into the box, speak into the recorder—for example, "Unopened package of guitar strings, box number one," or "Old cell phone, box number one." With five or six boxes open at the same time, you could do a general sorting. In other words, all magazines could go in the same box, clothing items in their same box, small miscellaneous items in the same box—but do not get carried away with the sorting process. Just pick up the item, determine if it is necessary to your immediate experience, and, if not, put it in a box, and speak into the recorder what the item was and which box you put it in. And, at a later time, you can take an hour or so and transfer the information from the recorder onto alphabetized index cards. In other words, under "A" you will write *abalone shell;* under "B," write *bathing suit;* under "C" write *cell phone. . . .*

Because you are not thoroughly sorting, this process will go very fast. You will find yourself feeling better as your space becomes less cluttered, and you will not experience your usual worry that you will not be able to find something, because you will have made a record of exactly where everything is.

Now, find a wall somewhere in your house or garage where these neat boxes can be placed, and be confident that you can retrieve anything that is important. If you do need the *unopened guitar strings,* your alphabetical card file will tell you which box you put them in.

After a few weeks, when you realize that you have not needed anything from box number 3, for example, you could then move that box out of the house, maybe to some outside storage facility, or you may even be willing to discard its contents, leaving box number 3 available for new clutter that may arise. And as you continue the process, you will begin to relax in the knowledge that you now have control of your environment.

Sometimes people will tell us that they are not bothered by clutter, so we tell them that this process is, then, unnecessary for them. However, since every piece of everything does carry a vibration, almost everyone really does feel better in an uncluttered environment.

Abraham, Speak to Us More about Clearing Clutter for Clarity

Physical Beings have a habit of gathering stuff around them. Most of you gather this stuff because it is the way you keep score; it is the way you fill time. In other words, you live in a physical world, and physical manifestation has become important to you, but then you get buried in the details of your manifestation.

Most of you spend much of your time just looking for things, and it is not only because you have too many things to sort through, but it is also because the gathering of the stuff is contrary to the freedom that is inherent within all of you. We have talked of the feeling of sadness that feels empty. People often try to fill that feeling of emptiness with *stuff*. They buy one more thing and bring it home, or they eat something; in other words, there are lots of creative ways in which you have tried to fill that void. And so, it has been our encouragement to some: *Discard everything from your experience that is not essential to your <u>now</u>.*

If you could just go through and release those things you are not wearing, release those things you are not using, release them and leave your experience in a clearer place, then the things that are more in harmony with who you are now will more easily flow into your experience. *You all have a capacity for attraction, and when your process is clogged with stuff that you no longer want, the new attraction is slower—and then you end up with a feeling of frustration or overwhelment.*

Imagine Yourself in a
Clutter-Free Environment

Jerry and Esther have been commenting recently that as Energy is moving faster, their ideas are also coming into fruition much more quickly—which means that they are buried in stuff. In other words, stuff is coming to them very fast. All kinds of stuff. And then it has to be dealt with. It has to be sorted or filed or read or discarded—something has to be done with it.

Never before has it been more important to get a picture in your mind's eye of your living space. So, imagine yourself in an environment of great clarity—a space with immense order—and imagine yourself knowing where everything is. Imagine organizing it in a way that it is very comfortable. In other words, just imagine. That is what you are shooting for here: The *feeling* of relief.

Esther, every now and again, will get a mental picture of her mother. Her mother worked full-time all of Esther's childhood, and they had a very large property. Her mother did most of the mowing of the huge lawn, and in those days there were no riding mowers—at least, they had never seen one, but Esther remembers her mother mowing. And then, the part that Esther remembers most is that once the lawn was all mowed and the sprinkler had been set to water it, her mother would sit on the porch and just sort of take it all in. And Esther would sit next to her mother and smell the freshly mown grass, and there was an overwhelming feeling of contentment that she was picking up on from her mother.

The day the lawn was mowed was always a happy day for Esther because there was something so satisfying that her mother felt once it was all done and she was sitting and taking it all in. Similarly, Jerry and Esther often feel this at the end of one of their workshops. It feels so good. It is like a job well done. It is as if everything is falling into alignment.

So what you want to do is, in advance, find that feeling-place. And if you do so, and the Energy lines up, then the clarity, ideas, and help will all come into making the physical reality fall into place for you.

In only an hour or two, you can box up the clutter from a room if you are just taking one thing at a time and putting it into a box. And since you have itemized where everything is, because it is all on your voice recorder, then some evening when you are doing something that does not require too much attention, you can listen to your recording. And with a small card file, you can indicate that the bathing suit is in box number 1, so that if you ever need it, you can find the index card and it will tell you which box it is in.

The power of this *Clearing Clutter for Clarity Process* is that you can do it very quickly. And there will be less resistance in it because everything that you want will be at your fingertips. In other words, you will have a record of where every bit of it is.

What we have noticed with the majority of people who have applied this system is that once they put something in the box, it is rarely something they ever need again. So, after you realize that you have had some item boxed up for a year or two and have not needed it at all, now you may feel freer to donate it to someone or to discard it in some way, but meanwhile, your life has been free of clutter and, therefore, free of that resistance for the entire period of time.

Process #15
The Wallet Process

When to Use This Process

- When you want to attract more money into your experience

- When you want to improve the way you currently feel about money in order to allow even more to flow into your life

- When you want to get your juices flowing regarding your specific desire

- When you feel that there is a shortage of money in your life

Current *Emotional Set-Point* Range

This *Wallet Process* will be of the most value to you when your *Emotional Set-Point* is ranging somewhere between:

(6) Hopefulness
and
(16) Discouragement

(If you are not sure what your current *Emotional Set-Point* is, go back to Chapter 22 and the *Emotional Guidance Scale*.)

Perhaps there are no more practiced vibrations in your culture than those related to the subject of money, for many see it as the means through which a good deal of their physical well-being flows.

Many people, however, without realizing it, are focused upon the *lack* of money rather than the *presence* of money in their experience. So even though they often identify things that they desire, they hold themselves apart from their own desires because they are more accustomed to noticing the lack of dollars than the presence of them. Again, it comes back to the fact that every subject is really two subjects: what is wanted, and the lack of it.

It is natural for all manner of abundance to flow easily into your experience, and the *Wallet Process* will help you offer a vibration that is compatible with the receiving of money instead of pushing it away.

Here is the process: First, obtain a $100 bill, and put it in your wallet or purse. Keep it with you at all times, and whenever you hold your wallet or purse, remember that your $100 bill is there. Feel pleased that it is there, and remind yourself often of the added sense of security that it brings to you.

Now, as you move through your day, take note of the many things that you could purchase with that hundred dollars: As you pass a nice restaurant notice that, if you really wanted to, you could stop in and have a delicious meal. As you see something in a department store, remind yourself that, if you really wanted to, you could purchase that because you have $100 in your wallet.

By holding the $100 bill and not spending it right away, you receive the vibrational advantage of it every time you even *think* about it. In other words, if you were to remember your hundred dollars and spend it on the first thing that you noticed, you would receive the benefit of really *feeling* your financial well-being only once. But if you *mentally* spent that hundred dollars 20 or 30 times in that day, you will have received the vibrational *feeling* advantage of having spent two or three thousand dollars.

Each time you acknowledge that you have the power, right there in your wallet, to purchase this or to do that, over and over again you add to your sense of financial well-being, so your point of attraction begins to shift.

You see, you do not have to actually *be* abundant in order to *attract* abundance, but you do have to *feel* abundant. A clearer way of saying it is that *any feeling of lack of abundance causes a resistance that does not allow abundance.*

So, by mentally spending this money again and again, you practice the vibration of Well-Being, of security, of abundance, and of financial security, and the Universe responds to the vibration you have achieved by matching it with manifested abundance.

Seemingly magical things will begin to occur as soon as you achieve that wonderful feeling of financial abundance: The money you are currently earning will seem to go further. Unexpected amounts of money in various increments will begin to show up in your experience. Your employer will feel inspired to give you a raise. Some product you have purchased will offer you a rebate. People you do not even now know will begin to offer you money. You will discover that things you wanted, things that you would have been willing to spend your dollars to have—will come to you even without an expenditure of money. You will be offered opportunities to be able to "earn" all the abundance that you can believe is possible. . . . In time, it will feel as if a floodgate of abundance has opened, and you will find yourself wondering where all that abundance had been hiding all along.

I could have that. I could have that. I have the ability to purchase that. . . .

And, because you really do have the means to do just that, because you are not pretending something that is not, there is now no hindering doubt or disbelief muddying the waters of your financial flow.

This is a simple but powerful process, and it will change your financial point of attraction. As your financial situation improves, your $100 stash or savings may grow to $1,000, then to $10,000, then $100,000, and more. Although there is no limit to what the Universe will yield to you, you have to feel good about money in order to allow it into your experience.

You have to feel good about great abundance before you will allow the pleasure of great abundance to flow into your experience.

Abraham, Speak to Us
More about the <u>Wallet Process</u>

Remember, you are on this sort of teeter-totter of balance, so you do not have to stop *all* thoughts of shortage because they are going to creep in; the influence is around you. All you have to do is deliberately offer more thought to tipping the Energies on the side of abundance; offer more deliberate thought—add more conscious use of the Non-Physical Energy toward the prosperity you want. And so, while you are moving through your day noticing how many things you could spend $100 on, you are deliberately utilizing the Non-Physical Energy to enhance your feeling of prosperity.

Someone once said, "Abraham, you obviously haven't been physical lately, for $100 won't go very far." And we said, *You missed the point. You spend $100 one thousand times a day, and you have spent the equivalent of $100,000. And that will bolster your feeling of prosperity, you see. It is the way you <u>feel</u> that is your point of attraction.*

Someone said to us, "Well, I haven't actually put the $100 in my wallet. I put an IOU in there, though." And we said, *Then you must not believe in your own IOU, because it is not fostering the feeling of prosperity. The IOU feels to you like another debt that you are carrying around.*

The *Wallet Process* is another means of giving deliberate attention to what makes you feel good.

Process #16
Pivoting

When to Use This Process:

- When you are aware that the statement you just made is the opposite of what you want to attract into your experience

- When you want to establish an improved point of attraction

- When you are feeling fairly good but know that you could feel even better, and you are willing to take the time to make that happen right now.

Current *Emotional Set-Point* Range

This *Pivoting Process* will be of the most value to you when your *Emotional Set-Point* is ranging somewhere between:

(8) Boredom

and

(17) Anger

(If you are not sure what your current *Emotional Set-Point* is, turn back to Chapter 22 and scan the 22 categories on the *Emotional Guidance Scale*.)

It is possible to be focused in vibrational opposition to what you really desire without knowing you are. It is like the opposite ends of a stick. When you pick up a stick, you pick up both ends. This *Pivoting Process* will help you be more aware of which end of your stick you are currently activating: the end that is about what you want, or the end that is about the *absence* of what you want.

The contrast of your time-space-reality is extremely useful, for contrast helps you focus your thoughts: Whenever you know what you do not want, you also know even more clearly what you do want; and whenever you know what you do want, you also know even more clearly what you do not want. And so, your exposure to contrast sharpens your focus and gives birth to new preferences and desires. In fact, this valuable contrast assures the eternal expansion of All-That-Is.

The process of *Pivoting* is often the first step in beginning to shift your habit of vibration, because this is a process that helps you more clearly define exactly what you desire. But because there is usually a wide variance in the vibration on one end of the stick and the vibration on the other end of the stick, you usually do not immediately shift your vibration just by making a statement of desire.

For example, when you are sick, you know very clearly that you want to be well. Or, when you do not have enough money, you know very clearly that you want more money. Now, by turning your attention to what you *do* want, and by holding your attention upon what you *do* want, you will begin to vibrate *there*.

At first, your awareness of what you do not want helps you identify what you do want; in other words, as you speak the words of your desire, your vibration may not match your words, but if you will continue the process of *Pivoting*—that is, if, whenever you feel negative emotion, which helps you know that you are focused upon something unwanted, you will stop and say, *I know what I don't want, so what is it that I do want?*—then in time, you will change your vibration on the subject. Little by little, you will redirect your vibration, and eventually the improved vibration will become your dominant thought.

See the process of *Pivoting* as a gradual shifting of your point of attraction, and enjoy the positive results that must follow. It is not possible for you to consistently give your attention to what you *do* want and not receive it, for the *Law of Attraction* guarantees that whatever you are predominantly focused upon will flow into your experience.

Abraham, Speak to Us
More about the <u>Pivoting Process</u>

The most important thing to remember is that you are the attractor of your experience, and that you are attracting it by virtue of the thoughts that you are offering. Thoughts are magnetic, and as you think a thought, it will attract another and another and another, until eventually you will have physical manifestation of the vibrational essence of whatever has been the subject of your thoughts.

If you have ever experienced (and we know you have) that which you would consider to be negative emotion (you may describe it as fear, doubt, frustration, or loneliness—there are many ways that you describe negative emotion), what you are experiencing in that negative emotion is the thinking of a thought that does not vibrate at a frequency that is in harmony with where or who your own *Inner Being* is.

You see, through all your life experiences, physical and Non-Physical, your *Inner Being,* or the *Total You,* has come to a place of knowing and to a place of wanting. And so, when you are in this physical body, consciously focused upon a thought that does not harmonize with that which your *Inner Being* has come to know, then the resultant feeling within you is one of negative emotion.

If you were to sit on your foot and cut off the circulation of the flow of blood, or if you were to put a tourniquet around your neck and restrict the flow of oxygen, you would see immediate evidence of this restriction. And, in like manner, when you think thoughts that are not in harmony with your greater knowing, the flow of Life Force—*the Energy that comes from your Inner Being into your physical apparatus*—is stifled or restricted. And the result is that you experience negative emotion. And if you would allow it to continue over a longer period of time, you would receive negative deterioration of your physical apparatus. That is why we say that all illness is a result of the allowance of negative emotion.

As you are understanding that a feeling of negative energy is an indicator that you are not in harmony with your greater knowing, many of you have reached the point of saying, *I want to feel good more of the time.* And we say that is a magnificent acknowledgment, because when you are saying, *I want to feel good,* what you are really saying is: *I want to be in the place of positive attraction,* or *I want to be in a place where the thoughts that I'm thinking as I'm feeling good are in harmony with my greater awareness.*

Pivot from What Is Unwanted to What Is Wanted

Many of you would not have such a difficult time feeling good if you were in an environment where there was not so much negative influence around you. (That was certainly true on the day that you emerged into this physical body.) But since you live in a dimension where there is much influence of thought that is abounding, it is of value for you to have some processes to assist you in getting from that place where you do *not* want to be, to the place where you *do* want to be, and the process of *Pivoting* is just such a process.

When you are feeling negative emotion, you are in a very good position to identify what you want. Because never are you more clear about what you do want than when you are experiencing what you do not want. And so, if you will stop in that moment and say, *Something is important here, otherwise I would not be feeling this negative emotion; I need to focus on what I want,* and then turn your attention to what it is that you want—in the moment of the turning of your attention, the negative emotion and the negative attraction will stop. And in the moment the negative attraction stops, the positive attraction will begin. And your feelings will change from not feeling good to feeling good. *That is the process of Pivoting.*

You will never be in a place where there is only the pureness of positive emotion or the pureness of positive Energy, because within everything that you want there is an automatic and natural counterbalance that is the lack of what you want. And so, your work is to define what it is you want, and then to, in a very deliberate way, hold your thoughts in the direction of your desires. And the emotional guidance that comes forth from your *Inner Being* that you feel in terms of negative or positive emotion will assist you in knowing which side of the equation you are on: Are you thinking of what you want or the lack of it?

A young father called and said, "Abraham, my son is wetting the bed, and he's too big for that. I've tried everything I know, and I'm at my wit's end. I don't know what to do." And we said, *When you come into the bedroom in the morning, what happens?* And he said, "I come in, and right away I know it's happened again; I can tell by the odor in the room." And we said, *And how do you feel at that point?* And he said, "I feel disappointed, and then angry, and then frustrated, because it keeps going on, and I don't know what to do about it."

And we said, *Aha, you are perpetuating the bed-wetting.* He asked, "What should I do?" And we said, *What do you say to your little boy?* And he said, "I tell him to get out of those wet clothes and get into the bathtub. I tell him he's too big for this; we've talked about it before." And we said, *When you enter the room and feel the negative emotion as you realize that what you do not want has occurred again, stop and ask yourself what it is you do want and get your thoughts focused upon that before you go further into the experience of your little one, and you will then see improvement in what happens.*

So, we asked this father what this experience had helped him recognize about what he wanted. He said, "I want my little one to wake up happy and dry and proud of himself, and not embarrassed." We said, *Good. As you are thinking those sorts of thoughts, then what is oozing out of you will be in harmony with what you want, not out of harmony. And you will be more positively, powerfully influencing your little one, also. And then, words will come out of you such as, "Oh, this is part of growing up. All of us have been through this. And you are growing up very fast. Now get out of those wet clothes and get in the bathtub."* This young father called very soon after that, within a few weeks, and said that the bed-wetting had stopped.

You see, it is really so simple. When you feel bad, you are in the process of attracting something that will not please you. And it is always because you are focused upon the lack of something you want. And so, the process of *Pivoting* is the conscious decision to identify what it is that you do want. We do not want to imply that the feeling of negative emotion is a bad thing, because, very often, in the feeling of negative emotion, you are alerted to the fact that you are in the process of negatively attracting. And so, it is like a warning bell. It is part of your guidance system.

We encourage you, very strongly, not to beat up on yourself when you recognize that you are feeling negative emotion. But as soon as you can, stop and say, *I'm feeling some negative emotion, which means that I'm in the process of attracting what I don't want. What is it that I do want?*

A very simple process of *Pivoting* would be to say, *I want to feel good.* Anytime you are feeling bad, stop and say, *What I want is to feel good.* And if you will offer that, then thoughts will begin to come to you on the positive side of the equation. And as one thought attracts another, attracts another, and attracts another, you will very soon be vibrating at the frequency that is in harmony with your greater knowing. And then you will really be rolling in terms of positive creation.

Thoughts Connect to Thoughts,
Which Connect to Thoughts

Our friend Jerry has offered us the most powerful analogy for the way your thoughts connect one to another. He described a large ship coming into the dock. It was to be tied with a rope that was very large, almost one foot in diameter, too big and bulky to throw across the expanse of water. And so, instead, a small ball of twine was tossed across, which was spliced into a little bigger rope, which was spliced into a little bigger rope, which was spliced into a little bigger rope. Until, eventually, the very large rope was easily pulled across the big expanse of water. And this is the way your thoughts dovetail into one another, with one connecting to another.

On some subjects, because you have been pulling on the negative rope longer, it is very easy for you to get off on a negative tangent. It can take just a little utterance from somewhere, a memory of something, or some suggestion to take you into a negative tailspin right away. And so, sometimes it is difficult for you to let go of that negative rope, for you have been holding on to it for a very long time. But if, whenever you are feeling negative emotion, you will realize that you are negatively attracting, and you will let your dominant intent be to feel good, then you can find yourself rather easily letting go of that rope.

And so, both the process of *Pivoting* and the process of the *Book of Positive Aspects* are offered to assist you in recognizing (in the early, subtle stages), that you are pulling on the very tips of that negative ball of twine, so that you may, right away, release it and reach for the positive twine.

As we are talking about the way thoughts connect to thoughts connect to thoughts connect to thoughts, we want to point out something that you may be missing: *It is much easier to go from a little thought of something that makes you feel good to more that makes you feel good to more that makes you feel good—than it is to be in a place where you are feeling bad, and then go right to a place where you feel good.*

Do Not Try to Save the World;
Save Yourself

Because thoughts are so *attractive* (meaning that they attract more unto them), once you get going on a thought that does not feel good to you, it is easier for you to stay focused in that train of thought until you have a great amount of negative energy going than it is for you to *pivot* away.

And for that reason, we would encourage the greatest exercise in *Pivoting* that we can offer you. In other words, rather than moving forward into your day, not having any clear ideas of what you want, and waiting until some influence touches you that you do not like, feeling the negative response, and deciding that you will *pivot*—it is so much more productive for you to go about your day with the decision to look for positive aspects.

Do not try to save the world; save yourself. That means that you need to focus on what makes *you* feel good. The process of *Pivoting* is the tool that will bring you to what you want. It is the process whereby you consciously decide: *Yes, I want to look for what I want, and I will no longer look in the direction of the lack of it.*

Pivoting is the continual, hour-after-hour, segment-by-segment process whereby you choose the positive. It is the way you get to feeling good—and it is a way that you can get whatever you want.

❧ ❧ ❧ ❧ ❧ ❧

Process #17
The Focus Wheel Process

When to Use This Process:

- When you realize that your current *Vibrational Point of Attraction* is not where you want it to be

- When you are aware that you are feeling negative emotion about something that is important, and you want to find a way of feeling positive emotion instead

- When something has just happened that is not to your liking, and you want to think about it while it is on your mind and change your point of attraction so that it does not happen again

- When you are reaching for a feeling of relief

Current *Emotional Set-Point* Range

This *Focus Wheel Process* will be of the most value to you when your *Emotional Set-Point* is ranging somewhere between:

(8) Boredom
and
(17) Anger

(If you are not sure what your current *Emotional Set-Point* is, turn back to Chapter 22 and scan the 22 categories on the *Emotional Guidance Scale*.)

Through exposure to life experiences, people often arrive at beliefs that hold them in a vibrational pattern that disallows their receiving of something they desire. And even though those beliefs are not serving them, many people defend their continual return to those unpleasant facts, arguing, "After all, they're true."

We want to remind you that the only reason anything has manifested into a physical, tangible, definable truth is because someone has given enough attention to it to make that so. But just because someone else has managed to create their *truth,* it does not mean that it has any relationship to you or to what you will create.

In your attempt to document the facts and events of your time, you often, without knowing you are doing it, hold yourself in patterns of vibrations that make it certain that you will confirm the "truth" (or some fact you are studying) with your own life experience. This is not because it is an undeniable truth that you are witnessing, but it is because, in your attention to it, you have achieved vibrational harmony with it, so the *Law of Attraction* brings a matching experience to you.

Sometimes someone will say to us, "But Abraham, I cannot ignore this, for it's true!" And we say, *It is only true because someone has made it true by giving their attention to it.* You see, what you are actually saying here is, "Because someone else has given attention to this and therefore, by the Law of Attraction, invited it into their own experience, I think I'll do the same. In other words, even though I don't want it, I'm obliged to create it in my own reality because someone else did."

There are many things that are true that you *do* desire. And there are many things that are true that you *do not* desire. It is our encouragement that you give your attention to the things that you *do* desire—and make *those* wonderful things the *truth* of your life experience.

Most people, however, have not deliberately guided their thoughts to those things that feel good, and so, without knowing they are doing it, they develop patterns of thoughts that they now continue to repeat.

Of course, some of your patterns of thought are extremely beneficial to you. Others are not. And so, this *Focus Wheel Process* is designed to assist you in changing your vibrational patterns on those specific subjects that are not beneficial to you. It is a process whereby you can literally practice your thoughts into a better feeling—and therefore into a better point of attraction.

We recommend that you spend 15 or 20 minutes with this process anytime you feel strong negative emotion about something that has happened, or whenever you wish to improve your feeling of clarity.

Your heightened negative emotion is always highlighting a good opportunity to shift your Energy on a subject, because something that you have been living has brought it to a particularly focused position. And so now, as you apply the *Focus Wheel Process* to it, you will be able to feel any improvement that you achieve in a more emphatic way. We recommend using this *Focus Wheel Process* in any moment when you are keenly aware of something that you do not want.

This is the process where you make a general statement that matches your desire. In other words, you're reaching for a match. And how do you know you have found one? Because you feel a sense of relief. In other words, the statement soothes you; the statement just feels a little better. And once you find it, if you can focus there for a little bit, even amplify it or exaggerate it, or remember something related to it . . . that is to say, if you can manage, once you find that gentle comforting statement, to stay there for at least 17 seconds so that you allow another thought to join it . . . it will then give impetus to your newly stated belief.

An Example of the Focus Wheel Process

Here's how to begin the *Focus Wheel Process:* Draw a large circle on a sheet of paper. Then draw a smaller circle, about two inches in diameter, in the center of the large circle. Sit back and look at the small circle and feel your eyes focus upon it.

Now, close your eyes for a moment and turn your attention to whatever has happened that has produced the negative emotion within you. Identify exactly what it is that you do not want.

At this point, say to yourself, *Well, I clearly know what I don't want. What is it that I do want?*

It is helpful if you try to identify what you do not want as well as what you do want in terms of the way you want to *feel* about it.

For example:

I feel fat, and I want to feel slender.
I feel poor, and I want to feel prosperous.
I feel unloved, and I want to feel loved.
I feel deceived, and I want to feel honored.
I feel ill, and I want to feel well.
I feel powerless, and I want to feel my power.

Next, try to write statements around the outside edge of your large circle that match what it is that you *do* want. When you find a statement that is a close enough match, you will know it. In other words, you will *feel* whether your statement does not match and throws you off the wheel into the bushes, so to speak, or whether it is a statement that is close enough to your desire that it sticks.

The reason the *Focus Wheel Process* is so effective is because the statements you are writing are those that you have deliberately chosen. They are general statements that you already believe, that match your desire. And the reason it works is because the *Law of Attraction* is so very powerful that when you hold a thought for as little as 17 seconds, another thought like it will join it; and as those two thoughts come together, there is a combustion that occurs that makes your thoughts even more powerful.

Whenever you make a general statement, you are more likely to be pure in your thought than when you make a specific statement, so the power of the *Focus Wheel* is that you are making general statements that you already believe, and as you hold each of them for 17 seconds or so, it gives you an opportunity to offer a pure vibration that is more and more specific to your desire.

So, let us say that you are preparing to do this process and you know that your intention is to eventually write: "I feel good about my body" or "My knee is well." But if you begin there, if the first little phrase you write is: "I feel good about my body," you can tell, by the way you feel, that the Energy is not lined up, because all it did was make you feel ornery and aggravate your awareness that you *do* feel fat or that your knee *does* hurt. So that statement was too specific.

In other words, it is sort of like trying to jump on a train that is going too fast, and all you do is just bounce back off of it. Can you imagine trying to get on a merry-go-round that is going too fast? You cannot quite get on yet, but if it slows down, you can— and then it can speed up, and as it does so this time, you can be comfortable on it. What you want to do is slow the "wheel" down, slow the belief down, so that you can get on. And then, once you do so, you can increase the speed of the vibration.

Now, just by trial and error, you can choose another statement. You might say something like, "I know that my physical body responds to my thoughts." Well, that is a softer statement, and you already believe that, but that makes you a little mad at yourself. So that was not a really good starting point either. You feel around for something else, and you say something like, "For the most part, my body's doing all right." Well, now, you believe that. That statement feels all right. You are able to stay on the merry-go-round.

As you write that around your circle and focus upon it, it feels pretty good. And then you make another statement. You might say something like, "I believe that the Universe matches our vibration." You absolutely believe that, so that statement sticks. Then you make a statement such as, "This physical body has been very good for me." You believe that. That statement stays. You are beginning to feel a little better. You are beginning to feel a little sense of relief. You are not quite so mad at yourself. Your vibration is lifting.

And so, let us continue to add power to this process of the *Focus Wheel:* As you find thoughts that feel good, continue writing them around the perimeter of your larger circle. Start at what 12 o'clock would be if you were looking at a clock, and then continue around to 1 o'clock, 2 o'clock, and so on, until you have 12 statements that feel good to you.

Since your thoughts are sometimes already spinning with such momentum that even though you want to change them you cannot find a place to jump in, this *Focus Wheel* game is about finding a thought that is close enough to where you are right now so that you do not end up thrown off in the bushes, but where you can gradually begin moving toward the way you want to feel. It is a wonderful vibrational bridging tool.

For example, let us say that you feel fat. Something has happened in your experience to bring that to the forefront of your mind, and you are, in this moment, feeling strong negative emotion about it. Take your paper, draw a circle in the center of the page, and within the circle you could write the words: *I want to feel slender.*

Now, focus upon the subject at hand and try to find thoughts that match how you want to *feel,* thoughts that feel good to you while you ponder them. Try to find a thought that does not throw you off in the bushes.

I can be slender again.

(This thought is too far from what you really believe, and while you want to believe it, you do not. And you can feel that you do not. And so, because this thought does not *feel* good to you, this is an off-in-the-bushes statement.)

My sisters are slender and beautiful.

(This thought does not feel good either. It points out their success and makes you feel your own lack of success even more. This thought throws you off in the bushes.)

I'll find something that will work for me.

(While this thought feels a little bit better than the previous ones, it still does not feel good. You have tried many things, but you believe that you have found nothing that works for you, so this thought just points out your past failures. This thought throws you off in the bushes.)

I know that there are others who have been where I now am who have found a way that works for them. (With this thought, you may feel a sensation of relief. You do feel a little bit better. Remember, you are not looking for the end-all solution here. You are only looking for a thought that feels good enough that it sticks. And this thought does not throw you off in the bushes. So, write it on your page at the 12 o'clock position, and now reach for more good-feeling thoughts.)

I don't have to do all of this today.
(That is another one that sticks. Write it at the 1 o'clock position.)
I'll find a diet that works.
(Off in the bushes.)
I don't feel good in my clothes.
(Off in the bushes.)
It will be fun to buy some new clothes. (2:00)
(That one sticks.)
My body will feel more refreshed. (3:00)
(Sticks.)
I will feel more vital. (4:00)
(Sticks.)
New ideas will come to me. (5:00)
(You're rolling now.)
I already know some things that will help. (6:00)
(Yes, feeling better.)
I like taking control of my own experience. (7:00)
(Sticks.)

I'm looking forward to making this change. (8:00)
(Sticks.)
I like feeling good.
(That one sticks. Write it on the 9:00 position.)
I like feeling good in my body. (10:00)
(Sticks.)
I feel good about my body. (11:00)
(Yes! Now, after writing that on the 11:00 position, emphatically circle the words you originally wrote in the center of your *Focus Wheel,* and notice that you now do feel a closer vibrational alignment with that thought, when only minutes before, you were nowhere near that vibration.)

Abraham, Speak to Us More about the <u>Focus Wheel Process</u>

You may have heard us say that your point of power is in the present because even though you may be thinking about the past, or you may be thinking about the now, or you may be thinking about the future—you are doing it all right now. You are vibrating now. The pulse is now. The vibrational offering is now. So what is happening is, any creative tension between the summoning of the Life Force and allowing of it to flow through you (the summoning and the allowing)—is all happening right here in the now.

So, here is the word that we want you to focus upon for the next few days. Here you stand in this *fresh* place. We love the freshness of where you stand. And now we want to show you how to stand in this *fresh* place and align your *fresh* Energy with *fresh* desire that will bring *fresh* and easy results.

The *Focus Wheel* is the best tool that we have found to help you bridge a belief so that it matches your desire. Now, this is what we mean by this: The formula for creating anything, even, let us say, joyful tax preparation, is: *Identify the desire and then achieve a vibrational match with it.*

Another Example of
a *Focus Wheel Process*

So, just begin by trying to find a phrase that will let you on the wheel. Write phrases that are close enough to what you already believe so that they do not throw you off in the bushes, so to speak. In other words, if you wrote, "I'm enjoying doing my taxes," you are off in the bushes. If you write, "I just think it is a wonderful thing that the government takes my money and squanders it in useless ways," you are off in the bushes. And so, the goal is to try to find something that matches your desire that feels better. So you could write something like, "I like to be on top of my life. It feels good to meet my commitments. I like it when I do things in a timely fashion. I love the feeling of order and organization in my experience."

Now, that might have been too strong a statement. You will know. You can tell by the way it feels whether it stays or whether it does not. So through trial and error, you just keep trying. So then you say something like, "I imagine that there are a whole lot of people who have felt like I'm feeling, who now have this thing handled." That got you on the wheel! "While the IRS taxing system isn't perfect, it's a mechanism through which our government runs." Now, did you end up in the bushes on that, or did you get on the wheel with it? "Every year I'm getting better at this. I'm managing things more comfortably. I'll find ways to make it more comfortable. My taxes are a good incentive to help me sort of get organized and figure things out."

The Better It Feels, the Better It Gets

Now, here is the thing we want you to hear: We have not solved anything. In other words, nothing has really changed. You still have your taxes to do, but the thing that we most want you to hear is that you are standing in a different place right now than you were before. In other words, clarity will come to you more easily than before. Memory will come to you more easily than before. An idea of where you left something will come to you more easily than before. In other words, all those scattered pieces of your life that are in piles and boxes and folders and bottoms of purses— all those pieces of information that are scattered here and there— are coming together in your mind. In other words, your Inner Mind will begin to feed you in a consistent way; in a way that did not happen before you took a little time to align your Energy with your desire.

Whether it is a castle or a button, if you are using it as your object of attention, it is summoning the Life Force, and it is the feel of the Life Force that life is about. The reason that you are summoning it is inconsequential. In other words, it is every bit as possible to feel as much joy in the preparation of your taxes as in the planning of an ocean cruise.

Now you might not believe that, but that is because you have not allowed the Energy to flow through you toward that object of attention without resistance. You summon the Energy because you want to do what you have to do, but then you divert the Energy, because you have all these habits or practiced statements that do not let it flow. When you have Energy flowing through you and you do not let it flow, it beats up on you pretty good. And now, because the *Focus Wheel Process* causes you to focus for a longer-than-usual period of time on a specific subject while you are deliberately reaching for thoughts that feel good, your point of attraction does change.

By applying this simple but powerful *Focus Wheel Process* to a variety of subjects as they come up in your life, you can effectively improve your point of attraction regarding everything that is important to you.

❧ ❧ ❧ ❧ ❧ ❧

Process #18
Finding the Feeling-Place

When to Use This Process:

- When you want to improve a situation

- When you want more money

- When you want a better job

- When you want a happier relationship

- When you want a better-feeling body

Current *Emotional Set-Point* Range

This *Finding the Feeling-Place Process* will be of the most value to you when your *Emotional Set-Point* is ranging somewhere between:

(9) Pessimism
and
(17) Anger

(If you are not sure what your current *Emotional Set-Point* is, turn back to Chapter 22 and scan the 22 categories on the *Emotional Guidance Scale*.)

Because you are generally giving much more attention to the aspects of your life that you are living right now, whatever you are living is carrying more vibrational weight, so to speak, than what you are desiring or imagining. In other words, if you have a desire to be slender even though you are considerably overweight at the moment, the aspects of your *now* experience are probably out-weighing the vibrations of your visualizations.

Often people will say, "I'm not happy over here. I wish I could be over there." But when asked what it is about over there that they desire, usually they will just explain to you what is wrong with being over *here*. Even though they use words such as, "I want to be over there," or "I want what is over there," their vibration is much more about over *here* where they now stand than about where they want to be.

As in our earlier "gas gauge" example of how unhelpful it would be for you to put a "Happy Face" sticker on your dashboard to cover the empty tank indicator, in like manner there is no value in using happy-sounding words if you do not *feel* happy. The *Law of Attraction* is not responding to your words, but instead is respond-ing to the vibrations that are radiating from you. It is quite possi-ble for you to use all the right-sounding words at the same time that you are in a state of powerful resistance to your own Well-Being, for the words you use are not important—how you *feel* is what matters.

The *Finding the Feeling-Place Process* is most helpful in making sure that you are radiating a vibration that will serve you, for this is a process that will help you realize what you are actually attract-ing. It is one of using your imagination to pretend that your desire has already come about and that you are now living the details of that desire.

As you focus upon what it *feels* like to be living your desire, you cannot, at the same time, be *feeling the absence* of your desire, so with practice, you can tip the scale, so to speak, so that even though your desire has not yet actually manifested, you are offering a vibration as if it has—and then it *must*.

Again, the Universe does not know if you are offering your vibration because you are living what you are living, or because you are imagining that you are living it. In either case, it answers the vibration—and the manifestation must follow.

For example, let us say that you go to your mailbox and you find the second notice of another unpaid bill, and as you open the envelope, you feel very uncomfortable because, right now, you do not know how you are going to pay it. This bill is already overdue, and there are several other overdue bills, so you feel overwhelmed and discouraged. "I want more money," you say. "I want a lot more money," you say, with even more emphasis. But you are offering empty, hollow words—that have no impact on your point of attraction whatsoever—because your words are not your point of attraction. Your point of attraction is your practiced vibrational offering, and the way you *feel* is the real indicator of what your point of attraction is. Right now you are pulsing with emotions that clearly match your state of not having enough money.

Your goal, in this process, is to conjure images that cause you to offer a vibration that *allows* money. Your goal is to create images that *feel* good to you. Your goal is to find the *feeling-place* of what it would be like to have enough money, rather than finding the *feeling-place* of what it is like to *not* have enough money.

Now, you could remember a time when you had more money, or even a time when, even though you did not necessarily have more money, at least you were not feeling the stress of too many bills. And when you find that memory, try to remember as many details as possible in order to try to feel it even more.

You could pretend that you have more money than you have any sensible use for; pretend that you have so much money you do not know where to keep it all, and imagine you have tons of it in the pantry and under the bed. See yourself going to the bank with buckets of change that you are converting to dollar bills. See yourself taking $5, $10, and $20 bills and having them converted to $100 bills, just for sake of more efficient storage.

You could pretend that you have a credit card with an unlimited balance that is easily paid, a sort of magic card that you use several times every day because it is very efficient, and then, once a month, you casually write a check that pays for all of the charges you have incurred. Pretend that the ratio of your money in the bank to this month's credit card balance is so great that paying the bill is inconsequential to your experience.

The more often you play this *Finding the Feeling-Place Process,* the better you will be at playing it, and the more fun it will become. When you pretend, or selectively remember, you activate new vibrations—and your point of attraction shifts. And when your point of attraction shifts, your life will improve regarding every subject for which you have found a new *feeling-place.*

Process #19
Releasing Resistance
to Become Free of Debt

When to Use This Process:

- When you want to experience the relief of being debt free

- When you want to create a larger spread between what you earn and what you spend

- When you want to feel better about money

- When you want to increase the flow of money through your experience

Current *Emotional Set-Point* Range

This process to *Become Free of Debt* will be of the most value to you when your *Emotional Set-Point* is ranging somewhere between:

(10) Frustration/Irritation/Impatience

and

(22) Fear/Grief/Depression/Despair/Powerlessness

(If you are not sure what your current *Emotional Set-Point* is, turn back to Chapter 22 and scan the 22 categories on the *Emotional Guidance Scale*.)

To begin the process of *Releasing Resistance to Become Free of Debt*, obtain a columnar writing pad with as many columns as you have monthly expenditures. Now, beginning in the far left column, write a heading that describes your largest monthly outgo. For example, if the largest check that you write each month is your house payment, then you would write as a header: "House Payment." And next, on the first line beneath the header, write the dollar amount of that house payment. Now, circle this amount, which represents the amount you are obligated to pay each month, and then, on the third line, enter the total outstanding debt for this "House Payment" category.

Next, enter your second largest payment in the second column, your third largest payment in the third column, and so on. And across the top of your columnar pad, write the following affirmation: *It is my desire to keep my promise regarding all of these financial obligations, and in some cases I will even do twice as much as is required.*

Each time you receive a bill, get out your columnar pad and adjust, if necessary, the minimum monthly amount that is required. If it stays the same, then write the same figure.

The first time you receive a bill, or when it is time to make the payment for the category that is on the far right column of your pad (in other words, the smallest payment you make each month), write the check for exactly twice what is required. And as you do so, write in the new amount of that outstanding balance.

This may seem a little strange to you when you first begin to play the game, but even if you do not have enough money to pay everything you owe in all of the columns, still double the payment in the far right column. And feel glad that you have kept your new promise to yourself to do your best to pay everything you owe, and to do even twice that amount in some cases.

Because you are looking at your finances in a way that is new, your vibration will begin to shift right away. As you feel even the slightest bit of pride for keeping your word, your vibration will shift. As you keep your promise about doubling up on payments, your vibration will shift. And with this shift, even if it is slight, things will begin to change in your financial condition.

If you will take the time to really enter everything you owe on the columnar pad, your newly focused attention will begin to positively activate circumstances around the subject of money for you. Instead of feeling discouraged as you find yet another bill in your mailbox, you will feel an eagerness to enter the bill on your columnar pad. And with this shift in attitude and vibration, things will begin to change in your financial picture.

Money that you were not expecting will appear in your experience. Bargains will reveal themselves, so your dollars will go further than you expected. All kinds of unusual financial things will occur, and when they do, be *consciously* aware that these things are happening in response to your newly focused attention and the resultant shift in your vibration.

As extra money appears, you will find yourself eager to apply another payment to the far right column. And soon, that debt will be paid, and you can eliminate that column from your pad. Column after column will disappear as your financial gap between what is coming in and what is going out widens. Your sense of financial well-being will improve on the first day you play this game. And if you will take the game seriously, your vibration around money will shift so significantly that you can be debt free in a short time, if that is your desire.

There is nothing wrong with debt, but if your debt feels like a heavy burden, then your vibration around money is one of resistance. When the burden has lifted, when you feel lighter and freer, your resistance has lifted, and you are now in the position to allow the Well-Being to flow abundantly into your experience.

Abraham, Speak to Us More about
Money and the Economy

As we mentioned in Process #17, it is as easy to create a castle as a button. It is just a matter of whether you are focused on a castle or a button, but it can also be as satisfying to create a button as a castle. And whether it is a castle or a button, if you are using it as your object of attention, it is summoning the Life Force, and the *feeling* of the Life Force is what life is about; the reason that you are summoning it is inconsequential.

So what about creating a very positive current of financial abundance? What about getting so good at visualizing that the money flows through you easily? What about expending money, and giving more people opportunity? What better way could anyone spend money than by putting it back into the economy that gives more people work? The more you spend, the more people benefit, and the more people get in on the game and dovetail with you.

Your role is to utilize Energy. That is why you exist. You are an Energy-flowing Being—a focuser, a perceiver. You are a creator, and there is nothing worse in all of the Universe than to come forth into the environment of great contrast, where desire is easily born, and not allow Energy to flow to your desire. That is a true squandering of life.

There is no high work or low work. There are just opportunities to focus. You can feel as fulfilled and satisfied in any task as in any other, for you are on the Leading Edge of thought, and Source is flowing through you—no matter what your endeavor is. You can be joyful at any endeavor where you decide to allow the Energy to flow. *Spiritual* versus *material* are not the choices. Everything about this physical, manifestational experience is spiritual. It is all the end product of Spirit. You have nothing to prove. Be the Spiritual You, and create like a physical fiend.

Your Financial Decline Will Not
Elevate the Impoverished

Think about what the economy was like in this nation a few hundred years ago. What has changed? Have more resources been trucked in from other planets? Or have there not been more people, over more time, who just identified more things that they desire and the Non-Physical Energy, which is endless and infinite, supplied that?

We never hear any of you say, "Well, I've been well for so many years that I've decided that I'm going to be sick for a while to allow some other people to be well," because you know that whether you are well or not does not have anything to do with others not getting enough wellness. You are not using up the wellness and depriving them of it. And it is the same thing with the abundance. People who have managed to find vibrational harmony with abundance—so that it is flowing to them and through them—are not depriving anyone else of that abundance. *You cannot get poor enough to help the impoverished people thrive. It is only in your thriving that you have anything to offer anyone. If you want to be of help to others, be as tapped in, tuned in, and turned on as you can possibly be.*

Feel appreciation for those who provide examples of well-being. How would you know that prosperity was possible if there was not some evidence of it around you? It is all part of the contrast that helps you sharpen your desire. Money is not the root of happiness, but it is not the root of evil either. Money is the result of how somebody lines up Energy. If you do not want money, do not attract it. But we say to you that your criticism of others who have money holds you in a place where things you *do* want, such as wellness, clarity, and Well-Being, cannot come to you either.

If the subject of money makes you uncomfortable when you think about it, it means that there is strong desire related to it, which means that it really, really, really matters. So finding a way to think about it and feel good is your work. But it is equally effective to think about anything else and feel good—and let it in. You do not have to think about money in order to let in money. You just cannot think about *lack* of money and let in money.

Success Is about the Joy You Feel

We love seeing you applauding someone else's success, because when you are genuinely thrilled by it, that means you are right on the track of your own. Many think that success means getting everything they want. And we say that this is what *dead* is, and there is no such thing as that kind of dead. Success is not about getting it done. It is about still dreaming and feeling positive in the unfolding. *The standard of success in life is not the money or the stuff—the standard of success is absolutely the amount of joy you feel.*

You can say things such as, "When I look at successful people—and by that I mean rich people, yes, and I mean happy people—sometimes they are rich *and* happy. When I'm talking about the successful ones, what I really mean is *the really happy people*—people who are really joyful, who are eager to get on with their day. Almost all of them, without exception, had a pretty rough beginning, which turned them into powerful rebels, initially. Then they found a way to relax into their natural birthright of Well-Being." (Success is about a happy life, and a happy life is just a string of happy moments. But most people do not allow the happy moments because they are so busy trying to get a happy life.)

Instead of "Earning" Abundance, "Allow" Your Abundance

Your action has nothing to do with your abundance! Your abundance is a response to your vibration. Of course your belief is part of your vibration, so if you believe that action is part of what brings you abundance, then you have to unravel that. We would like you to release the word *earn* from your vocabulary and your understanding altogether, and we would like you to replace it with the word *allow*. You want to *allow* your Well-Being; it is not something that you need to earn. All you have to do is decide what you would like to experience, and then allow it in order to receive it. It is not something you have to struggle or try for. You are all worthy Beings, and you are deserving of this Well-Being.

All the resources you will ever want or need are at your fingertips. All you have to do is identify what you want to do with it and then practice the feeling-place of what it will be like when that happens. There is nothing you cannot be, do, or have; you are blessed Beings, and you have come forth into this physical environment to create. There is nothing holding you back other than your own contradictory thoughts. And your emotion tells you whenever you have such thoughts. Life is supposed to be fun—it is supposed to feel good! You are powerful creators, and you are right on schedule.

Savor more; fix less. Laugh more; cry less. Anticipate positively more; anticipate negatively less. Nothing is more important than that you feel good. Just practice that and watch what happens.

⋙ ⋙ ⋙ ⋙ ⋙ ⋙

Process #20
Turning It Over to the Manager

When to Use This Process

- When you feel you have too much to do

- When you want more time to do more things that you enjoy

- When you want to become the powerful creator that you were born to be

Current *Emotional Set-Point* Range

This *Turning It Over to the Manager Process* will be of the most value to you when your *Emotional Set-Point* is ranging somewhere between:

(10) Frustration/Irritation/Impatience

and

(17) Anger

(If you are not sure what your current *Emotional Set-Point* is, turn back to Chapter 22 and scan the 22 categories on the *Emotional Guidance Scale*.)

Imagine that you are the owner of a very large corporation and that there are thousands of people who work for you. There are people who assist in the manufacturing and marketing of your products; and there are bookkeepers, accountants, and advisors. There are artists, advertising experts—thousands of people, all working to make your company successful.

Now, imagine that you do not personally work with any of these people, but you have a manager who does, and your manager understands them, advises them, and directs them. So, whenever you get an idea about something, you express it to your manager, who says, "I'll take care of that right away." And he does. Efficiently. Effectively. Precisely. Just the way you like it.

You may be saying to yourself right now, "I'd love to have a manager like that—someone I can count on, someone who would work on my behalf."

And we say to you, *You do have a manager who is that and much more. You have a manager who works continually on your behalf called the Law of Attraction, and you have only to ask in order for this Universal Manager to jump to your request.*

But most of you do not see this manager in this way. You have this manager, but you continue to hold the responsibility in your own heart. In other words, you say, "Oh yeah, the *Law of Attraction* is out there, but I've got to do all the work." And we say, *Well, then, what good is the Law of Attraction?* That would be like having a manager that you pay $500,000 a year to who just asks you, "Is there anything you want from me?" And you reply, "No, no, no. I'm happy just to pay you to have that title." Meanwhile, you are out there scrambling around, doing all the computer stuff and all the building stuff . . . you work yourself into oblivion and are exhausted all the time, while your manager is basking on the beach somewhere.

You would not do that, would you? You would put your manager to work. You would delegate to him or her, making requests with an expectation of receiving. And that is the way you must treat the *Law of Attraction.* Make requests with the attitude of expecting results. And when you delegate in that way, you are doing the only two things that are required in *Deliberate Creation:* You are identifying your object of desire, and you are allowing the Universe to yield it to you.

So, setting goals is like delegating to the Universal Manager. And achieving the vibration of *allowing* is like standing back and trusting your manager to set things into place, trusting that when something is required of you, your manager will bring your attention to it. In other words, when another decision is needed from you, you will be aware of it.

You are not *delegating* your life—you are *creating* your life. You are becoming the visionary, in the creation mode, rather than the "actionary." But there will still be plenty of things that you will want to do. We in no way want to steer you away from action. Action is fun. There is not anything in all of the Universe more delicious than to have a desire that you are a vibrational match to, and—in that alignment of your being connected to Source Energy—being inspired to an action. That is the furthest extension of the *Creation Process—there is no action in all of the Universe that is more delicious than inspired action.*

❧ ❧ ❧ ❧ ❧ ❧

Process #21
Reclaiming One's
Natural State of Health

When to Use This Process:

- When you do not feel well

- When you have been given an unsettling diagnosis

- When you are feeling pain

- When you want to feel more vital

- When you feel a vague fear associated with your body

Current *Emotional Set-Point* Range

This *Reclaiming One's Natural State of Health Process* will be of the most value to you when your *Emotional Set-Point* is ranging somewhere between:

(10) Frustration/Irritation/Impatience
and
(22) Fear/Grief/Depression/Despair/Powerlessness

(If you are not sure what your current *Emotional Set-Point* is, turn back to Chapter 22 and scan the 22 categories on the *Emotional Guidance Scale*.)

Do this process while lying in a comfortable place—the more comfortable, the better. Choose a time when you have approximately 15 minutes when you are not likely to be disturbed by anyone.

Now, write this short list in a place where it will be easy for you to read, and when you first lie down, read it slowly to yourself.

- *It is natural for my body to be well.*

- *Even if I don't know what to do in order to get better, my body does.*

- *I have trillions of cells with individual Consciousness, and they know how to achieve their individual balance.*

- *When this condition began, I didn't know what I know now.*

- *If I had known then what I know now, this condition couldn't have gotten started.*

- *I don't need to understand the cause of this illness.*

- *I don't need to explain how it is that I'm experiencing this illness.*

- *I have only to gently, eventually, release this illness.*

- *It doesn't matter that it got started, because it's reversing its course right now.*

- *It's natural that it would take some time for my body to begin to align to my improved thoughts of Well-Being.*

- *There's no hurry about any of this.*

- *My body knows what to do.*

- *Well-Being is natural to me.*

- *My Inner Being is intricately aware of my physical body.*

- *My cells are asking for what they need in order to thrive, and Source Energy is answering those requests.*

- *I'm in very good hands.*

- *I will relax now, to allow communication between my body and my Source.*

- *My only work is to relax and breathe.*

- *I can do that.*

- *I can do that easily.*

Now, just lie there and enjoy the comfort of the mattress beneath you—and focus upon your breathing—in and out, in and out. Your goal is to be as comfortable as possible.

Breathe as deeply as you can while still remaining comfortable. Do not force it. Do not try to make anything happen. There is nothing for you to do other than to relax and breathe.

You will very likely begin to feel soft, gentle sensations in your body. Smile, and acknowledge that this is Source Energy specifically answering your cellular request. You are now feeling the healing process. Do nothing to try to help it or intensify it. Just relax and breathe—and allow it.

If you were experiencing pain when you laid down, follow the same process. However, if you were feeling pain, it would be helpful for you to add these words to your written and spoken list:

- *This sensation of pain is an indicator that Source is responding to my cellular request for Energy.*

- *This sensation of pain is a wonderful indicator that help is on the way.*

- *I will relax into this sensation of pain because I understand that it's indicating improvement.*

Now, if you can, drift off to sleep. Smile in your knowledge that All-Is-Well. Breathe and relax—and trust.

Abraham, Speak to Us
More about <u>Reclaiming One's Natural State of Health</u>

The next time you feel any discomfort, stop in the middle of it and say to yourself, "This discomfort that I'm feeling is nothing more than my awareness of resistance. It's time for me to relax and breathe, relax and breathe, relax and breathe." And you can, in seconds, bring yourself back into comfort.

Every cell in your body has a direct relationship with Creative Life Force, and each cell is independently responding. When you feel joy, all the circuits are open, so the Life Force can be fully received. When you feel guilt, blame, fear, or anger, the circuits are hindered and Life Force cannot flow as effectively. Physical experience is about monitoring those circuits and keeping them as open as possible. Your cells know what to do; they are summoning the Energy.

There is no condition that you cannot modify into something more, any more than there is any painting that you cannot repaint.

There are many limiting thoughts in the human environment that can make it seem that these so-called incurable illnesses or unchangeable conditions cannot not be changed. But we say that they are only "unchangeable" because you believe they are. Someone asked us recently, "Is there any limitation to the body's ability to heal?" And we said, *None, other than the belief that you hold.* And he asked, "Then why aren't people growing new limbs?" And we said, *Because no one believes they can.*

But What about an Unhealthy Little Baby?

The question that often arises is: "Well, what about the little ones? What about the unhealthy babies?" And we say that they have been exposed to a vibration, even in the womb, that caused them to disallow the Well-Being that would have been there otherwise. But once they are born, no matter what their disability, if they could be encouraged to the thought that would allow the Well-Being, then even after the body is fully formed, it could be regenerated into something that is well.

It is natural for you to be absolutely well. It is natural for you to be abundant. It is natural for you to feel good. It is natural for you to feel clarity. It is not natural to feel confusion or to not have enough or to feel lack or blame. These are not natural to the you that is really You. But they seem to be sort of natural to the human patterns that most of you have picked up along your physical trail.

Anytime you have physical discomfort of any kind, whether you call it emotional or physical pain within your body, it always, *always* means the same thing: "I have a desire that is summoning Energy, but I have a belief that is not allowing, so I've created resistance in my body." The solution, every single time, to the releasing of discomfort or pain is the relaxation and the reaching for the feeling of relief.

We are asked, "If there is no source of illness, then why are there so many sick people?" It is because they have found lots of excuses to hold themselves in vibrational discord with wellness. They are not letting it in. And when they do not let Well-Being in, the absence of it looks like sickness. And when enough of them do it, you say, "Oh, there must be a source of sickness. In fact, let us give it a label. Let's call it cancer. Let's call it all kinds of terrible things, and let's imply that it jumps into people's experience." And we say that it never jumps into anybody's experience. It is just that people learn, through trial and error and through banging around with each other, patterns of thought that do not let Well-Being in.

As you do not allow the Well-Being in, it shows up in shadows in your life that are illnesses in your body, and deprivation of things that you want. Then, over time, you come to believe that that is a reality that has a source somewhere. And then you develop whole bodies of information to protect yourself from the "evil source" that never existed to begin with.

If You Have Received
a Frightening Diagnosis

If you get a diagnosis that is not what you want to hear, the tendency is to say, "Oh my God! How did I get so far away from something I want so much?" And we say that it is not a big thing at all—it is just a series of little things. It is the, "I could choose this thought that feels good, or this thought that does not feel so good, but I've developed a pattern for what *does not* feel good. So it's the daily dose of not being in the receiving mode that keeps me out of the receiving mode."

And that is all that it is! So, do not let any place that you are standing frighten you. All it is, is a by-product of some Energy alignment that only gives you stronger clarity about what you want—and, most important, greater sensitivity about whether you are in a receiving mode or locked off from it.

Wellness that is being allowed, or the wellness that is being denied, is all about the mind-set, the mood, the attitude, or the practiced thoughts. There is not one exception in any human or beast because you can patch them up again and again, and they will just find another way of reverting back to the natural rhythm of their mind. *Treating the body really is about treating the mind. It is all psychosomatic—every bit of it. No exceptions.*

There is nothing that cannot be reoriented to Well-Being. But it does take the determination that you are going to put your thoughts upon something that feels good. So here we are going to make a very bold statement: *Any disease could be healed in a matter of days—any disease—if distraction from it could occur and a different vibration dominate—and the healing time is about how much mix-up there is in all of that, for any malady in your physical body was a lot longer in coming than it takes to release it.*

Illness As an Extension of Negative Emotion

Physical pain is just an extension of emotion. It is all the same thing; there are two emotions—one feels good and one feels bad. This means that you are *connected* to your Energy Stream or you are *not allowing* your Energy Stream. Illness or pain is just an extension of negative emotion, and when you are no longer feeling any resistance to it, it is a non-issue.

Do you have to think specific positive thoughts about your body in order for it to be the way you want it to be? No. But you have to not think the specific negative thoughts. If you could never again think about your body and, instead, just think pleasant thoughts, your body would reclaim its natural place of wellness.

You can live comfortably, joyfully, resiliently, and healthfully as long as you have desire that summons life through you. People do not die because they pass through time. They die because they do not allow this arena to stimulate decisions. The only reason people ever die is either because they have stopped making decisions about being here, or they have made decisions about being Non-Physical.

You Could Remain
in These Bodies Indefinitely

Are we saying that you could reach what you consider to be a prime human physical condition and that you could maintain it for as long as you remain physically focused in this body? The answer is . . . absolutely yes. And it does not mean reaching your prime and then jumping off a cliff the same day either. It means reaching your prime and basking in the deliciousness of that. Now, why is anything other than that the more consistent experience? Because almost everybody is looking around and vibrating in response to what they are seeing. So what is the solution? Look around less. Imagine more. Look around less. Imagine more. Until your imagery is the most familiar vibration that you have.

You could remain in these bodies indefinitely if you would allow your environment to continue to produce new, continuing, life-summoning, pure, unresisted desire. You could be one who opened your vortex to continually find new things to want, and those desires would continue to summon the Life Force through you. In other words, you are living raucously; you are living joyously; you are living rambunctiously, and you are living passionately . . . and then, from that same framework, you make a conscious decision to make your transition.

Every Death Is Self-imposed

The best reason to make your transition into the Non-Physical is not because the physical is miserable. It is because you have a sense of completion in physical—and you are looking for another vantage point. Death is a withdrawal of Consciousness; it is like taking attention from here and putting it there.

Every death is brought about by the culmination of the vibration of the Being. There is not an exception to that. No one, beast or human, makes their transition into the Non-Physical without it being the vibrational consensus that is within them, so every death is a suicide because every death is self-imposed.

You are an eternal Being always projecting from Non-Physical, and sometimes that projection is into a physical personality. When the physical personality is complete for this time, then there is a withdrawal of focus. It is sort of like: Here you sit, and sometimes you go into a movie, and sometimes you come back out of the movie, but you are always the you that went into the movie, whether you are in the movie or not.

Here is a rule of thumb that will help you: If you believe that something is good, and you do it, it benefits you. If you believe that something is bad, and you do it, it is a very detrimental experience. There is nothing that you can do that is worse for yourself than to do something that you believe is inappropriate, so get clear and happy about whichever choice you make, because it is your contradiction that causes the majority of the contradiction in vibration.

Make a decision about what you want, focus your attention there, and find the feeling-place of it—and you are there instantly. There is no reason for you to suffer or struggle your way to or through anything.

⚜ ⚜ ⚜ ⚜ ⚜ ⚜

Process #22
Moving Up the Emotional Scale

When to Use This Process:

- When you feel bad and are having a difficult time feeling better

- When something has happened to you or someone close to you that has knocked you back on your heels (that is, someone died, your lover left you, your dog got run over, and so on)

- When it has been necessary for you to deal with a crisis

- When you have been diagnosed with a frightening illness

- When someone you love has been diagnosed with a frightening illness

- When your child, or someone very close to you, is experiencing a trauma or crisis

Current *Emotional Set-Point* Range

This *Moving Up the Emotional Scale Process* will be of the most value to you when your *Emotional Set-Point* is ranging somewhere between:

(17) Anger
and
(22) Fear/Grief/Depression/Despair/Powerlessness

(If you are not sure what your current *Emotional Set-Point* is, turn back to Chapter 22 and scan the 22 categories on the *Emotional Guidance Scale.*)

So, the contrast of your life experience has helped you identify your preferences and desires. And whether you speak them out loud or not, Source has heard each of your preferences and desires—no matter how large or small they may seem—and has answered them. And the manager, called the *Law of Attraction,* has lined up circumstances, events, other people, and all manner of things to assist in the fulfillment of your desires. In other words, you have asked, and it is given—but now you must let it in.

Remember, there is no Non-Physical Source of darkness, sickness, confusion, or evil. There is only the Stream of Well-Being, and it is flowing toward you at all times. And unless you are offering resistance of some kind, you are the full receiver of it, and your emotions help you understand to what extent you are allowing or resisting the Stream. In other words, the better you feel, the less you are resisting; the worse you feel, the more you are resisting.

The process of *Moving Up the Emotional Scale* will assist you, no matter where you stand, no matter what you are creating, and no matter how you feel, to lower your state of resistance and therefore improve your state of *allowing*—and every feeling of relief will be an indication of your release of resistance.

We want to help you understand that *Deliberate Creation* is really about *deliberately* achieving an emotional state. For example:

- When you do not have enough money, you want more. But we want you to understand that the distance you will be traveling is not the distance between not enough money to enough money, but instead is the distance between a feeling of insecurity to a feeling of security. *Once you practice the thought that makes you consistently feel more secure—the money must follow.*

- When you are sick, you want to be well, but the distance you are traveling is not from sickness to wellness—but from fear to confidence. *Once you practice the thoughts that make you feel more confident, the physical improvement must follow.*

- When you have no mate and want to find one, the distance you are really traveling is from the feeling of being lonely to the feeling of excitement or satisfaction. *Once you practice the thoughts that make you feel excitement or anticipation, the perfect mate must follow.*

You may say, *I want a new car,* but what the Universe is hearing is:

I am not happy with my current car.
I feel embarrassed by my current car.
I feel disappointed that I don't have a better car.
I feel jealous that my neighbor has a much better car.
I feel angry that I cannot afford a better car.

You may say, *I want to be well,* but what the Universe is hearing is:

I'm worried about my body.
I'm disappointed with myself.
I'm worried about my health.
I'm afraid that I will have a bad experience like my mother had.
I'm angry that I didn't take better care of myself.

You may say, *I want to find another job,* but what the Universe is hearing is:

I'm angry because my employer doesn't see my value.
I feel bored.
I feel unhappy with my current salary.
I'm frustrated that I can't make them understand.
I'm overwhelmed, with too much to do.

There is nothing that you or anyone else has ever wanted that exists for any other reason than you think you will feel better in the achieving of it. Once you consciously identify your current state of emotion, it becomes easier for you to understand whether you are choosing thoughts that move you closer to your desired destination or further from your desired destination. *If you will make the improved feeling or emotion be your real destination, then anything and everything that you want will quickly follow.*

The following is the basic list of emotions (also found in Chapter 22), beginning with those that hold the least resistance, all the way down to those that hold the greatest resistance. Whenever emotions have very similar vibrations, we have indicated them on the same line. These emotions range from the extremes of strongly allowing of your Source Energy to strongly disallowing of your Source Energy—and they are indicated by the words of *Empowerment* or *Joy,* on one end of the scale, all the way down to *Depression* or *Powerlessness* on the other end.

The words, or titles, that have been given to these emotions are not absolutely accurate because different people feel different about emotions even when they are using similar words. However, the Universe is not responding to your words; it is responding to your vibrational offering that is accurately and always accompanied by your emotions.

So, finding the perfect word to describe the way you feel is not essential to this process, but feeling the emotion is important—and finding ways to improve the feeling is even more important. In other words, this game is strictly about discovering thoughts that give you feelings of relief.

A scale of your emotions would look something like this:

1. Joy/Knowledge/Empowerment/Freedom/Love/Appreciation
2. Passion
3. Enthusiasm/Eagerness/Happiness
4. Positive Expectation/Belief
5. Optimism
6. Hopefulness
7. Contentment
8. Boredom
9. Pessimism
10. Frustration/Irritation/Impatience
11. Overwhelment
12. Disappointment
13. Doubt
14. Worry
15. Blame
16. Discouragement
17. Anger
18. Revenge
19. Hatred/Rage
20. Jealousy
21. Insecurity/Guilt/Unworthiness
22. Fear/Grief/Depression/Despair/Powerlessness

Here is the way we would apply this powerful process:

When you are aware that you are feeling some rather strong negative emotion, try to identify what the emotion is. Consciously think about whatever is bothering you until you can pinpoint the emotions that you are feeling.

Considering the two extreme ends of this emotional scale, you could ask yourself, *Do I feel powerful, or do I feel powerless?* While you may not actually be feeling either one of these emotions precisely, you will be able to tell which way your emotional state of being is leaning right now. So, in this example, if your answer is *powerless*, then shorten the range that you are considering, and ask yourself,

Does it feel more like powerlessness or frustration? Still more like power-lessness. Then shorten the range still further. *Does this feel more like powerlessness or worry?* As you continue (there is no right or wrong approach to this), eventually you will be able to state with accuracy what you are really feeling about the situation you are addressing.

Once you have found your place on the emotional scale, your work is to try to find thoughts that give you a slight feeling of relief from the emotion you are feeling. A process of talking out loud or writing down your thoughts will give you the best reading of the way you are feeling. As you make statements with the deliberate intention of inducing an emotion that gives you a slight feeling of relief, you will begin to release resistance, and you will be able to move up the vibrational scale to a place of feeling much better. Remember, an improved feeling means a releasing of resistance, and a releasing of resistance means a greater state of *allowing* what you really want.

So, using the emotional scale, and beginning with where you are, look at the emotion that is just about where you believe you are, and try to fashion some words that lead you more into a slightly less resistant emotional state of being.

For example, a woman found herself in a state of tremendous resistance and pain because of the death of her father. Even though he had been seriously ill and his death was expected, when it hap-pened she found herself in the deepest *depression.* She felt *powerless* and *grief stricken* in response to her focus upon the uncontrollable death of her father.

During the days before her father's death, this woman had barely left his side, but he slipped into unconsciousness during one of the rare times when she was not with him, and he did not awaken again before he died. As she thought about not being there to have just one last conversation, tremendous thoughts of *guilt* washed through her. And while she did not consciously recognize the slight improvement in the way the guilt felt, it was a very important vibrational transition for her. And then her thoughts turned to a powerful *anger.* She focused upon the woman who had been with her father when he had slipped into unconsciousness, and she felt *rage* that this woman had given her father such a strong dose of medication (for the purpose of making him more comfortable), and then she *blamed* the woman for having deprived her of her last conversation with her father.

She did not realize it at the time, but the feelings of guilt, rage, anger, and blame were each definite improvements over her grief-stricken vibrational state of resistance. She did feel better in her blame—much better, in fact. At least she could breathe, and she was now able to sleep.

Of course, it is always better when you achieve the improved state of emotion deliberately. But even, as in this case, when the improved emotions were discovered naturally and unconsciously, *each improvement now gives you access to something even more improved.*

Once you find the relief that anger and blame can offer from those suffocating emotions of powerlessness and grief, you can move even more quickly up the vibrational scale. And while it may even take a day or two to move up even one vibrational level, from (22) *Grief* to (21) *Guilt* to (18) *Revenge* to (17) *Anger* to (15) *Blame*, you can reclaim your connection to your Source and to your feeling of empowerment in a much shorter time than almost anyone realizes.

Here is an example of conscious statements that this woman could have offered to improve the way she felt:

I did everything I could think of doing to help my father,
but it wasn't enough.
(Grief)

I miss him so much. I can't stand him being gone.
(Grief)

How will I be able to soothe my mother?
(Despair)

Every morning when I awaken, the first awareness that
I have is that Daddy is gone.
(Grief)

I shouldn't have gone home to shower.
(Guilt)

I should have stayed right there so I could have told him good-bye.
(Guilt)

I should have realized how close he was to going.
(Guilt)

I was there day and night, day and night, and I still didn't get to say good-bye.
(Rage)

The woman who was with him knew very well what was happening.
(Rage)

How would she like it if the shoe was on the other foot and I put her father into a coma?
(Revenge)

She has seen many people die, and she should have warned me that it was close.
(Anger)

I think she knew and didn't want me to be there.
(Anger)

She gave him more medication than he needed just to make it easier for her.
(Blame)

I wish I could have said good-bye.
(Disappointment)

There are too many details to attend to, and I don't really feel like doing anything.
(Overwhelment)

I've been neglecting so many things in my life; I need to regroup and get organized.
(Overwhelment)

The health-care professionals are insensitive to the families of sick and dying people.
(Frustration)

They're more concerned about picking up the oxygen tanks than about how I feel.
(Irritation)

It will be good to spend more time with my own family.
(Hopefulness)

It will feel good to get back into the swing of things at work.
(Positive Expectation)

I know that in time I'll get to feeling better.
(Positive Expectation)

I don't know if I'll ever feel the way I felt before, but I know I will feel better in time.
(Positive Expectation)

There are so many things to do, and so many things that I want to do.
(Positive Expectation)

I'm so looking forward to smiling and meaning it, and laughing and really feeling it.
(Positive Expectation)

*I appreciate my husband so much. He's been helpful in so
many ways.*
(Appreciation)

*I do appreciate all of those people who have cared for my
father and mother.*
(Appreciation)

*I appreciate my sisters. We all love our parents, and we
love each other.*
(Appreciation) (Love)

*All things considered, we have lived, and are living, really
wonderful lives.*
(Appreciation) (Love)

Death is a part of life.
(Knowledge)

*Since we are really Eternal Beings, there really is no such
thing as "death."*
(Knowledge)

Daddy is not gone, because there's no such thing as death.
(Knowledge)

He's in a place where sadness doesn't exist.
(Knowledge)

That is truly a wonderful place to be.
(Joy)

I love knowing that he's in a place of utter joy and understanding.
(Joy)

I so adore this glorious Earth experience.
(Joy)

I love knowing how all of this fits together.
(Joy)

I loved having this wonderful man as my father.
(Joy)

This has all been good.
(Joy)

This is all good.
(Joy)

Remember, you do not have access to emotions that are far from where you are currently vibrating. Although you may spend an entire day beating the drum of the emotion where you are, on the next day, try to establish a different set-point even if it is only a slight improvement.

If the negative emotion you are feeling is slight, you will quickly move up the emotional scale. If the negative emotion you are feeling has begun only recently, you will quickly move up the emotional scale. If you are experiencing something extremely serious, or it is something that you have been living with for many years, it is conceivable that you could spend 22 days moving up this emotional scale, each day deliberately choosing the improved emotion just above the one you are currently feeling. But 22 days from *Powerlessness* to *Empowerment* is not a long time at all when you compare it to people you know who have been in a state of *Grief, Insecurity,* or *Powerlessness* for many years.

Now that you understand that your goal is to reach a better-feeling emotion, it is our expectation that this process will free you from troubling negative emotions that you have been experiencing for years. And as you gently and gradually release the resistance you have unknowingly gathered, you will begin to experience improvements in your life experiences . . . in all troubling areas of your life.

One Last Thing

Be easy about all of this. You tend to take life so seriously. Life is supposed to be fun, you know.

As we watch you in the creation of your life, we feel only love for you and appreciation for all that you are. You are Leading-Edge creators, sifting through the wonderful contrast of this Leading-Edge environment, and coming to new conclusions that summon the Life Force forward. There are not adequate words to explain the value of that which you are.

It is our powerful desire that you return to your state of self-appreciation. We want you to feel love for your life, for the people of your world, and most of all, for yourself.

There is great love here for you.

And . . . for now . . . we are complete.

Glossary

All Is Well: The basis of All-That-Is, is Well-Being. There is no source of anything that is other than Well-Being. If you believe you are experiencing something other than Well-Being, it is only because you have somehow chosen a perspective that is temporarily holding you out of reach of the natural Well-Being that flows.

Allowing: The state of alignment with the Well-Being that flows from Source. The focusing of your attention upon things that cause you to offer a vibration that "allows" your connection to your natural source of Well-Being. Tolerating is very different from allowing. Tolerating is seeing what is not wanted, feeling the vibrational evidence of that perspective, but deliberately taking no action. Allowing is deliberately giving your attention only to that which causes a vibration of alignment with Source. When you are in the state of allowing, you always feel good.

All-That-Is: The Source from which all things flow; and all things that flow from that Source.

Art of Allowing: The practiced process of deliberately choosing your subjects of attention, with a keen awareness of how that perspective feels to you. By deliberately choosing thoughts that feel good, you achieve vibrational alignment with your Source of Well-Being.

Being (noun): Source energy that is focused into a definite perspective. Non-Physical Being is Consciousness perceiving from Non-Physical perspective. Physical Being, or human Being is Non-Physical Energy perceiving through the physical perspective.

Collective Consciousness: All thoughts that have ever been thought still exist. All who perceive have access to all that is, and has been, perceived. This body of thought exists as Collective Consciousness.

Connection: Being in vibrational alignment with your Source.

Consciousness: Awareness.

Creative Energy: The electrical current at the basis of everything that exists.

Creative Life Force: The electrical current at the basis of everything that exists.

Creative Process: The electrical current at the basis of everything that exists, flowing specifically toward topics or ideas.

Creator: One who focuses Creative Energy.

Deliberate Creation: Focusing on what is intended while being consciously aware of one's vibrational state of being and connection to one's Source.

Desire: The natural result of living in a contrasting environment. (which includes *all* environments).

Emotion: The body's physical, visceral response to the vibrational state of being caused by whatever you are giving your attention to.

Emotional Guidance: Awareness of your state of attraction because of the way you feel as you give your attention to different things.

Emotional Set-Point: The emotion most often practiced.

Energy (Non-Physical): The electrical current at the basis of everything that exists.

Energy Stream: The flow of the electrical current at the basis of everything that exists.

Essence: Having matching vibrational properties.

Guidance System: The comparative feeling of your energetic state of being when you are aligned with your Source or when you are not aligned with your Source.

Inner Being: The Eternal part of you that perceives all that you have ever been and all that you currently are. A perspective always available to you if you will "allow" it.

Law of Attraction: The basis of your world, your Universe, and All-That-Is. Things of like vibration are drawn to each other.

Law of Deliberate Creation: The deliberate focusing of thought with the intention of feeling alignment with one's own desire.

Laws: Eternally consistent responses.

Leading Edge of Thought: A state of relaxed and deliberate consideration of ideas with the intention of new discovery.

Life Force: Eternal Consciousness specifically focused.

Mass Consciousness: The combined awareness of a large body of perceivers. Usually referring to the physical earth's human awareness.

Meditation: The state of quieting one's mind, and therefore stopping any resistant thoughts that would disallow vibrational alignment with one's Source.

Non-Physical: Eternal Consciousness, which is at the basis of all that is physical and all that is Non-Physical.

Overwhelment: The state of simultaneously focusing upon what you want and your inability to achieve it at the same time.

Receiving Mode: A vibrational state of being, absent of resistance, and therefore in absolute alignment with Source.

Self: Any point of awareness. The point from which all perception flows.

Source (noun): The eternally expanding vibrational stream of Well-Being from which all that is, flows.

Source Energy: The eternally expanding vibrational Stream of Well-Being from which all that is, flows.

Stream of Consciousness: The eternally expanding vibrational stream from which all things flow.

Stream of Well-Being: The eternally expanding vibrational stream from which all things flow.

Total You: You, in your human form, in a state of feeling good, and therefore offering no resistance that causes separation from who you really are.

Universe: A somewhat quantifiable spatial experience.

Vibration: The response of harmony or discord of all things to all things.

Vibrational Alignment: Harmony of perspective.

Vibrational Frequency: A state of vibration.

Vibrational Harmony: Harmony of perspective.

Vibrational Match: Harmony of perspective.

Wanting: Natural desire born from any comparative experience.

Well-Being: The universal natural state of feeling good.

You: An Eternal Consciousness who perceives from your broader Non-Physical perspective, your physical perspective, and even your cellular perspective.

About the Authors

Excited about the clarity and practicality of the translated word from the Beings who call themselves *Abraham,* **Jerry and Esther Hicks** began disclosing their amazing *Abraham* experience to a handful of close business associates in 1986.

Recognizing the practical results being received by themselves and by those persons who were asking meaningful questions regarding finances, bodily conditions, and relationships . . . and then successfully applying Abraham's answers to their own situations—Jerry and Esther made a deliberate decision to allow Abraham's teachings to become available to an ever-widening circle of seekers of answers to how to live a better life.

Using their San Antonio, Texas, Conference Center as their base, Jerry and Esther have traveled to approximately 50 cities a year since 1989, presenting interactive *Art of Allowing Workshops* to those leaders who gather to participate in this progressive stream of thought. And although worldwide attention has been given to this philosophy of Well-Being by Leading-Edge thinkers and teachers who have, in turn, incorporated many of Abraham's concepts into their best-selling books, scripts, lectures, and so forth, the primary spread of this material has been from person to person—

as individuals begin to discover the value of this form of spiritual practicality in their personal life experiences.

Abraham—a group of obviously evolved Non-Physical teachers—speak their broader perspective through Esther Hicks. And as they speak to our level of comprehension through a series of loving, allowing, brilliant, yet comprehensively simple, essays in print and in sound—they guide us to a clear connection with our loving Inner Being, and to uplifting self-empowerment from our Total Self.

The Hickses have now published more than 600 Abraham-Hicks books, cassettes, CDs, and videos. They may be contacted through their extensive interactive Website at **www.abraham-hicks.com** or by mail at Abraham-Hicks Publications, P.O. Box 690070, San Antonio, TX 78269.

Hay House Titles of Related Interest

Books

Angel Therapy, by Doreen Virtue, Ph.D.

Contacting Your Spirit Guide (book-with-CD), by Sylvia Browne

Experiencing the Soul, by Eliot Jay Rosen

How to Get from Where You Are to Where You Want to Be,
by Cheri Huber

I Can Do It® (book-with-CD), by Louise L. Hay

The Power of Intention, by Dr. Wayne W. Dyer
(also available as a card deck, calendar, and CD program)

Trust Your Vibes, by Sonia Choquette

Wisdom of the Heart, by Alan Cohen

Card Decks

Comfort Cards, by Max Lucado

Empowerment Cards, by Tavis Smiley

Kryon Cards: *Inspirational Sayings from the Kryon Books,*
channelled by Lee Carroll

Mars/Venus Cards, by John Gray, Ph.D.

Miracle Cards, by Marianne Williamson

Organizing from the Inside Out Cards, by Julie Morgenstern

Women's Bodies, Women's Wisdom Healing Cards,
by Christiane Northrup, M.D.

ᴓ ᴓ ᴓ

All of the above are available at your local bookstore,
or may be ordered by visiting Hay House (see next page).

ᴓ ᴓ ᴓ

To:

HAY HOUSE, INC.
P.O. Box 5100
Carlsbad, CA 92018-5100

Tune in to Hay House Radio to listen to your favorite authors: **HayHouseRadio.com**™

Yes, I'd like to receive:

☐ **a Hay House catalog**   ☐ *The Louise Hay Newsletter*
☐ *The Christiane Northrup Newsletter* ☐ *The Sylvia Browne Newsletter*

Name_____

Address_____

City_____ State_____ Zip_____

E-mail_____

Also, please send:

☐ **a Hay House catalog**   ☐ *The Louise Hay Newsletter*
☐ *The Christiane Northrup Newsletter* ☐ *The Sylvia Browne Newsletter*

To:
Name_____

Address_____

City_____ State_____ Zip_____

E-mail_____

If you'd like to receive a catalog of Hay House books and products, or a free copy of one or more of our authors' newsletters, please visit **www.hayhouse.com**® or detach and mail this reply card.

HAY HOUSE